BEYOND THE BROKEN YEARS

Peter Stanley recently retired as Research Professor at UNSW Canberra. He has published over forty books, many in Australian military history, among which *Bad Characters* jointly won the Prime Minister's Prize for Australian History in 2011. He was formerly Principal Historian at the Australian War Memorial, where he worked from 1980 to 2007. He has been a crucial participant in the field for over forty years, known as mentor, supervisor and examiner of doctoral theses, reviewer, critic, exhibition curator, and collaborator. He was inaugural President of Honest History and is a Principal of Defending Country, a coalition dedicated to encouraging the War Memorial to keep its undertaking to acknowledge Frontier Conflict fittingly.

'An unflinching and insightful tour through the evolving landscape of Australian war history, led by one of the country's most trusted guides. This impressive blend of scholarship and reflection is crucial reading for anyone wanting to understand the place of war in Australian history.'

Kate Ariotti, University of Queensland

'All historians of Australian military history will be indebted to Peter Stanley for this virtuoso commentary on the books of the field, written with his characteristic flair, insight and delight in controversy.'

Emeritus Professor Joan Beaumont, Australian National University

'Peter Stanley's evocation of Australia's military history is not to be missed. Half a century after Bill Gammage's superb book *The Broken Years* was published, Stanley has cleverly drawn on the cream of Australian military historians to underline the key elements of Australia's military past. However, it is Stanley's own analysis of the importance of Australia's military past that has given new meaning to the importance of Australians at war. Remarkably, Stanley has researched 1300 books written by Australian authors since 1974. The result is a gripping overview of our military history that should not be missed.'

The late Tim Bowden AM, author, radio and television broadcaster, producer and oral historian

'Peter Stanley is surely the military historian's historian. This book is an extraordinary achievement, both knowledgeable and eminently readable. It should take pride of place in any military history library.'

Mike Carlton, author, broadcaster and journalist

'In engaging prose, and with a light touch, Stanley analyses the military history boom of the last fifty years, pondering the rise and rise of Anzac commemoration, and making a strong claim for better representation of frontier wars at the Australian War Memorial. *Beyond The Broken Years* will be devoured by those who enjoy military history and will endure as the authoritative account of how Australians have understood our experience of war.'

Carolyn Holbrook, Deakin University

'For more than a century Australia's military experience has been central to the nation's identity, and the bedrock of understanding that experience has been the published histories, academic studies and personal stories. Peter Stanley's book is a brilliant, erudite, and insightful examination of the books that have enlightened, strengthened and at times challenged our understanding of Australia's military history in the past fifty years. *Beyond The Broken Years* is a reminder that there are multiple strands to Australia's military history. This is not just because Australia continues to go to new wars, but also because our understanding of the impact of war continues to grow.'

David Horner, Emeritus Professor, Australian National University

'As an exceptional historian and a generous patron and mentor, Peter Stanley is ideally placed to analyse the last 50 years of Australian military historiography. This brilliant and original book will entertain and inform readers at all levels of expertise. *Beyond The Broken Years* will inspire all readers to read (or write) more Australian military history.'

Mark Johnston, Head of History and Classics, Scotch College Melbourne

'Aficionados of Australia's rich military history will enjoy reading this latest work by prolific military author and historian, Peter Stanley. *Beyond The Broken Years* will stimulate reading, and further analysis and research on Australia's military history, which is important, as Australia's military history reveals much about us. I commend this book to you.'

Paul Irving, MAJGEN (Ret'd) AM PSM RFD, Manager, Royal United Services Institute NSW Ursula Davidson Library

'Another Stanley original. Inspiring, thoughtful, provocative and personal, this book will have you reaching for your pencil to jot down titles for your next library visit. Essential reading for all Australian military history enthusiasts.'

Professor Emerita Melanie Oppenheimer, Australian National University and Flinders University

'A spirited romp through the annals of Australian military history. Searching, sceptical, self-reflexive and engaging, Peter Stanley vigorously ponders the past and future of the discipline.'

Professor Bruce Scates, Australian National University

Also by Peter Stanley

What did you do in the war, Daddy? (ed.) (1984)
Australians at War, 1885–1972 (with Michael McKernan) (1984)
Bomber Command (1985)
But Little Glory: The New South Wales contingent to the Sudan, 1885 (ed.) (1985)
Anzac Day 70 years on (with Michael McKernan) (1986)
A Guide to the Australian War Memorial (1986)
The Remote Garrison: The British Army in Australia, 1788–1870 (1986)
Air Battle Europe 1939–45 (1987)
Rosemary and Wattle (1993)
Tarakan: An Australian tragedy (1997)
White Mutiny: British Military Culture in India, 1825–75 (1998)
Alamein: The Australian story (with Mark Johnston) (2002)
Stolen Years: Australian prisoners of war (with others) (2002)
For Fear of Pain: British surgery 1790–1850 (2003)
Whyalla at War 1939–45 (2004)
Quinn's Post: Anzac, Gallipoli (2005)
Borneo, 1942–1945 (2006)
Invading Australia: Japan and the battle for Australia, 1942 (2008)
A Stout Pair of Boots: A guide to exploring Australia's battlefields (2008)
Men of Mont St Quentin: Between victory and death (2009)
Commando to Colditz: Micky Burn's journey to the far side of tears (2009)
Bad Characters: Sex, crime, mutiny, murder and the Australian Imperial Force (2010)
Simpson's Donkey (2011)
Digger Smith and Australia's Great War (2011)
Black Saturday at Steels Creek: Fire and an Australian community (2013)
Lost Boys of Anzac (2014)
The Cunning Man (2014)
A Welch Calypso (ed.) (2014)
Die in Battle, Do Not Despair: The Indians on Gallipoli, 1915 (2015)
The War at Home (with John Connor & Peter Yule) (2015)
Armenia, Australia & the Great War (with Vicken Babkenian) (2016)
The Crying Years: Australia's Great War (2017)
Charles Bean's Legacy (ed.) (2017)
Victory on Gallipoli (ed.) (2017)
Jeff Grey: A life in history (ed.) (2018)
'Terriers' in India: British Territorials 1914–19 (2019)
Alienation (2020)
The Devil's Uncle (2020)
The Weight of Light (2022)
Golden Pagoda (2022)
On Private Affairs (2022)
Hul! Hul!: The Suppression of the Santal Rebellion, Bengal, 1855 (2022)
Falklands/Malvinas 1982: A war of two sides (with Maria Inez Tato and others) (2022)
John Company's Armies: The military forces of British India 1824–57 (2024)
The Sherrin (2025)

BEYOND THE BROKEN YEARS

AUSTRALIAN MILITARY HISTORY IN 1000 BOOKS

PETER STANLEY

NEWSOUTH

UNSW Press acknowledges the Bedegal people, the Traditional Owners of the unceded territory on which the Randwick and Kensington campuses of UNSW are situated, and recognises the continuing connection to Country and culture. We pay our respects to Bedegal Elders past and present. The author acknowledges the Ngunnawal people, on whose land this book was written.

A NewSouth book

Published by
NewSouth Publishing
University of New South Wales Press Ltd
University of New South Wales
Sydney NSW 2052
AUSTRALIA
https://unsw.press/

First published 2024

10 9 8 7 6 5 4 3 2 1

NATIONAL LIBRARY OF AUSTRALIA
A catalogue record for this book is available from the National Library of Australia

ISBN: 9781761170140 (paperback)
9781761179044 (ebook)
9781761178146 (ePDF)

Design Josephine Pajor-Markus
Cover design Peter Long
Cover images Peter Long and iStock / LeventKonuk
Printer Griffin Press

UNSW SYDNEY

I dedicate this book to Bill Gammage, fifty years after *The Broken Years*, in recognition of all he has done for our understanding of Australia's history, and to the next generation of historians of our sadly seemingly unending involvement in war.

CONTENTS

PART V POST-1945

PART VI THEMES IN AUSTRALIAN MILITARY HISTORY

INTRODUCTION: FROM MEMORY TO HISTORY

Fifty years ago, ANU Press published a book based on the 1970 PhD thesis of a 31-year-old historian, Bill Gammage: *The Broken Years*, sub-titled *Australian soldiers in the Great War.* It was almost certainly the first doctoral thesis written in Australian military history, and certainly the first to be published. Military history was unfashionable. In universities, especially at the tail end of the Vietnam war, Bill had struggled to get a supervisor, but found one in Bruce Kent, a political historian with whom he'd played football. Bill Gammage went on to become among the most respected, even revered, figures in the field of Australian history. He has since written books which have challenged, enriched and often transformed areas of Australia's understanding of its past – the colonisation of Papua New Guinea (*The Sky Travellers*), the complex history of country towns (*Narrandera Shire*); the environmental changes following the continent's settlement (*The Biggest Estate on Earth*). *The Biggest Estate* places the Aboriginal environment at the heart of the story of Australia's history, but *The Broken Years* had a startling impact on the way Australians write about their military history.

And it's had an impact on me. I remember opening the Adelaide *News* in 1974 (my Matric year) on 24 April and reading extracts of this new book on the First World War. In 1978, as a student teacher, I used that book to make worksheets for the pupils in Year 10 history at Campbell High School. In 1980, I drew on it to write speeches for Noel Flanagan, the Director of the War Memorial. In the 2000s, I re-read it while researching what became *Quinn's Post* and *Men of Mont St Quentin*. One or another edition of *The Broken Years* has always been on my bookshelves.

In 1994 (the 20th anniversary of the publication of *The Broken Years*), the editors of the *Journal of the Australian War Memorial* (my colleagues in the Memorial's former Historical Research Section) asked Bill to reflect on his book's genesis: already we thought of it as a 'classic'. Bill wrote an elegy to the Australians who had experienced the Great War, many of whom he had come to know both in growing up in Wagga Wagga, and through researching the PhD thesis which became the book. He remembered visiting the Memorial as a schoolboy in January 1960, meeting Bruce Harding, a Wagga-ite working there, who showed him filing cabinets full of soldiers' letters. Bill's honours thesis in 1965, inspired by buying volumes of Charles Bean's official history at a jumble sale, drew on some of those letters. He then began the doctoral thesis which used and quoted hundreds of those letters and diaries, working in an institution so unused to visiting researchers that it had no reading room, and served him tea at the spare desks at which he sat.

Bill recalled those far-away years and the people he met with pleasure and gratitude, conscious that he had been vouchsafed an opportunity which no one now can replicate. He later reflected on how he had come to know the generation which had lived through, and often died in, the Great War, from their writings, and from conversations with men who were glad to speak to this young man from the country who came with questions no one else thought to ask. Bill reflected that he was 'part of the generation which took them from memory to history'. That phrase is central to the conception of this book. It's mostly not about how those who experienced war remembered or described it: it's about how those who have mostly not experienced war have sought to understand and write about it.

Although he remained interested in military history, Gammage did not much return to the trenches of Gallipoli and the Western Front. (Perhaps because, I surmised from his comments about his relationship with the men he met, he found re-visiting such a powerful experience as an historian emotionally draining.) But *The Broken Years* lived on, going through four editions with three publishers, and many reprintings, reportedly selling perhaps 50 000 copies over four decades, for reasons which will soon become clear. Over the course of his career, Gammage witnessed the revitalisation, perhaps the invention, of a part of Australian history which historians had until then disdained or dismissed. Of all the books published in Australian military history, the vast majority appeared after *The Broken Years*. That explains this book's sub-title and focus.

Except for several review articles (notably Lloyd Robson's 'Behold a Pale Horse' in *Australian Historical Studies* in 1988 and perceptive surveys by Jeff Grey in *History Compass* (2008) and Joan Beaumont in *Australian Historical Studies* in 2002 and *War & Society* in 2022), *Beyond The Broken Years* is, I think, the first general account of the writing of Australian military history.* When I conceived this book, I guessed that about a thousand books had appeared in Australian military history since 1974, but I found over 1300. Its brevity precludes any deep or sustained analysis: it's very much both a personal view and one intended to stimulate reading and further research and writing. Looking at books like this in other fields, I found a critic disapproving of a book which merely 'rattles through titles, authors and genres'. Gulp, I thought ... But I hope I've done more than that. If I've prompted you to find a book on a shelf, in a library, in a second-hand shop or off the internet, to read or re-read, then I'll be happy.

I should explain that this book is structured partly more-or-less chronologically but also deals with important themes in the field. It's based on a bibliography of over a thousand titles published since 1974 which I compiled while thinking about its themes and arguments and mentions almost exactly a thousand books and films. It's not intended to be anything like an annotated reading list, and it can't hope to even notice everything in what's been a torrent of writing in the field. For example, just about every Australian book on the Boer war mentions the Morant-Handcock murders: I mention a handful of them.

* Just as I delivered the manuscript, I discovered Richard Travers's *Above the Mists of Ages* (2023), an essay of 30 000 words on *The Anzac Legend and Historical Practice*. Its virtue is that it examines Australian military history in international and intellectual contexts, but it actually discusses only about twenty Australian military historians, all of whom appear in this book, along with many others.

It deals essentially with books, but discusses films and memoirs because of their importance to how historical interpretation is conveyed. I'll mostly ignore articles and published chapters, no doubt to the dismay of my academic colleagues, though I'll notice some influential articles and a few important edited collections. (Because many academics publish chapters and articles rather than books – partly because of the absurd pressures the tertiary sector imposes on them – focusing largely on books somewhat understates the productivity and contribution of many colleagues, for which I apologise.) I also don't discuss school texts, children's books, exhibition catalogues, or technical works. Nor do I deal with coffee-table or picture books, so leaving out books like Robert Nelson's *Pictorial History of Australians at War* (1970), from which I first learned my Australian military history as a 14-year-old British migrant, and *Australians at War 1885–1972*, which Michael McKernan and I published in 1984 to showcase the Memorial's photographic and documentary collections).

Despite my frequent criticisms of Australian military history as 'unduly parochial', *Beyond The Broken Years* deals with the military history of Australia, not with Australian military historians, so I'll largely ignore Australians who write wider military history, such as my UNSW colleagues, Richard Dunley, James Goldrick, Eleanor Hancock, Debbie Lackerstein or David Stahel. Nor do I deal with debates in current defence policy and strategy, so cutting out a raft of scholars, such as Des Ball, Michael Evans, David Kilcullen, Russell Parkin or Al Palazzo, except when their work has been explicitly historical. Nor do I treat postgraduate theses, though I could have written much lamenting theses that should have been published but weren't, such as Janette Bomford on prisoners of war and their families, Jack Clear on the Wiradjuri wars, Kevin Fewster on censorship, Martin Ball on Bean's writing, Bryan Egan on medical officers in the Great War, or Kerry Neale on facial wounds, among many. I include overseas authors who have contributed to the subject, such as Lida Mayo or Yuki Tanaka, and Australians who have spent much time away, such as Kevin Blackburn (Singapore), John Moremon (New Zealand) and Carl Bridge, Alexia Moncrieff and Philip Payton (Britain). I don't use authors' titles or post-nominals, and there are no footnotes or publication details besides years. And I don't use the high falutin' 'historiography' except in this sentence.

To borrow Bill Hudson's praise for John McCarthy's *Australia and Imperial Defence* in 1977, this is intended to also be 'a short pungent book for the educated layman' – obviously a time-bound bit of unthinking misogyny. It's based on decades of reading, research, writing and, often, contact with authors or their sources, but it's not a scholarly book as such – I'm retired, I don't have to do that stuff any more. Above all, this is a personal history: that means that I'm also responsible for any mistakes.

Note on the text

I refer to the Australian War Memorial as 'the Memorial'. Military historians revel in abbreviations, most obscure, many unnecessary. I don't, but several are needed, so often do the names of services and institutions recur:

AIF	Australian Imperial Force
RAAF	Royal Australian Air Force
RAN	Royal Australian Navy
RAR	Royal Australian Regiment
RMC	Royal Military College (Duntroon)
UNSW	University of New South Wales*

Dealing with a field which has produced well over a thousand books has involved making some severe choices. The full bibliography on which

* RMC Duntroon acquired a History Department in 1967, under the auspices of the University of NSW. It moved to the new and adjacent Australian Defence Force Academy in 1983, where it remains. Because it then existed under several names, now UNSW Canberra, for convenience and clarity I'll call it RMC before 1983 and UNSW Canberra after.

I largely based this book can be found at <https://unsw.press/beyond-the-broken-years-full-bibliography/>. If you want to chase up anything, author and title will find it for you. I've made judgments that I think reflect their strength or focus and which across such a span of years and themes gives a reliable basis for my analysis; not to mention that it's based on almost fifty years of familiarity with the field to which I've devoted my career.

PART I
A SHORT HISTORY OF AUSTRALIAN MILITARY HISTORY

1

THE STORY OF ANZAC: AUSTRALIAN MILITARY HISTORY TO 1974

When did Australian military history begin? Surely both First Nations and convict campfires were enlivened by stories of fighting with spear and musket: but tales, even if formalised as 'oral history', do not count as the sort of history with which this book deals. Craig Wilcox, doyen of Australia's early military history, found in the Mitchell Library, Sydney, the papers of Grace Hendy-Pooley (1864–1947). A British officer's daughter, Miss Hendy-Pooley became something of a force in Sydney antiquarian circles, joining the Australian Historical Society (later the Royal) in 1902, soon after its establishment. She published papers in its journal and articles in newspapers, going on to work on the *Historical Records of Australia* and in the Parliamentary Library, a single career woman at a time when most young ladies did no paid work. Miss Hendy-Pooley so devoted herself to assisting other researchers (creating, for example, an index to the *Sydney Gazette*, sadly published with her name mis-spelled on the title page) that she neglected to publish her own work. In researching his *For Hearths and Homes*, Craig Wilcox discovered in her papers plans for and drafts of a two-volume history of British soldiers in Australia. Had Miss Hendy-Pooley's book been published, it would have been the earliest book of Australian military history not written by a participant. As it was, primacy seems to belong to what might be called 'participant historians' – those who write about a conflict they witnessed at first hand. In that case, the first Australian military historian might be regarded as John West, missionary, educator and journalist, whose *The History of Tasmania* (1852) described the Indigenous inhabitants of the island as having been 'a people in arms'.*

While writing on what Australians called 'The War' – the Great War – appeared regularly in what became clear was the interval between the world wars, the great bulk of it was written by those who had experienced war. Some of it was of high quality – why would readers pay for anecdotes they could hear in the pub or at home? (Or read in the regular 'Unofficial History of the AIF' column in 'the Digger's Paper', *Smith's Weekly*.) The best memoirs were of lasting value – Harold Williams's *The Gallant Company* (1933) or Rowland Lording's *There and Back* (1935). Every few years, another volume of the official history appeared (received with respectful reviews in many newspapers, along with reports of the appearance of battalion histories), while Memorial salesmen travelled door-to-door hawking volumes of the official history. But all those writing, selling or reviewing these works remembered The War: almost no one looked at it historically.

The first book-length history of Australia's Great War was not Charles Bean's official history or Monash's *The Australian Victories in France* (1920) but Miles Staniforth Smith's *Australian Campaigns in the Great War* (1919). Smith had already served as a senator and an administrator in Papua before he volunteered in 1916, aged 47, becoming the intelligence officer of the 4th Battalion. For much of the period until the 1970s the history of Australia's wars was written by men like these – participants and survivors. Australia's South African war was likewise arguably not accorded a secondary account until Max Chamberlain's *To Shoot and Ride: The Australians in the South African War* (1967). For decades history by other than those who had served was practically unknown: those who had not served had no right to write.

Much of what might look like contemporary history published in wartime was, of course, propaganda. Books like the war correspondent George Johnston's *Grey Gladiator: H.M.A.S. Sydney with the British*

* But already, James Bischoff, entrepreneur, had quoted Governor George Arthur describing Tasmania's 'blacks' as 'an open and accredited enemy' in his *Sketch of the History of Van Diemen's Land* (1832). Arthur was assuredly a participant.

Mediterranean Fleet (1941) or *New Guinea Diary* (1942), while still useful as contemporary sources, were so constrained by the scrutiny of the Department of Information that they hardly qualified as history. The blurred line between history, reportage and propaganda is exemplified by the 'Christmas books' written mainly by authors in uniform and published by the Memorial as one of its contributions to the war effort. Its director, John Treloar, then heading the army's Military History and Information Section, proposed publishing illustrated popular compilations. The first, *Active Service*, appeared late in 1941, with 94 000 copies printed – Australia's largest print run to that time. Families eager to know more about their sons and husbands' war bought them in huge numbers – *Jungle Warfare* (1944) sold over 268 000 copies. By the time the series closed in 1950, twenty titles had appeared, selling nearly two million copies. Many volumes related to particular services: four each for the RAN and RAAF, one for the Volunteer Defence Corps, though, curiously, none for the women's services. Five titles, all called *As You Were*, appeared after 1945 (though reprints appeared into the 1950s). They especially might be considered a first draft of history, perhaps the only thing many people read.

Official history (see chapters 13 and 24) prompted what might be called 'demi-official' history, such as Colonel Eustace Keogh's *South-West Pacific, 1941–45* (1965). Keogh had served in both world wars and his book appeared at a time when all of the army's senior officers had served in the second. Keogh's other publishing achievement (besides editing the *Australian Army Journal*) was to write a little guide to the Shenandoah campaign of 1862, a subject familiar to generations of aspiring majors when the army insisted on officers demonstrating a proficiency in military history as part of their fitness for promotion. (Keogh also acted as advisor to the TV series *The Sullivans*.)

Readers of a certain generation – say those coming to the subject between the mid-1950s and the mid-1990s – will have read the books written by John Laffin, a prolific author who had served in the 2/31st Battalion in Papua. Laffin became one of the few Australian authors after 1945 to make a quid out of writing non-fiction history, and then only by living in Britain and writing and publishing, it has to be said, indiscriminately. As a teenager living in a remote provincial city in South Australia in the period 1966–74, I certainly borrowed half-a-dozen of Laffin's books from school or council libraries, and they formed a part of my education in military history. The books I read included *Digger: The Story of the Australian Soldier* (1959), *Scotland the Brave* (1963), *Anzacs at War* (1965), *Boys in Battle* (1966), and *Surgeons in the Field* (1970). Many will recall other Laffin books: he published about 130.

But except for eccentrics and enthusiasts, military history largely remained the province of 'Returned Men', who produced and read mainly memoirs and unit histories. The 1950s saw the foundation of the first of several historical societies whose members were typically ex-servicemen. A Military Historical Society of Australia was established in 1957, but in 1962 its New South Wales branch seceded for reasons no one now can recall, though the breach remains. An Aviation Historical Society was formed in 1959 and in 1970 a Naval Historical Society. But except for occasional bestsellers such as Russell Braddon's *The Naked Island* (1952) or Alan Moorehead's *Gallipoli* (1956) military history remained a minority interest.

Bill Gammage, though favourably reviewing Alec Hill's *Chauvel of the Light Horse*, pointed out that Hill wrote for 'the old soldier and the military historian'; and Bill was neither. Academic historians in Australia, Alan Gilbert of RMC wrote in the Memorial's *Journal* in 1984, 'have been condescending, hostile, or preoccupied with other themes'. Those who had noticed military history, he continued, had approached it as social history, by which he presumably meant Gammage's *The Broken Years*, which was not esteemed by the serious military historians in the RMC History tea-room. Len Turner of RMC, one of South Africa's official historians and one of Bill's PhD examiners, insisted that *The Broken Years* was not military history as he understood it, and Bill dutifully included a note in the first edition accepting the censure.*

* This niggle continued for some years: in reviewing Peter Pedersen's *Monash as Military Commander* in 1986, Jeff Grey commented that there was 'more work to be done on the AIF but it will require historians to distance themselves from concentration on the private soldier to the virtual exclusion of all else'.

Twenty-odd years after 1945, military history began to change, surprisingly, perhaps, at first through the academic historians who had for so long disdained it. In 1965 the RSL chartered a Turkish passenger ship, the *Karadeniz*, to carry 300 Great War veterans to the peninsula most had last seen fifty years before. With them went Ken Inglis, a 35-year-old historian of religion in Victorian Britain (of all things), curious to see how they reacted and willing to send occasional bulletins to the *Canberra Times*. Though Inglis did not publish the manuscript he produced reflecting on the trip, his insights influenced his thinking about the importance of Anzac, and all that that meant.

At the time, it meant less and less, with Anzac observance dwindling and military history moribund. The book review pages of the main Australian historical journal (*Historical Studies: Australia and New Zealand*, and then re-named *Historical Studies* (1967–1987) for five decades from the 1960s to the 2000s) reveal that it reviewed almost nothing relating to war before the late 1960s. The first war book reviewed (in October 1967) was *Sydney's Burning*, Ian Turner's study of the socialist 'Wobblies' who caused Billy Hughes so much grief – and that really reflected Australian historians' interest in the labour movement. In 1968, Roy Forward and Bob Reece's *Conscription in Australia* appeared, a product of the continuing turmoil over Vietnam – the reviewer, Lloyd Robson, of the University of Melbourne, concluded that 'the instinct which leads people to distrust conscription is a sound one'.

Ken Inglis's Gallipoli pilgrimage had prompted further thought. In 1970 he published a major, two-part article, 'The Australians at Gallipoli': the first time an academic writer (a rising historian, now at the University of Papua New Guinea) had considered any aspect of Australia's Great War. Quoting soldiers' words provided by Gammage, it was based on a paper he had presented at the 1969 ANZAAS Congress, then Australia's main 'scientific' meeting. At the same time, Lloyd Robson had never evinced any interest in military history, but his work analysing *The Convict Settlers of Australia* (1965) led him to a brief 1969 narrative study of *Australia and the Great War* and in 1970 *The First A.I.F.: A study of its recruitment*. A reviewer marked

Robson as 'the first scholar to investigate [the subject] since Scott wrote his volume of the *Official History*' – in 1936. Robson was motivated by an awareness of 'an episode ... which bites more deeply into the nation's psyche than anything else in its history'. Australia's military history was about to be re-discovered and re-invented

2

THE BROKEN YEARS: AUSTRALIAN MILITARY HISTORY RE-DISCOVERED

The decisive step in the re-invention of Australian military history came in 1974 with the publication of Bill Gammage's *The Broken Years*, launched with an 18-gallon keg at the University of Papua New Guinea on Anzac Day.* Its success was a puzzle, and not just because though a thesis, much of it comprised quotations from letters of men, many killed in the war, their words dormant for decades. It had been written by a relatively young man but, as Michael McKernan later noted, 'a new breed of historian'; not a Returned Man, as were so many historians of the post-war generation (Geoffrey Serle, Eric Fry, Ian Turner), but 'a doctoral student'. No other doctoral thesis had yet been completed in Australian military history. Geoffrey Serle (later Monash's biographer) declared it to be 'not a military history but an evocation of what it was like to be an Australian fighting soldier in the 1914–18 war'. He found it 'a searing, a scarifying book', but also one which, far from challenging the interpretation of forty years before was notable for 'its general verification of and respect for C.E.W. Bean's work'. In fact, Serle thought, RSL members would approve of *The Broken Years*. (But not everyone did – the younger Jeff Grey sniffed that 'his actual argument does not add anything much to ... Bean'.)

---

* In yet another link in the Great Chain of Being, Manning Clark, the nation's best-known historian, sent a characteristically worded telegram to Bill (whom he had known at ANU): 'GLORY TODAY TO THE BOY FROM WAGGA AND THE CHILD OF HIS HEART'.

But even Jeff acknowledged that Bill's greatest service was not so much what he wrote, but what he effectively discovered – the Lasseter's Reef of Australian military history. As then War Memorial historian Anne-Marie Condé's research revealed, John Treloar, the head of the Australian War Records Section and later the Memorial's longest serving director, had assiduously collected hundreds of letters, diaries and other documents. Though gathered ostensibly for Bean's official history, they were never used for it, and with the Memorial a little-visited back-water and military history unexplored, they lay untouched until Gammage came knocking on the door of Arthur Bazley, Bean's former assistant. 'Baz', still at the Memorial in the late 1960s, became Bill's guide, a serendipitous link in the Great Chain of Being in our little field.

At the time, Len Turner of RMC Duntroon said, 'in the serious study of war, Australia lags far behind'. *The Broken Years* invigorated a generation of scholars. In his *Regional Australia and the Great War* (2012), Philip Payton recalled that as a postgraduate at Adelaide in the mid-1970s he had been attracted by its 'democratic' approach, 'its reliance upon the testaments of those who had fought' and for whom 'ever since ... it has remained a favourite and a yardstick'. Meanwhile, popular interest in war history, seemingly suppressed by the ferment of the Vietnam years, received the further stimulation of *The Anzacs* (1978) by Patsy Adam-Smith, a freelance author and sometime field officer for the State Library of Victoria. Adam-Smith, already known for her celebration of rural battlers, became inspired by the records she collected for the library, and produced *The Anzacs*, published and energetically promoted by Thomas Nelson, then an emerging firm in Australian publishing. *The Anzacs* was less a formal history than a series of short pieces, each based on the letters, diaries, memoirs and photographs she had collected. It became the *Age* Book of the Year and sold probably more copies than any book in the field since Monash's memoirs and the Memorial's Christmas books. Patsy Adam-Smith acted as John the Baptist, inspiring John Dixon to make the television mini-series also called *The Anzacs* (see chapter 37). The multi-pronged advance by serious historians, popular writers and film-makers, supported by the re-invigoration of the Memorial, started a boom which is only now diminishing.

When *The Broken Years* had appeared military history was, Geoffrey Serle wrote, 'controversial [largely because of Vietnam], confusing and underworked'. In the ensuing decades that would dramatically change – Serle himself would publish the single most substantial study of John Monash, the senior Australian general of the Great War. From the late 1970s academic historians increasingly recognised the value of books on war. From 1982 to 2004 all but five issues of the twice-yearly journal *Australian Historical Studies* contained reviews of war books. Australian military history was about to enter its boom-time, creating a wave on which historians of all varieties and stripes would surf for several decades.

Comparative figures based on the bibliography created for this book are persuasive. In the 1970s, after the appearance of *The Broken Years*, an average of seven-and-a-half titles appeared in Australian military history annually. In the 1980s that more than doubled to nearly twenty; in the 1990s to twenty-six. In the next century they increased to thirty in the 2000s and to over forty in the 2010s. It's too early to say definitively how the trend will go in the 2020s, but so far it's back to where it was in the 2010s, at around thirty titles per year. Of course, the figures are pretty rubbery, but I think that the trend is clear.

The Broken Years, and particularly the reaction it aroused, did not simply emerge from the imagination of a young PhD candidate who had the happy inspiration to seek a rapport with elderly Returned Men. It had been written in the late 1960s and published at the mid-point of the Whitlam years, touched by a rising sense of nationalism, and informed by Lloyd Robson and Ken Inglis's questions about the effects of the Great War on Australian society. Gammage was part of the first generation to enjoy the boon of wider tertiary education and was guided by supervisors imbued with a curiosity about an aspect of Australian history that had impinged upon their lives and their communities. *The Broken Years* arose from a complex combination of circumstances, of Gammage's personality, of the community and the nation in which he lived; at a time of conscious exploration, questioning and celebration of an Australian identity. But it can rightly be regarded as a distinctive starting point, the second Big Bang in Australian military history. (Assuming that Bean's insights on Gallipoli and expressed in *The Anzac Book* and *The Story of Anzac* constituted the first.)

It would soon be clear from the footnotes and bibliographies of the books which began to appear in greater numbers that one explanation for this boom was that the archives were opening up. (This was itself novel. At the time archives were routinely closed for fifty years, and the Archives Office, as it then was, had primitive research facilities – it occupied temporary buildings beside Lake Burley Griffin, where the National Gallery now stands.) Nor was the Memorial accustomed to hosting researchers or even helping them. When Raymond Paull approached John Treloar in his final years as director for help with *Retreat from Kokoda*, he was told that the Memorial was 'restrained by public policy from giving assistance in the preparation of a private venture', a reaction that to a generation accustomed to institutions offering support sounds simply perverse. (The attitude soon changed: the Memorial from the 1980s saw the support of initiatives intended to foster research as worthy.)

Gammage's *The Broken Years* led others to follow, excited to use the 'letters and diaries' which became the stock sources for many books, and theses which often became books. This was helped by the greater organisation and accessibility of major archival collections, especially the Memorial's, under dedicated archivists and curators, including Michael Piggott, Bill Fogarty, Paul Macpherson and Anne-Marie Schwirtlich.* Piggott himself produced the first *Guide to the Personal, Family and Official Papers of C.E.W. Bean* (1983). The passing of an *Archives Act* the same year indicated the opening up of Australian Archives (from 1974; from 1998 National Archives of Australia). In 1970, the 'fifty-year-rule' was reduced to thirty, meaning that the archives of the Second World War soon also opened. Awareness of newly released or described records suggested entire books. Awareness of the manuscripts of Bean's

* If you don't know these names, you should. They comprise the leading members of the dedicated tribe of archivists who enabled writers to produce the flood of books over the following decades.

Anzac Book, for example, led David Kent to question the origins of the Anzac legend, while learning of the richness of the 'troopship serials' in the Memorial resulted in his *From Trench and Troopship* (1999), a study of the social history of the AIF as presented through its informal magazines.

In the space of a decade, military history in Australia passed from being ignored to become one of the leading genres in academic research and teaching and in popular and scholarly publishing.

3

THE MYTH OF THE DIGGER: ANZAC INVESTIGATED

As late as the bicentennial year of European settlement, military history remained relatively unimportant. A list of the 101 'best Australian books' published in *The Bulletin* magazine in 1991 included just two post-1974 military histories – Bill Gammage's *The Broken Years* and Henry Reynolds's *The Other Side of the Frontier* (see chapter 5). In 1988, Lloyd Robson, one of the pioneers of the boom in writing about war, published a review article in the former *Historical Studies*, now called *Australian Historical Studies*. He surveyed more than a dozen books which had appeared over the previous several years. Robson noted that serious study of war in Australian history had long been left to official and battalion histories. He thought that Alan Seymour's iconoclastic play *The One Day of the Year* (1958) represented the first challenge to the RSL's monopoly over what war meant to Australians. That may have been so, but it took a while for curiosity and criticism to work its way into historians' writings, which necessarily take time: for thought; for research; for writing; for publication; for reaction. He acknowledged Ken Inglis's 1965 Gallipoli pilgrimage (even if it seemingly produced only newspaper articles). Robson himself rightly claimed credit as 'the first academic historian to produce a full-length study of the first AIF'. He then analysed why so many had followed the lead offered by him and Inglis.

Robson acknowledged the recently reinvigorated Memorial and its suite of grants and scholarships, and what had over the previous decade become an annual conference. Then there was the Memorial's own *Journal* (1982), soon followed by *War and Society*, published by historians at what became UNSW Canberra. He also pointed to the growing number of university courses on 'Australians at War' which in turn stimulated postgraduate theses which often fuelled both new academic courses and the sorts of books he was reviewing. The university courses in turn attracted school students primed, as it were, by the increasing attention paid to conflict in high schools, though that would vary over the decades.

Robson discussed the effects of the Vietnam war which if, as Carolyn Holbrook later showed, it depressed interest in Anzac commemoration, paradoxically sparked interest in issues such as conscription, as important in 1967 as it had been in 1917. Robson reported at Melbourne University 'a sudden huge increase' in enrolments in his Great War course. All this meant that by 1988 it had become 'difficult to keep up with publications in the field of Australian war studies', noticing 'dozens of books' of all kinds, including memoirs, in the late 1980s now encompassing reminiscences of former prisoners of war (see chapter 18). Moreover, the boom turned seeming dross into gold. Battalion histories 'command very high prices on the antiquarian book market when once they could be picked up in the op. shops for a shilling or two'.

Among the many insights Robson offered was to muse on the two world wars, which he described as 'gigantic mountains towering above the plains and gentle foothills in the Australian historical landscape'. Why, he asked, had a nation which had made 'a bloody defeat on foreign soil' its national day, even protecting its name by law and elevating returned men into 'a cult', taken so long to analyse that landscape? By 1988, twenty years after Bean's death, Australians were at last confronting that history.

This impulse to investigate and analyse stimulated novel research and books which advanced understanding, sometimes in durable ways. Jane Ross's *The Myth of the Digger* (1985), the first attempt to deconstruct the Anzac legend sociologically, deserved to be remembered and used for longer than it was: the unjustified fate of many books opening up a field. Lloyd Robson thought her seeming 'acceptance of the myth ... curious', but scholars approached revered national beliefs warily, and with a fitting scepticism. Joan Beaumont, reviewing John Barrett's last book, *We Were There: Australian Soldiers of World War II tell their stories* (1987), while questioning how representative was the self-selected (male) sample, concluded that it was large and diverse enough to be useful. (Barrett's original questionnaires, now in the Memorial, have unfortunately barely been used by other historians.) Reviewing it for *Labour History*, I described its selection of extracts variously as informative, wry, revealing, disgusting, poignant and even beautiful. Its main shortcoming, I thought, was that Barrett did not ask these men what it felt like to fight.

The revival in Australian military history introduced differences between interpretations, especially in the 'social' rather than the 'operational'. Bill Gammage, for instance, in reviewing Michael McKernan's *Australian Churches at War* (1980) reiterated a theme from *The Broken Years*, asserting that 'religion had some place in ritual but little in life'; especially in the AIF he knew so well. By contrast, Daniel Reynaud, a practising Christian, argued in his *Anzac Spirituality* (2018) that, based on a study of 1000 soldiers' diaries (like Gammage before him) a large minority of soldiers manifest spiritual concerns. But Gammage also hoped that 'historians of faith and historians of other things will one day start talking to each other'.

Those conversations became more likely because of the resurgence of institutions and agencies. The Memorial's revival from the late 1970s included related research grants and scholarships, conferences and a journal. Gradually, other agencies also began scholarship schemes (notably the National Library and National Archives), while the Army History Unit opened a research grants scheme and a conference which, though focusing on army history, provided funds and opportunities to conduct and present research. The Army History Unit's head, Roger Lee, formed a particularly effective relationship with academic historians Peter Dennis and Jeff Grey. They programmed a series of Chief of Army conferences, each exploring historical themes relevant to the army, each producing valuable published proceedings of papers by Australian and overseas historians. The RAN and RAAF also mounted conferences, though less consistently than the army: the other two services seemingly lacked the army's resolve, while Lee fought the corner of history repeatedly as his superiors changed, some with less regard for its value.

The 1990s were fecund years; 1990 saw the publication of the first edition of Jeff Grey's *A Military History of Australia*, the first time anyone had surveyed Australian military history from 1788, a scope so wide that when it was reviewed in the *Journal of the Australian War Memorial* we commissioned reviews by no fewer than four specialists. (They were Eric Andrews on the early 20th century, David Horner on the Second World War, Bob O'Neill on post-1945, and me, on the colonial period). The Memorial celebrated its 50th anniversary in Canberra in 1991. (Though it had first opened in Melbourne in 1922.) The celebration saw the publication of a history of the Memorial, *Here Is Their Spirit*, by Michael McKernan, its assistant director, and a special issue of the Memorial's *Journal*, offering a comprehensive analysis of the state of the field after the first intensive decade of the boom.

At that time, I headed the Memorial's Historical Research Section, and in that special issue I analysed the Research Grants Scheme which it had operated since 1976. In yet a further example of the chains of influence in the field, in looking into the scheme's files, I found that the idea had been proposed by Gavin Long, twice, in 1954 and in 1966, finally accepted by the Memorial's Board of Trustees. The first intermittent grants went to Bill Gammage, then a postgraduate; Peter Burness, an amateur military historian yet to join the Memorial's staff, where he became its longest-serving member of staff and an authority on the charge at *The Nek* (1996); and to Alec Hill, for his *Chauvel* biography. The scheme soon became an annual program, attracting increasing numbers of applications – twenty-eight in 1979, forty-nine in 1980 and sixty-three in 1981.* It always supported a range of researchers – a breakdown of its first fifteen years showed about a quarter were academic, and 40 per cent 'non-institutional researchers', though the proportion of academic historians grew as the scheme became

* I was an applicant in 1979, deservedly unsuccessful in seeking a grant for what became *The Remote Garrison*, but a year later I was responsible for running the scheme as the junior clerk in the History and Publications Section.

more competitive. Among dozens of worthwhile projects, I singled out a representative selection: Peter Pedersen's *Monash as Military Commander* (1985), Suzanne Welborn's *Lords of Death* (1982), Alan Powell's *The Shadow's Edge* (1988), David Hay's *Nothing Over Us* (1984), Michael McKernan's *The Australian People and the Great War* (1980), Robin Gerster's *Big-Noting* (1987) and Joyce Thomson's *The WAAAF in Wartime Australia* (1991). These, I wrote:

> have made a distinctive contribution to Australian military historical writing, and have enhanced the Memorial's position as a sponsor of quality. Grantees are also a mainstay of the Memorial's *Journal* and its annual conference, and now form the core of the network of expert researchers on whom the Memorial depends to advance knowledge in our field.

Sadly, over the following decade, under Steve Gower as Director, the grants scheme, the conference, and the journal would all end.

In November 1997 the Memorial launched a new popular magazine, *Wartime*. (I would have liked Peter Londey's whimsical *Beanstalk*, one of the alternatives proposed in an informal naming competition, but it was dismissed as too frivolous.) Its progenitor, Londey, one of the Memorial's senior historians, sold the idea of extending the understanding of potential visitors to the Memorial, so that they came already knowing something of the subject matter. With a popular focus, reviewing just a few books each quarterly issue, *Wartime* propagated awareness but did not foster a community of interest, and sadly the attention it needed effectively strangled the *Journal*. (And in 2024, *Wartime* itself was 'paused'. True to the spirit of the times, the announcement of the cancellation of the print edition was described as an 'exciting change'.)

Reading the book review pages of the Memorial's *Journal* in its final phase suggests how the field had matured. The April 1994 issue included, besides pieces reflecting on the interment of the Unknown Australian Soldier, which had been held at the Memorial the previous November, no fewer than twelve pages of book reviews covering twenty-four books. The reviews, almost all by historians who themselves had produced books, reveal generosity of insight which may surprise those who see historians as wary rivals. The books they reviewed included two on the Burma–Thailand railway (reviewed by Joan Beaumont), Chris Coulthard-Clark on John Mordike's *An Army for a Nation*, Kate Darian-Smith on two books on the 'home front' in the Second World War, official historian Peter Edwards on two books on the Vietnam war (including a positive reading of John Murphy's *Harvest of Fear*), Bryan Gandevia on Michael Tyquin's *Gallipoli: The medical war* (not so favourable), John McCarthy on Tom Frame's *Pacific Partners*, James Goldrick on the RAN's 1992 Coral Sea conference and Peter Dennis on John Moses's claim (in *Australia and the Kaiser's War*) that Germany threatened Australia in 1914. The books reviewed covered every period of Australian military history. (Bryan Gandevia, a Sydney thoracic surgeon who had served as a medical officer in Korea and, as a member of the Memorial's Council 1967–83, had urged it to embrace research and scholarship. A memorial bequest allows the Memorial to offer a prize to assist developing scholars in Australian military history.)

The review pages showed practitioners speaking to each other: Libby Stewart (of the Vietnam official history team) voiced disappointment over Siobhán McHugh's *Minefields and Miniskirts* (1993, on Australian women and Vietnam), and Hank Nelson explained why James Burfitt's history of the 2/18th Battalion (*Against All Odds*, 1991) was so unusual (because its members mostly spent their captivity on Blakang Mati, an island off Singapore where extraordinarily few PoWs died). George Parsons, who had himself researched the New South Wales Corps for years, praised Pamela Statham's *A Colonial Regiment* (1992, in the process reminding readers of the pioneering work of Maurice 'Bunny' Austin). Kay Saunders, herself an historian of the Second World War's effects on Australia, praised the book of the ABC radio series *When the War Came to Australia*, appreciating Joanna Penglase's skill as an interviewer. The field had almost become too fecund to even document – by the time it went 'EJ' (became an electronic journal, as the National Library's jargon had it) the *Journal* was also 'noticing' another dozen books unable to be reviewed fully. Tragically, while the *Journal* struggled on as a digital periodical (becoming ever more so, with lengthy delays in publication) the book reviews ceased, and soon so did the *Journal* in 2007. There is no longer a single forum for Australian military historians to review each others' work; and soon, there was an even wider range of books needing review and criticism.

4

HELLFIRE: RISE OF THE 'STORIANS

The mid-1990s saw further developments. Under Con Sciacca, the charismatic Labor Minister for Veterans' Affairs 1994–96, Australia embarked on a massive celebration marking the 50th anniversary of the end of the Second World War, under the rubric of 'Australia Remembers'. Fervently promoted by Sciacca and generously funded, Australia Remembers comprised an ambitious program of official pilgrimages, exhibitions, reunions, memorial dedications and other events, in which veterans of the Second World War were feted, culminating in a parade and performance in Brisbane on VP Day, 15 August 1995. (My small part in it was to curate a 50th anniversary exhibition at the Memorial, *1945: War & Peace*, out of which grew my book *Tarakan*.) Australia Remembers also revived the lowly ranked and clearly declining Department of Veterans' Affairs, which though losing veterans took on commemoration as a new program, one which has long survived 1995 itself. Though Sciacca claimed Australia Remembers to have been *Bigger than Gallipoli* (the title of Liz Reed's 2004 study of it based on her PhD) his focus was essentially on events and spectacle: besides stimulating many memoirs and family histories, relatively few books came out of it. The 50th anniversary of the war's end also saw a portentous development with implications for the future of the Pacific war, in the creation of the Australia-Japan Research Project.

Contrary to persistent Australian popular belief that 'Japan has never apologised', in fact, at least twenty formal apologies had been offered when in August 1994 Murayama Tomiichi, Prime Minister 1994–96, delivered a speech in which he expressed 'deep remorse' for the war's excesses and announced a 'Peace, Friendship and Exchange Initiative' under which Japan funded extensive research projects in collaboration with several former enemies, notably Australia. The Japanese Embassy accordingly approached the Memorial, seeking its collaboration in hosting an Australia–Japan Research Project which bravely risked public obloquy by accepting Japanese money, though in the event its academic character dampened concern. Though it was never fully jointly funded – the Memorial contributed little but housing and managing it – the project survived from 1996 to 2009, located in the Memorial's Military History Section, which I had the pleasure to head for most of that time.

Besides digitising and translating records and publishing books and articles, the Australia–Japan Research Project facilitated many exchanges between historians in the two countries. Its staff, notably Steve Bullard and Keiko Tamura, produced books (in parallel texts in English and Japanese). They included *From a Hostile Shore* (2004), which comprised essays on the war in New Guinea from both sides, and *Blankets on the Wire* (2006), which offered new insights on the Cowra outbreak. Steve Bullard's translation of the Papua volume of the Japanese official history (2007) profoundly influenced serious Australian writing on the Pacific war. From then on, no one writing about, say, Kokoda, could exclude Japanese records, and the results became clear through a succession of books, including Phillip Bradley's and Peter Williams's on the campaign. The Australia–Japan Research Project hardly influenced populist books, but a researcher's willingness to engage with the Japanese sources became a measure of their desire to reach a justifiable interpretation.

Another major development from the turn of the 20th century was symbolised by the publication of *Gallipoli* (2001) by sporting journalist Les Carlyon. Journalists have always been prominent in writing Australian military history: the two greatest official historians, Charles Bean and Gavin Long, both came out of the *Sydney Morning Herald* (an example of patronage if not apostolic succession). Journalists wrote what was to them long-form contemporary history, or journalism in hard covers, in wartime little different from officially sanctioned propaganda, such as Hector Dinning's *Nile to Aleppo* (1920) or George Johnston's *Pacific Partner* (1944), though a respected friend rates Osmar White's *Green Armour* (1945) 'one of the best Australian war books'. While journalists continued to write about conflict, official histories became the preserve of academic historians. In the 21st century they increasingly turned to write popular, if not always serious, military history.

Carlyon's *Gallipoli* was responsible, practically single-handedly, for profoundly changing the Australian perception of Gallipoli. Carlyon's version was based on surprisingly superficial research, and he grounded his portrayal largely on what he heard while visiting Turkey. Despite its length (600 pages), his *Gallipoli* was actually not really about the campaign, but about the tragically flawed British commander, Ian Hamilton, in contrast to the genius of Mustafa Kemal, later Atatürk, the father of the modern Turkish republic. In his book, Anzacs and Turks shared the ordeal of the trenches and their common enemy was the arrogant and ineffectual British. Captivated by the presentations of his Turkish guides, Carlyon paved the way for what has become known in the trade as the 'Atatürk quote', the one beginning 'Those heroes ...'. Although represented as Atatürk's words, Honest History researchers later established that it had been concocted, each for their own reasons, by a Light Horse veteran and Turkish diplomats, one wishing to reconcile with his former adversaries, the others eager to restore Turkey's reputation in and relationship with the West, battered after a succession of military coups.*

Many Australians, including public servants who should have sought advice, embraced its 'Kemalist' message of reconciliation. Supposedly addressed to Anzac mothers in 1935, it asked them to 'wipe away your tears' because 'your sons are now lying in our bosom and are in peace'. Carlyon died in 2019. By then, ironically, just as the 'Kemalist' interpretation he had fostered had come to dominate

* For over a decade from 2013, I was an active member of Honest History, a lobby group dedicated to the proposition that 'Australian history is and always has been more than Anzac', formed in anticipation of the jingoism of the 'Centenary of Anzac' and providing a counterweight to it.

Australian understanding of Gallipoli, the rise of the fundamentalist Islamic-nationalist Erdoğan regime supplanted it in Turkey. Australian visitors to Gallipoli may be the last of the Kemalists. Carlyon's *Gallipoli* can be seen as the most pernicious book in Australian military history. One sign of its influence is the proliferation of the Atatürk quote on memorials across the country, and its recitation in Anzac Day ceremonies. It is beautiful poetry, but it is not history. Still, Carlyon's *Gallipoli* won the inaugural Prime Minister's Prize for Australian History in 2007, awarded by a divided panel and on the insistence of John Howard himself. Or so the gossip said.

Carlyon followed Gallipoli's commercial success with his massive (860-page) *The Great War* (2006), which struggled to encompass the Western Front, more sentimental rhetoric than substantial research, with an absurdly low ratio of sources to text. Carlyon's successor (in both the bestseller lists and on the Memorial's Council), was the former Wallaby and also a sporting journalist, Peter FitzSimons, who extended his reach to war. After the publication of *Nancy Wake* in 2001 (*A Biography of Our Greatest War Heroine*) he published a further eight war books: *Kokoda* (2004), *Tobruk* (2006), *Gallipoli* (2014), *Fromelles and Pozières* (2014), *Victory at Villers-Bretonneux* (2017), *Breaker Morant* (2020), *The Battle of Long Tan* (2022) and *The Last Charge of the Australian Light Horse* (2023). At 250 000 words, *Tobruk* was two-and-a-half times longer than the PhDs of the academics populists often disparaged.

FitzSimons coined the term ''storian', explaining in his *Breaker Morant*, 'I have tried to bring the *story* part of this hi*story* alive by putting it in the present tense, and constructing it in the manner of a novel' (and similar sentences appear in other books). 'I want to make my account read like a novel', he explained in *Fromelles and Pozières*, admitting to bending words, tenses and times: 'I have taken documented detail from one time frame and placed it in a slightly later time'. He took 'the liberty of using that dialogue, to help bring the story to life' – his *Nancy Wake* opens with Nancy's birth, giving details as a novelist rather than an historian. Equally telling is his boast that when confronted with a conflict between a contemporary document and an elderly participant's memory, FitzSimons preferred the memory, an extraordinary admission to a professional historian.

I reviewed *Tobruk* at length in *The Australian* in 2006, to the displeasure of my boss, the Memorial's Director, Steve Gower, who would have preferred to see his Principal Historian not publicly joust with Australia's beloved sporting journalist. I described Fitzy's style as 'ocker grandioso', because of his tendency to combine Aussie slang and purple passages. I decried his lack of command of the detail – he made many errors – his tendency to resort to playground insults against the Italians and his claim, contrary to the facts, that the story 'hasn't been told before'. I also criticised his anti-British bias – actually describing British officers in the siege as 'Pommy pooftas', and his venerating Rommel but presenting Churchill (the man who did most to win the war) as the chief villain. In this prejudice he was not alone: Churchill has often been the scapegoat for nationalist Australians writing about both world wars.

FitzSimons was forward scout for a platoon of other journalist-historians, including Cameron Forbes, John Hamilton and Patrick Lindsay. Forbes produced *Hellfire: The story of Australia, Japan and the prisoners of war* (2005) and *The Korean War: Australia in the giants' playground* (2010). Hamilton published *Goodbye Cobber, God Bless You* (2004), on the charge at the Nek. Lindsay's books expressed a common theme, emphasising 'spirit': *The Spirit of the Digger* (2003), *The Spirit of Kokoda* (2003), *The Essence of Kokoda* (2005), *The Spirit of Gallipoli* (2006), *Kokoda Spirit* (2009) and *Fromelles* (2016), which banged the doomed digger drum. These authors were all accomplished writers – some had won Walkley awards for journalism – but virtually all wrote too much based on too little, and typically made too much of what they found.

Roland Perry, a protégé of Les Carlyon, has published more than twenty books, many about sport. I reviewed Perry's first war book, *Monash: The outsider who won a war* (2007), observing that my only disagreement with it was that Monash wasn't an outsider (he literally walked with prime ministers) and he didn't win the war (he was the most junior corps commander on the Western Front). It didn't stop the adulation heaped on his *Monash*, and it certainly didn't deter Perry. He went on to write further war books, including *The Australian Light Horse* (2009), actually a comparison of Harry Chauvel and TE Lawrence, culminating in 'race for Damascus' (which the Light Horse won). He also wrote *Bill the Bastard* (2012), like FitzSimons's billed as 'dramatised non-fiction'; not the first biography of an animal at war, because Ion Idriess had published *Horrie the Wog Dog* in 1945. Perry reprised that story too, but as *Horrie the War Dog* (2013), the title softened for modern sensibilities. Perry's later books also dealt with the Second World War, including *Pacific 360°* (2012). He too seemed to be driven by stories rather than history. His *Red Lead* (2020) dealt with HMAS *Perth* ship's cat. The naval historian Greg Swinden described it as setting 'a new low standard ... without a doubt the worst of the "pulp history" that has been trotted out in Australia in the past decade'. (Someone put this quotation on Perry's Wikipedia page.)

One of the key differences between the academics (or perhaps the serious historians) and the 'storians is that the latter rarely discuss the nature of the evidence, perhaps the key distinction in a distinctly democratic enterprise, in which knowledgeable 'amateurs' can hold their own with professionals. 'Storians value the story above the evidence, emphasising personalities, drama and action, leading to Fitzy's 'rat-a-tat-tat' and 'kapow!'.

As with earlier decades, journalists also wrote good books; that is, books which sought to comprehend and explain as well as to celebrate nationalist myths or sensational stories. Just as journalists have always contributed strongly to understanding Australia's wars, both at the time and later, so several writers made significant contributions, based partly on their willingness to do the necessary research. Paul Ham had been the London *Sunday Times*'s Australian correspondent for fifteen years when in 2004 he published his breakthrough book, *Kokoda*. He followed it with *Vietnam* (2007), *Hiroshima–Nagasaki* (2011) and *Passchendaele* (2016). Though long, Ham's books were at least based on his own research, if sometimes rushed; an inevitable pressure on the freelance writer.

After four decades in the Canberra press gallery, journalist Peter Rees produced a string of well-researched and well-written books on war history, including the most substantial biography of Charles Bean, *Bearing Witness*, though like previous biographies, the Great War years occupied most of the book. Rees was unusual in writing a book, *Desert Boys* (2011), on Australians in the Middle East spanning the two world wars, which explained why it was over 700 pages long. But he also produced good books on a range of war subjects. The most sophisticated of the journalist-historians was Paul Daley, now of the *Guardian* Australia, whose *Beersheba* (2010) offered not just a ride through the Light Horse's campaigns, but also a meditation on Australia's involvement in the complexities of the Middle East's history. *Beersheba*, sensitively accompanied by Mike Bowers's photographs, was short-listed for the Prime Minister's Prize for Australian History in 2011. Among the best of the former journalists-turned-historians was Mike Carlton, whose three naval history books have been highly regarded by naval enthusiasts, inclined to be somewhat discerning (see chapter 33).

Just as Bill Gammage's *The Broken Years* marked a distinct turn in Australian military history, so Jeff Grey's *A Military History of Australia* (1990) offered an opportunity to evaluate what had been achieved. In this, and in revised editions in 1999 and 2008, he traced the growing maturity of a field which in the early 1970s had barely existed separately to political and diplomatic history, generally ignored by academic historians and regarded as fit only for hobbyists and old soldiers.

Much changed in the decades following Grey's *Military History*. The Memorial revitalised its former Library, re-named a Research Centre in the mid-1980s, and increasingly opened its collections in ways which led to international researchers acknowledging its superb standards of service and accessibility. Both official and private records were catalogued and cleared (archivists sometimes finding series which had lain unsuspected in storage for decades), and later led in digitisation and the 'dissemination' enjoined in the Memorial's Act. Its website (in concert with parallel innovations by the National Archives) accelerated the popular use of military records. Its historians became players in the field, and the Memorial hosted four official history projects (see chapters 25–28). Under the same managerial impulses, its galleries were progressively and repeatedly re-developed, a process which, though begun under Brendon Kelson, reached its apogee under Steve Gower, who was director 1996–2012.

With the appointment as director of former Liberal minister Brendan Nelson in 2013 the gains of the previous three decades eroded. Formerly the product of a judicious balance between commemoration, exhibitions and research, Nelson's evangelical belief in Anzac and the nationalist impulses of the Anzac centenary made it increasingly the propaganda arm of the Defence Force (devoting disproportionate attention to the post-2001 conflicts) and diminishing the engagement of Memorial staff in the wider field. Nelson's legacy (when he left in 2018 to take up a position with an arms manufacturer donor to the Memorial) was a protracted and controversial 're-development'. It involved a massive expansion at a cost of over half a billion dollars and entailed demolishing the 20-year-old, award-winning Anzac Hall, a process approved by the Morrison government even before it was announced, and which saw a cynical disregard of public opinion. (The Memorial's standing as a trusted institution allowed it to represent public acquiescence as approval.) This did not just distort the character of a formerly revered institution – one which before 2013 had been fulfilling exactly the functions expected of it by the Australian Parliament and the people it served – but actually harmed the field it was enjoined to foster.

How did we get here? First, let's trace how Australian military history has been written, from Sydney Cove in 1788 to Uruzgan in 2014.

PART II
BEFORE ANZAC

5

BLOOD ON THE WATTLE: THE AUSTRALIAN WARS

In 1967, in a landmark referendum, Australians voted by an overwhelming majority to change the Constitution so that what are now called Aboriginal and Torres Strait Islander or First Nations peoples would be counted in the federal census and the Commonwealth Parliament could legislate for them (enabling it to challenge discriminatory state laws). The following year, the anthropologist William Stanner delivered the Australian Broadcasting Commission's prestigious annual Boyer Lectures, which he entitled After the Dreaming. Stanner spoke about what he called a 'cult of forgetfulness', in which Australians had colluded in a 'Great Australian Silence'. They neither acknowledged nor even thought of the European conquest of the Australian continent from 1788.

Charles Bean claimed in his distillation of his official history, *Anzac to Amiens*, that in 1914 Australians were proud that 'war never had happened there'. Though in the previous decade Bean had as a journalist written apprehensively of a 'race war' in the Pacific between the 'Anglo-Saxon' and the 'Oriental', he was oblivious to the fact that a 'race war' had once consumed his birthplace of Bathurst fifty years before his birth.

As the 1967 referendum suggested, Anglo-Celtic or settler Australia, itself increasingly facing demographic change from waves of non-British migration, was changing. It signified that at last, just as the 'Silence' had been named, it was to end.

Australia's Indigenous people had, of course, always known of the conflict which had led to what Charles Rowley, another pioneering scholar, called *The Destruction of Aboriginal Society* (1970), his most influential book. Following the 1967 referendum, a generation of younger historians ended white Australia's silence. Henry Reynolds, who was 30 in 1968, researched the history of colonialism in north Queensland, where he taught. He and his post-graduates led what was to become over the ensuing forty years a wave of scholarship which decisively changed our history. White Australians had traditionally venerated what they called explorers and pioneers, representing the settlement of Australia as a heroic struggle against a harsh and unforgiving environment. The continent's original inhabitants were a colourful and inconvenient irrelevance, who had impeded settlement before being 'dispersed'. Reynolds's *The Other Side of the Frontier* (1982) comprehensively showed for the first time that 'settlement' had been anything but peaceful, and had seen violence virtually everywhere, effectively a war, or a series of small wars, in which First Nations peoples had, sooner or later and with degrees of devastation, always lost. In the meantime, other historians discovered and wrote about episodes in the conflict, such as the Tasmanian-born Lloyd Robson, who in 1980 published a children's book, *To the Last Breath*, a book of just 120 pages which documented 'The Coming of the Invaders', 'The Black Line' and 'Tales of Atrocities'. Surprisingly, Bruce Elder, a freelance author of travelogues and Australian editor of *Trivial Pursuit*, published what might be seen as the first mainstream book in the field, *Blood on the Wattle*, in 1988.*

Over the succeeding decades Reynolds became the premier scholar, followed both by white academics and historians and increasingly by Indigenous researchers, all discovering, or re-discovering, the long and tragic history of the conflicts which followed British settlement in 1788. This unprecedented boom in research has produced a huge literature of dozens, perhaps hundreds of books. The explosion traced the course of those conflicts across the continent as the frontier moved beyond the initial colonial footholds, and through more than a century until,

* Wikipedia advises that *Blood on the Wattle* was 'listed as one of the ten most influential Australian works of non-fiction in the twentieth century' in a poll conducted by the *Sydney Morning Herald* and *The Age*.

around 1900 (on the eve of the federation of the six British colonies of Australia) most of the continent could be said to have been occupied. Conflict continued, as did the degradation of Indigenous people into the 20th century.

Not that everyone accepted that the conflict that punctuated the expansion of the frontier deserved the description of a 'war'. In 1981, as a young researcher who'd been at the Memorial for less than a year, I gave a paper at one of its early history conferences in which I described how (British military) Mounted Police had attacked and massacred Kamilaroi on the banks of a creek on the Gwydir River, 'while acting under orders' (as its commander, Major James Nunn, wrote). Many present (including scholars I came to admire, such as Alec Hill) rejected my argument that this was war, quoting Carl von Clausewitz's text *On War*. Some continue to hold the view, arguing that (if they accept that it happened at all) violence between spear-wielding tribal warriors and (often) stockmen, squatters or policemen cannot be seen as war.

The deniers are now very much a recalcitrant rump, and it is now accepted by virtually all Australian historians that between 1788 and about 1928, First Nations peoples and settlers fought an intermittent but extensive series of small-scale conflicts as settlement extended across the continent. Beginning with Watkin Tench's clumsy expeditions to seize the heads of defiant Eora around Botany Bay in 1788, frontier conflict continued until in 1928 at Coniston Station, 160 miles north-west of Alice Springs, Territory police killed at least thirty Walpiri people in retaliation for the murder of a dingo shooter who had abused Aboriginal women. With this, the last officially sanctioned massacre on the frontier, the killings might be seen to have ended, although the dispossession, impoverishment and structural disadvantage of Australia's Indigenous people was to continue, sadly, up to the present.

The past forty years, accompanying the revival of interest in and research on frontier violence, have seen many attempts to commemorate the events of frontier conflict, and memorials have been created at many places, especially the scenes of massacres. Increasingly, tentative commemoration, oral history and storytelling by Indigenous communities has combined with traditional scholarship to create a comprehensive picture of their course and consequences. Many of these books are painful to read, recording as they do the deaths by violence of an unknown number of First Nations people but it's probably comparable to Australia's deaths in the two world wars. Estimates range from 20 000 – almost certainly too low – to 100 000 – perhaps too high. But between 40–60 000 deaths over a century makes what are increasingly called 'the Australian Wars' among Australia's most costly.

An important element in the evolving story of frontier conflict is the way in which it has been gradually accepted by Australian historians, by communities, by university and school curricula and by historical institutions such as museums. Key steps in the period 1990–2005 were the publication of three works by authors who could not in any sense be seen as long-haired pinko ratbags: Jeff Grey's pioneering *A Military History of Australia* (1990) included a chapter placing frontier violence at the beginning of Australia's military history. His colleague John Connor clinically analysed *The Australian Frontier Wars 1788–1838* as a series of counter-insurgency conflicts. In 2006 John Coates documented frontier massacres as the opening section of his *Atlas of Australia's Wars*. All three authors came from UNSW Canberra. Books on frontier conflict are now seen as Australian military history's single most fertile aspect.

A crucial strand in this saga has been the attitude of the Australian War Memorial. From the early 1980s the Memorial received requests to recognise frontier conflict, from within its staff and outside. For many years lobbying made no impression on an institution which sought to protect the 'Anzac legend' from supposedly being sullied by an association with a discreditable racist conflict. Arguments have continued for decades over whether the conflict should justifiably be described as war, and over aspects of its representation in a commemorative museum. During the tenure of Brendan Nelson as director (2013–19) change seemed imminent. Though in 2013 Nelson had proclaimed that frontier conflict would never appear in the Memorial 'on my watch', in 2020 Stephen Gapps's *The Sydney Wars* won the Memorial's inaugural Les Carlyon prize. At the same time, Nelson had acquired expensive works of Indigenous art depicting massacres, perplexingly displayed in the galleries without comment.

In 2022, the argument passed a decisive point. Rachel Perkins's documentary series *The Australian Wars* aired. Featuring a range of both Indigenous and non-Indigenous testimony and expertise, it framed the long-running debate around a new title, one swiftly gaining favour in the field. Months later, Kim Beazley, the chair of the Memorial's Council, publicly accepted that frontier conflict should be accorded 'substantial representation' in exhibition galleries presently under development. How thoroughly the Memorial acts upon that intent remains to be seen: members of Beazley's Council, notably Major-General Greg Melick, soon publicly contested the idea, without being disciplined.* In the meantime, David Marr's *Killing for Country* (2023) appeared, mounting a powerful argument for facing the truth.

The field is swiftly changing, with new scholarship supporting assertive remembrance within First Nations communities. An historical conference in Bathurst in August 2024, hosted by Wiradjuri elders, marked the bicentenary of Governor Brisbane's declaration of martial law. In a session chaired by Stephen Gapps (author of the recently published *Gudyarra*, on the Bathurst war of 1824) three researchers spoke, each offering new contributions. Mina Murray, an emerging Wiradjuri scholar, had published her work in the magazine *Wartime* (a sign of the Memorial's ambivalence, its historians bravely fostering scholarship while its Council dodges and weaves). Jack Clear discussed his recent PhD thesis, on the extent of Wiradjuri resistance – his interest sparked by an article Bill Gammage published forty years before on the 'Narrandera wars'. Ray Kerkhove summarised his ground-breaking work on Aboriginal tactics, based on his *How They Fought* (2023). Later, David Marr spoke, linking the 1824 Bathurst war to the wider saga of resistance and repression. The argument over the Australian Wars continues.

---

* The Memorial's most recent responses to representations from the lobby group Defending Country's (in August 2024) continue to insist that frontier conflict will be included in a projected 'Pre-1914 gallery', one that occupies just 1.1% of its massively expanded galleries. That conflict fundamental to the continent's settlement which cost tens of thousands of lives should be accorded such a derisory proportion of its galleries undermines its Chairman's undertaking that it be accorded 'substantial representation'.

6

BUT LITTLE GLORY: COLONIAL MILITARY HISTORY

The 'British' period in Australia's colonial military history has always been its Cinderella. Not until 'Bunny' Austin published *The Army in Australia 1840–50* in 1979 did any book-length study appear, and when it did, it was on the British garrison's least significant decade. Austin, a regular officer who had had served in the Second World War and Korea, devoted his retirement from 1971 to researching military history, and especially the period before 1850. Another army officer, Clem Sargent, Colonel-in-Chief of the Royal Australian Survey Corps, pursued a deep interest in regiments which served in Australia after fighting in the Peninsular war. He collected scarce books (the only copies in Australia of some rare books were in Clem's study), bought their medals (also rare and expensive) and in 1996 self-published *A Colonial Garrison*, on the 48th Regiment in New South Wales and Van Diemen's Land.

Both Bunny and Clem encouraged my own interest in this subject, which I began while an unemployed teacher in 1979 and which produced *The Remote Garrison: The British Army in Australia 1788–1870* (1986), which was particularly aimed at family researchers. It was illustrated by Lindsay Cox, himself an authority on Victoria's élite horse artillery. The most subtle and perceptive book on colonial military history must be Craig Wilcox's *Redcoat Dreaming* (2009), a delightfully innovative exploration of aspects of the relationship between what Wilcox's mentor, Ken Inglis, had called *The Australian Colonists* (1974) and the red-coated soldiers that they thought of when anyone talked of 'the army'.

Apart from Aboriginal resistance and the pursuit of runaway convicts and bushrangers (from the 1820s largely left to the military

Mounted Police, which awaits a history) the largest action fought by British soldiers was the attack on the Eureka Stockade, on the Ballarat goldfield at dawn on 3 December 1854. Though Eureka remains a profoundly important event in Australia's political history, and though it has been the subject of dozens of books, only one study, Greg Blake's *To Pierce the Tyrant's Heart* (2009), has addressed the event as a military history. Otherwise, for the most part, the British troops remain a shadowy presence, as suggested by the title of my book on them, *The Remote Garrison*.

The six colonies' military (and for some naval) forces each have enthusiasts, most amateurs, and most colonies remain surprisingly neglected. DH Johnson's *Volunteers at Heart: The Queensland Defence Force 1860–1901* appeared in 1975, expected to 'lead to more histories of colonial defence forces': it did not. The only general survey is Bob Nicholls's *The Colonial Volunteers* (1988), but book-length histories of some aspects include Lindsay Cox's *The Galloping Guns* (1986), Winty Calder on *Colonel Tom Price and the Victorian Mounted Rifles* (1985) or George Ward's *Victorian Land Forces 1853–1883* (1989). Tasmania has several studies of some of its units, mostly by Doug Wyatt (*A Lion in the Colony*, 1990), representative of the expert amateurs who remain the mainstay of colonial military history, but Victoria has only gained its most recent military history in Bob Marmion and Andrew Dagg's *Gibraltar of the South* in 2024. Astonishingly, no general history of New South Wales's forces has appeared, and Hans Zwillenberg's thesis on South Australia's forces was only partly published, but in the amateur journal *Sabretache* forty years ago.

If the colonial armies have been poorly served, their navies still have only one general history, though it is an excellent one, in Colin Jones's *Australian Colonial Navies*, one of the first books published by the reinvigorated Australian War Memorial, in 1985. It deals with the despatch of the Victorian colonial warship, *Victoria*, to the Taranaki war in 1860, colonial Australia's first, and bloodless, overseas commitment.

Colonial Australia's trans-Tasman connections have seen its most innovative approaches. In 1984, RAAF padre Frank Glenn dealt with the Australians who joined the Waikato Militia in the 1860s serving *For Glory and a Farm*. In 2009 Jeff Hopkins-Wiese published *Blood Brothers: The Anzac genesis*, arguing unconvincingly that an 'Anzac spirit' began not on Gallipoli but in 'shared military struggles' against Māori resistance to British settlement. In 2022 Craig Wilcox's *Australia's Tasman Wars* authoritatively presented the episode in an imperial and colonial context.

Colonial Australia engaged in three larger overseas expeditions: to the Sudan in 1885, to China against the nationalist rebels dismissively nicknamed 'Boxers' in 1900, and the conflict remains Australia's third most costly external war, in South Africa, 1899–1902.

The Sudan contingent has barely attracted new work since three books produced to coincide with the expedition's centenary in 1985. The two rival military historical societies, of New South Wales and the larger national body, each published histories, in Ralph Sutton's quaintly titled *Soldiers of the Queen: War in the Soudan* and the Military Historical Society of Australia's *But Little Glory* (which I edited). (A New South Wales officer wrote that the contingent entailed 'much sweat, but little glory'.) More significantly, Ken Inglis, already one of the country's most notable historians, perhaps surprisingly published *The Rehearsal*, in which he treated the eccentric little expedition seriously, examining not just its comic opera formation and its virtual unemployment once in the Sudan, but revealed its significance as a harbinger of overseas wars to come (a view that Lloyd Robson found unpersuasive). The Sudan contingent makes clear the extent to which colonial military history was and largely remains neglected. In *But Little Glory*, Paul Macpherson, a Memorial librarian, contributed a bibliography. He found that in the half-century after 1885 only twenty-five pieces had appeared. (Curiously, not a single item of the ninety-six he found used the word 'forgotten' in the title.)

The Australian colonies' contribution to the suppression of the 'Boxer' rebellion was entirely a naval affair, documented by former sailor Bob Nicholls in *Bluejackets and Boxers* (1986) and more authoritatively by schoolteacher Justin Corfield in his *Australian Illustrated Encyclopaedia of the Boxer Uprising 1899–1901* (2001).

The largest of the imperial conflicts, in South Africa, has attracted a suitably large body of work, like other colonial subjects a mixture of expert amateurs with a few professional or academic authors. Despite its scale, South Africa was long overshadowed by the world wars. Its earliest chroniclers were of course memoirists, but even its supposed 'official records', compiled by a staff officer, Pembroke Murray in 1911, was merely a statistical summary and nominal roll of Australian contingents. Later in the 20th century it attracted serious amateur attention, by authors such as Max Chamberlain, a Melbourne accountant, who published one of the earliest of the new wave, *To Shoot and Ride* (1967). His mantle was taken up by Robin Droogleever, who, as well as convening an active Anglo-Boer War Research Group and publishing several histories of individual contingents, collaborated with Chamberlain on *The War with Johnny Boer* (2003), effectively an encyclopaedia of Australia's part in the war.

John Barrett, reviewing Bob Wallace's *The Australians at the Boer War* (1976) in *Historical Studies*, praised him as 'one of those amateur historians who frequently give professionals cause to stop and think' (Wallace had worked for 'the PMG' – what became Australia Post and Telecom), writing 'informatively and fairly'. Barrett later reviewed Laurie Field's *The Forgotten War* (1979) and judged that it 'does not add much to our understanding as it might have'; compared to Wallace. Barrett, a Methodist minister as well as an academic historian, valued Wallace's factual integrity while Field was 'an anti-imperialist who cannot escape his point of view'.*

The Memorial's contribution to the centenary of the South African war was to commission a quasi-official history of Australia's part in it. The historian chosen was Craig Wilcox, who had completed a PhD with Ken Inglis on citizen soldiering, published through the Army History Unit. Wilcox, who used a wider range of sources than any previous author on the war, brought to what became (at the publisher's

* Laurie Field had served with 460 Squadron in the bomber offensive and researched a history of it, his hopes of publication foiled by his untimely death. Peter Rees used his papers (in the AWM) in writing *Lancaster Men*.

request) *Australia's Boer War* (2002; the Memorial's historians had previously preferred 'South African' or 'Anglo-Boer' war – because it wasn't entirely the Boers' fault). Wilcox offered sharp and fresh insights into the war and the Australian colonies' contribution. He structured his book in a novel way, alternating narrative chapters with discussions of aspects such as logistics, the supply of horses and opposition to the war. One of the pleasures of managing the project (which I did as the Memorial's Principal Historian) was that the distinguished historian Geoffrey Blainey, a member of Council, advised Wilcox, a relationship from which both Craig and I benefited, not least in connecting the war to colonial society.

Australian interest in the Boer War has been unduly skewed by the crimes and executions of Harry 'Breaker' Morant and Peter Handcock, who were convicted of murdering up to a dozen civilians, and were then executed by firing squad in Pretoria in February 1902. Interest in 'Breaker Morant' (Handcock was often left out) was piqued by Bruce Beresford's 1980 film of that name. While (as the film acknowledged) their trial was flawed, it also made clear that they were guilty of multiple murders. The film was based on the 1978 play *Breaker Morant* by Kenneth Ross. *The Breaker* (1973) by freelance writer Kit Denton also presented the pair as victims of British injustice, and accordingly sold well to readers excited by the new nationalism of the Whitlam years. When in 1983 Denton published the non-fiction *Closed File*, his re-think of the case (which presented them much less sympathetically), it was remaindered.

For a couple of decades several enthusiasts have conducted a campaign to secure a pardon for Morant and Handcock. This has been mounted by an ex-naval lawyer, James Unkles, who bases his case on legal technicalities, and by the 2002 book *Shoot Straight, You Bastards!* In it, television producer Nick Bleszynski purported to tell *The Truth Behind the Killing of 'Breaker' Morant*, which, lacking definitive evidence, bizarrely imagined dialogue in heaven between Lord Kitchener (the villain of the piece) and Morant. (Handcock was again overlooked.) Craig Wilcox offered a more temperate view in his *Australia's Boer War*.

Curiously, when the nationalist-republican 'storian Peter Fitz-Simons turned his squad of researchers to the Morant-Handcock case, though he called his 2020 book *Breaker Morant* (*'The Epic Story of the Boer War and Harry "Breaker" Morant: Drover, Horseman, Bush Poet, Murderer or Hero?'*) he actually declared for the Morant-as-villain camp. (He reached this conclusion: 'a killer he was', related on p. 498, accepting the unanimous verdict of his tribe of research assistants.) The turmoil continues: in 2024 the Adelaide City Council faced advocates lobbying for and against adding Morant's name to South Australia's Boer War memorial. They failed. The Council unanamously rejected the proposal, rightly – surely, Australian soldiers who kill civilians unlawfully forfeit any claim to honourable commemoration.

Colonial military history remains largely an amateur ghetto. The reason, of course, is that Australian military history has long been associated with the idea of national identity, and pith helmets and imperial wars sit oddly with that cause.

7

LION AND KANGAROO: THE FEDERAL YEARS

By the time the Boer War had ended, the six Australian colonies had federated. Fifty years of colonial anxiety bequeathed to the new nation a fundamental sense of insecurity, one sharpened by the rise of Japan as a naval power. Despite Japan's alliance with Britain from 1902, Australians remained apprehensive (such as Charles Bean, who anticipated a race war in the Pacific). Neville Meaney explored this crucial period in his *The Search for Security in the Pacific, 1901–14* (1976). Though criticised as making a more explicitly nationalist case than the evidence warranted, Meaney's book has rightly influenced those seeking to understand why in the decade after federation Australia created both a large citizen army intended for defence (supposedly against Japan) and a large 'fleet unit' which played a part in British naval strategy in and beyond Australian waters. The federal period is notable for the foundation of what became the Royal Australian Navy, a subject of compelling interest to naval historians.

The tension between an Australian agenda and duty to the empire is explicitly the core of John Mordike's *An Army for a Nation* (1992). Mordike, another soldier–scholar, found evidence that Australian governments secretly but willingly signed up to commit troops to an imperial war, which is exactly what happened in 1914. Mordike's bland sub-title, *A history of Australian military developments 1880–1914*, belied the profundity of his argument. It sparked one of the few genuine controversies in Australian military history, contested with verve by Craig Wilcox, author of *For Hearths and Homes*, a history of Australian citizen forces, which were explicitly directed to home defence. Ten years on, Mordike persuasively substantiated his argument in *We Should Do This Thing Quietly* (2002).

The new nation grappled with how it should meet the challenge of defending a small, self-consciously 'white' nation, anxious about a 'race war' with Japan. Chris Coulthard-Clark's *The Citizen General Staff* (1976) showed how the nation's military intellectuals anticipated an inevitable conflict (though with Japan, not imperial Germany). Thomas Tanner's *Compulsory Citizen Soldiers* (1980) and especially John Barrett's *Falling In* (1979) revealed the expedient of conscripting youths. Michael McKernan described Barrett's as a 'frankly revisionist' book because it challenged the assumption, stemming from a projection of the defeat of conscription in 1916 and 1917, that Australians were independent-minded: Barrett showed the conformist reality.

The federal period is little studied in itself, invariably seen as the precursor for the great trauma that the nation and its people faced from 1914. It saw the growth and consolidation of the sense of Australian identity, often expressed by phrases like 'Australasian Britons', a feeling explored by the prolific and respected journalist Gavin Souter in his *Lion and Kangaroo: The initiation of Australia 1901–1919* (1976). Spanning the decades before and of the Great War, it reminds us of the artificiality of what historians call 'periodisation' (but which I'm following in this book). The idea of 'race' infused the federal period, and Peter Cochrane's brilliantly argumentative *Best We Forget: The war for white Australia, 1914–18* (2018) showed how closely the defence of a 'White Australia' was connected to Australia's compliance. And that brings us to the Great War itself, a seismic event not just in Australia's military history but a trauma with which the nation and its people lived over the succeeding century.

PART III
THE GREAT WAR AND AFTER

8

ANZAC BATTLEFIELD: GALLIPOLI

The twenty-fifth of April is the day upon which Australians formally remember all those who served and died in war, but especially those who landed on – invaded – the coast of Ottoman Turkey in 1915. It is without doubt the single most intensively researched day in Australian military history – but only since about 1970. In considering the re-discovery of the Australian history of Gallipoli, then, we need to start not with Bean's official history *The Story of Anzac*, nor with classic battalion histories like Cyril Longmore's *The Old Sixteenth* (1929) or memoirs such as *Jacka's Mob* (1933, by Edgar Rule, a decorated officer of the 14th Battalion). Rather, the re-discovery goes back to the journalist and war correspondent Alan Moorehead. Educated at Scotch College, Melbourne, between the wars he had, as biographer Ann Moyal explained in her *Alan Moorehead*, 'stood through the ceremonies each Anzac Day', thinking when he left Australia in 1936 that he would 'never again expose myself to the idea of Anzac'. A chance meeting in Italy with a visiting Anzac veteran in the early 1950s left him 'captivated' by a subject he had disdained and, after visiting Turkey and steeping himself in the published sources, he wrote *Gallipoli*. Published in 1956, it was an immediate international success. In Australia, bookshop windows were cleared to display it and Charles Bean declared it 'brilliant and sympathetic'. Since Moorehead's *Gallipoli*, another of his biographers, Thornton McCamish, wrote, a 'great cairn of Anzac books have piled up'.

One of the strengths of Moorehead's *Gallipoli*, the journalist's seizing on the fitting individual story, reflected a peculiarly Australian attitude to understanding war, one quite distinct from that prevailing especially in Britain, whose official history, unlike Bean's, rarely mentioned any but officers. As David Kent put it in the preface to his *From Trench and Troopship* (1999), 'I have learned more about the Gallipoli misadventure from Private Albert Facey than from General Sir Ian Hamilton …'. (That it later became clear, from his AIF file, that Facey's account of the landing at Anzac was entirely imagined, makes Kent's faith somewhat ironic: see chapter 32.) A counter view emerged only when Alec Hill's disciples, scholars mainly associated with the Australian army, began to pursue generals' biographies purposefully. This contest has been won handsomely by those favouring personal stories over synoptic insights.

In the 1990s Gallipoli studies in Australia gained the boost of the film *Gallipoli*, for which Bill Gammage was Peter Weir's advisor. Joan Beaumont observed that for a decade, every university tutorial she led saw students (when they could be induced to speak) comment on the Great War by referring to the film. Despite the film's popular influence, however, relatively few books appeared on the campaign, with the exceptions of Kevin Fewster's *Gallipoli Correspondent* (1983, based on Charles Bean's diary) and Phil Taylor and Pam Cupper's *Gallipoli: A battlefield guide* (1989), which surely helped the authors of later books in visiting the peninsula. A decisive step was the publication of John Robertson's magisterial and sadly posthumous *Anzac and Empire* (1990), surprisingly for an academic book sub-titled *The tragedy and glory of Gallipoli*. Robertson's book put what might be regarded as the classic post-Bean account, one which the succeeding decades would elaborate and even distort.

Denis Winter, a British schoolmaster historian who had produced the iconoclastic *Death's Men* and *The First of the Few* (which presented the grim reality of life in the trenches and in the air during the Great War) arrived in Australia as a PhD candidate to write the biography of Charles Bean. The biography was unfortunately never published, but by-products included his selections of the best-of-Bean, *Making the Legend* (1992) and *25 April 1915* (1994), the first book-length re-evaluation of the invasion since Robert Rhodes James's *Gallipoli* of 1965. Winter also published *Haig's Command* (1991), a revisionist book on the Western Front denounced by those outraged at Winter's claims that archival records had been 'filleted'. The extremity of Winter's claims made his Gallipoli book suspect, and despite what I called his 'unjustifiably casual approach to sources' in *25 April* he produced the first serious revision of the landing, arguing that it was not made in the wrong place. (A throwaway line in Bean's first volume – 'The damn fools have landed us a mile too far north!' – had derailed the story for a century.) Winter implicitly endorsed Chris Roberts's pioneering revision of the invasion, published in the Memorial's *Journal* in 1992, the subject of his book *The Landing at Anzac* (2013). Gallipoli was coming under sustained scrutiny, though in the hands of the 'storians, the myth retained its power.

In the early 21st century a distinct difference grew between the popular nationalists and the academic internationalists. A flood of Gallipoli books appeared – at least two dozen in the decade after Carlyon's blockbuster, *Gallipoli*, including my own *Quinn's Post*. Although Robin Prior of UNSW Canberra had jokingly proposed awarding grants to writers *not* to produce more books about Gallipoli, he wrote another, *Gallipoli* (2009), optimistically sub-titled *The end of the myth*. This pious hope could not stand against the impulse of the centenary, and even I published two more explicitly Gallipoli-focused books, in 2014 and 2015, *Lost Boys of Anzac* (tracing the fates of the men of the first wave to land who died on the 25th) and *Die in Battle, Do Not Despair*, the first book on Indians on Gallipoli, which drew crucially upon Anzac evidence.

Several developments in Gallipoli studies became apparent as the 'Anzac Centenary' approached. First, more popular books than ever appeared, with many 'storians such as Peter FitzSimons, John Hamilton and Jonathan King essentially re-telling the familiar national epic. Second, paradoxically, scholarly Gallipoli studies went 'transnational': having begun rooted in national stories, it evolved to address the relationships between the contending forces, a synthesis best evident in the work of Rhys Crawley, author of *Climax at Gallipoli* (2014). An early melding of the 'personal stories' and international approaches came in *Men of Gallipoli* (1976) by Peter Liddle, who then worked at Sunderland Polytechnic in Britain. Liddle's book was (as Lloyd Robson wrote), based on a simple idea: 'you gather all the diaries and letters ... and organise the material into a chronological order'. The result, Robson wrote in 1978, was an 'indispensable' book. Unfortunately, Liddle induced aged Gallipoli veterans from Australia and New Zealand to part with their records, which are now in the Liddle Collection in Leeds. His foray led Bill Gammage to beseech the Alexander Turnbull Library in Wellington to start collecting Great War records. In this my own Gallipoli work was representative. My *Quinn's Post* explicitly dealt with the Australians *and* New Zealanders who held the post. Two companion books sponsored by the Army History Unit, Chris Roberts's *The Landing at Anzac* (2013) and Mesut Uyar's *The Ottoman Defence Against the Anzac Landing* (2015), offered complementary views from both sides of the hill. Thirdly, the physical study of the landscape of Gallipoli came under scrutiny (and again, *Quinn's Post* offered the first 'biography of a place' on the peninsula). This trend produced Antonio Sagona and colleagues' *Anzac Battlefield* (2016), a massive international and interdisciplinary collaborative study, involving historians and archeologists including Richard Reid of Veterans' Affairs. In the perhaps inevitable slump after the centenary (the decade after 2015 saw many fewer books than the one before) its impact has yet to be seen, but we might suspect that Gallipoli, annually refreshed, will regain its former prominence.

9

DIGGERS IN FRANCE: THE WESTERN FRONT

From mid-1916 to the war's end, Australian troops fought on the Western Front, the theatre in which the war was decided. The five Australian infantry divisions served as part of a huge British empire force: not the usual story told by the hundreds of Australian books on the subject. Forty thousand Australians died in France and Belgium, the most intense slaughter the nation has ever endured, an ordeal explaining its prominence in Australian military history. The reasons for the often exaggerated presentation of the AIF's part lies in its losses, the drama of the experience, in the perennial nationalism inherent in most nations' war history, and in the natural tendency of participants to seek to find meaning in their part in such a tragic conflict.

Anticipating the official history, the AIF's survivors were of course the first to describe their war in memoirs and histories, notably John Monash, the commander of the Australian Corps in 1918. Monash's *The Australian Victories in France*, hastily written in 1919, became a bestseller, anticipating Bean's official history volumes on 1918 by two decades. Monash's account set the pattern for virtually all later interpretations, in which a citizen force of unrivalled skill under exemplary leadership – Monash's – surpassed the uneven and often ineptly led British to prevail. Staniforth Smith's *Australian Campaigns in the Great War*, though (as Ernest Scott, professor of history at Melbourne wrote in its Preface) 'different in design and scope from any which have yet been published', faded from memory. Smith had sought to avoid the 'purple' writing which had coloured wartime reportage.

He offered 'a sincere endeavour to describe battles ... tersely, accurately and clearly': but not to the public taste.

Although all but the final months of the war had seen a succession of costly failures, the litany of the AIF's battles, inscribed on memorials across the nation – Pozières, Bullecourt, Messines, Ypres and Villers-Bretonneux – became a saga of triumph. The AIF's main chroniclers were its aging members, as if only participation entitled commentary. Battalion histories collectively constituted a communal remembrance of shared achievement and loss. Though celebrated every April, with 'Returned Men' a fixed, venerated and powerful part of Australian society, the AIF's history remained unexplored except in the volumes of the official history and in unit histories.

The outbreak of a second world war eclipsed interest in what became the First World War. One measure of the atrophy of enquiry is that of the 132 books cited in Patsy Adam-Smith's *The Anzacs* (1978), fewer than one in five had been published after 1945. Until the 1980s, the sheer authority of Bean's history tended to deter inquiry: for all the respectful commemoration of Anzac Day and Remembrance Day there seemed to be no impetus to research. Even the fiftieth anniversary of the Great War brought no weighty re-evaluation, though it impelled some Australian historians to start to think about it. Most, preoccupied with colonial history, national identity, the history of the labour movement and political history, remained indifferent to the war that had in many ways dominated their lives. Ken Inglis, having been born in 1929, the son of a father too young to serve, later realised that, like Australia as a whole, he 'forgot Anzac for some years'. The Western Front, Australia's most intense ordeal in war, remained for over fifty years respected and commemorated but increasingly marginal to Australian life and its history. Gammage's *The Broken Years* did not by itself break that drought. Lloyd Robson's *The First AIF* (probably stimulated by turmoil over conscription during the Vietnam years) had appeared in 1970 – but it both prompted interest in a neglected facet of Australian history, and alerted researchers to unexploited riches in the Memorial's collection especially.

The Queensland journalist Peter Charlton published *Pozières* (1986), one of the first of a new wave of Western Front histories. Lloyd Robson found Charlton's book 'simplistic', but those wishing to understand the 'haemorrhaging' of Australia in the Great War thought it 'as good a place to start as any' – not, note, Bean's volumes. As with Gallipoli, the succeeding revival of interest in the Western Front saw from the 1980s an explosion of studies of all kinds – unit and battle studies, biographies and works of social history, many combining those approaches – and at all levels from academic works to popular, amateur and family history books and articles.

There is a standard narrative of the AIF's service in France, most recently set out by Richard Travers's *Diggers in France* (2008). In the orthodox view, based on a great range of (it has to be said, published) sources, Travers 'describes the experience of the diggers in the authentic voice of the young soldiers who offered their lives in service of their country'. But Travers's references, like many populists', read 'Monash, *Australian Victories* ... ' and then twelve '*ibids*' – it was his first book. It's hard to escape the orthodox narrative – almost every popular or amateur book dealing with 1918, for example, quotes the all-too familiar passage in Monash's book in which he compares the co-ordination required to launch attacks using 'all arms' with an orchestra (with Monash as the conductor). The problem is that none of these admirers have looked beyond the boundaries of the Australian Corps, quoting Monash as if he invented combined-arms offensive tactics. In fact, by 1918 the methods Monash applied – skillfully – were standard in the British armies in France. Thirty years of British Western Front research – usually summed up as the 'learning curve' interpretation – has established this beyond dispute, but it's a view Australian popular writers have yet to accept or even discover.*

* A good example of the boosting so often expressed in Australian writing about 1918 especially is the sub-title of Stephen Dando-Collins's *Heroes of Hamel* (2018): *The Australians and Americans whose WWI victory changed modern warfare.* On the scale of the Western Front, Hamel was a minor raid. It straightened out a German salient; that's all.

Who has gone beyond this parochial view? The answer is an impressive clutch of historians: Dale Blair, David Coombes, Craig Deayton, Meleah Hampton, and especially Peter Pedersen and Robin Prior, representing academic and non-institutional writers, albeit academically trained. (Although enthusiasts can contribute to serious history, the complexity of substantial operational research especially demands specialist knowledge and levels of research skill not easily acquired on weekends and evenings.)

Dale Blair, author of a penetrating history of the 1st Battalion (*Dinkum Diggers*, 2001), also wrote both *The Battle of Bellicourt Tunnel* (2011) and *No Quarter* (2005), a study of *Unlawful killing and surrender* in the Great War. David Coombes, like Blair a non-institutional historian, has published several biographies (of Talbot Hobbs and Leslie Morshead, and of Australian PoWs on the Western Front). His *A Greater Sum of Sorrow* (2016) deals with the two battles of Bullecourt, which remain oddly neglected. Craig Deayton, author of a well-regarded history of the 47th Battalion, published *At Any Price*, a study of *The Anzacs in the Battle of Messines 1917* (2017). Though essentially dealing with the Australian part in the battle, Deayton (as his title suggested) included the New Zealanders – surprisingly, perhaps, one of the few battles in which the two dominions' troops fought together. Like many authors of 'battle' books, Deayton adapted his research for a volume of the 'Campaign' studies published by the Army History Unit. Meleah Hampton, formerly of the Memorial, wrote (under Prior's supervision) a revisionist PhD published in 2016 as *Attack on the Somme: 1st Anzac Corps and the Battle of Pozières Ridge, 1916*. She produced a dispassionate and detailed study of a battle in which the scale and pathos of loss is traditionally emphasised (but it was published in Britain: the National Library doesn't have a copy of it, though it does have the 'Campaign' book she also produced). Peter Pedersen, author of *Monash as Military Commander*, later commanded 5/7 RAR, and then joined the Memorial as head of its Research Centre. He produced both the detailed and insightful *The Anzacs* (2007) and a battlefield guide to *Anzacs on the Western Front* (2011), written in collaboration with Chris Roberts, a retired brigadier and the most energetic proponent of the idea that military training makes better military history. Robin Prior of UNSW Canberra, with his University of Adelaide colleague, Trevor Wilson, produced *Passchendaele: The untold story* (1996) and *The Somme* (2005), reminders that although not writing centrally in the field of Australian military history, Australian historians could make decisive contributions to the understanding of a subject of international significance.*

Episodes in the Great War have attracted uneven and disproportionate attention. The action at Noreuil in 1917 (one of the 'outpost fights' in the advance to the Hindenburg Line) was not treated until Andrew Faulkner published *Guts, Glory and Blunders: Noreuil, 1917* (2024), for once justified in describing it as *The Forgotten Fight*. This contrasts with the attention paid to the one night of battle at Fromelles (admittedly Australia's most costly), which has been the subject of a score of books, virtually all popular. (Except for Roger Lee's *British Battle Planning in 1916 and the Battle of Fromelles* (2015), another of the relevant books not in the National Library.) Lee's thesis, written under the supervision of Jeff Grey, argued that Fromelles was part of the evolution of British command methods, eschewing the sensational exceptionalism of almost all other Australian books on the battle.)

The claim by Victorian schoolteacher Lambis Englezos that an undiscovered mass grave lay beside Pheasant Wood within the German lines in 1916 turned out to be true. Building on Robin Corfield's authoritative *Don't Forget Me, Cobber* (2000) Englezos pressed his campaign in the face of what he called 'active discouragement and incredulity from the authorities'. Bill Gammage accepted Lambis's argument, but I was one of the sceptics. We had to accept the truth of his claims when in 2008 remains were found: I ate humble pie on the front page of *The Australian*. But claims that 'Fromelles' had been 'forgotten' – the perennial plaint of populist writers and especially publishers' blurb-writers – were unjustified. Bean's Volume III had devoted two

* Prior and Wilson would be the first to insist that although military historians working *in* Australia, they did not write the military history *of* Australia. Wilson produced a massive history of Britain in the Great War, *The Myriad Faces of War* (1986), while Prior has published several iconoclastic books on Britain in the world wars.

chapters to 'The Battle of Fromelles'. Still, Fromelles became the subject of more books, with Geoffrey Benn's *Fromelles: 100 Years of Myths and Lies: Analysing the background to, the treatment of, and setting the record straight* (2021) representative of their accusative tone. (At over 500 pages it reflected the dedication, not to say obsession of what came to be called the 'Fromelles families' – there were no 'Pozières families', for example – who 'sought out every piece of material they could find referring to 'Fromelles'.) The Pheasant Wood investigation crucially occurred in the years preceding the Great War centenary, and the new cemetery was dedicated in 2010.

The centenary saw both sentimental, populist panegyric, but also a scholarship representing a depth and maturity of research. Jean Bou's edited collection, *The AIF in Battle* (2016), demonstrated the strength of a developing corpus of serious research, including chapters by ten authors (Bou, Rhys Crawley, Damien Finlayson, Meleah Hampton, David Horner, Roger Lee, Michael Molkentin, Aaron Pegram, Garth Pratten and Robert Stevenson), most of whom published their own books on the subject. Bou observed that many books on the AIF on the Western Front dealt with 'individual experiences ... or uncover some supposedly "forgotten" aspect', but that 'books that examined the way the AIF actually went about what it was created for – fighting' were relatively scarce.

Though the largest and most costly episode in Australian military history, the AIF's contribution to the fighting on the Western Front has aroused relatively few controversies. Arguments periodically recur over the trivial question of 'who shot down the Red Baron?' More substantial has been the running controversy over whether John Monash was either the war's greatest soldier or merely a talented but junior corps commander. Largely through the influence of populists, such as the three sporting journalists Roland Perry (*Monash*, 2004), Grantlee Kieza (*Monash*, 2015) and Peter FitzSimons (*Victory at Villers-Bretonneux*, 2017), it became an article of faith to accept that Monash had overcome prejudice against his Jewish background to become the war's best general (in contrast to the *British Butchers and Bunglers of World War One* whom John Laffin had stigmatised in 1989). The adulation of Monash complemented Tim Fischer's case for his posthumous promotion to field marshal in *Maestro John Monash* (2014). Professional military historians derided Fischer's special pleading and, surprisingly, perhaps, the proposal failed. Monash's admirers had to be content with watching the documentary *Monash: The forgotten Anzac* (2008). Interestingly, while Monash's contribution had already been judiciously considered by Peter Pedersen (*Monash as Military Commander*, 1985) no one ventured to correct the boosters, presumably because no publisher would risk a book being seen as 'knocking' the forgotten hero of the $100 note.

While the social history of the AIF remained relatively undeveloped – there were few studies besides sociologist Jane Ross's work and historians such as Nathan Wise *Anzac Labour* (2014), on 'workplace cultures' and the AIF and my book on its discipline (*Bad Characters*, 2010) – a serious argument persisted over the composition of the AIF. Since Bean's *Anzac Book* of 1916 admirers had connected its undoubted value in war to its 'bush' ethos, a connection celebrated repeatedly. Notably, Gammage's *The Broken Years* had implicitly endorsed the bush ethos, and one of his doctoral candidates, Lucas Jordan, did an impressive job in his *Stealth Raiders* (2018) showing that the most enterprising proponents of 'Peaceful Penetration' in 1918 were indeed men from the bush. Peter Dennis and Jean Bou's volume of the Oxford *Centenary History of Australia and the Great War*, on *The Australian Imperial Force* (2015), offered a different interpretation to Gammage, based on Peter Dennis's massive AIF database.

The coda to Australia's Great War was the brief and ineffectual contribution to the 'Relief Force', which saw about 150 Australians (either naively regretful at missing out on the Somme or men who knew no calling but war) fighting Bolsheviks in the Russian arctic. This tiny contingent, actually part of the British army, periodically attracts attention, each time unveiling a 'forgotten' story. They include Bruce Muirden's *The Diggers Who Signed on for More* (1990), Peter Quinlivian's *Forgotten Valour: The story of Arthur Sullivan VC* (2006) and Michael Challinger's *Anzacs in Arkhangel* (2010) (billed as 'untold' despite its precursors). Damien Wright's *Australia's Lost Heroes: Anzacs in the Russian Civil War 1919* (2024) continues the tradition.

10

HORSEMAN, PASS BY: SINAI, PALESTINE AND BEYOND

Long before the Great War, the mounted rifleman became the quintessential Australian soldier: a bushman, able to shoot and ride. While the AIF included only fifteen regiments of light horse (compared to sixty (larger) infantry battalions, which suffered much heavier losses) its often triumphant story offered a counterpoint to the slaughter of the Western Front. In 1919 Henry Gullett's popular *Australia in Palestine* anticipated the official history he would produce four years later.

In a familiar pattern, except for histories of most light horse regiments little appeared besides memoirs or novels. Ion Idriess, the champion of outback Australia, wrote about forty books, including *Flynn of the Inland*, *Lasseter's Last Ride* and *The Cattle King*. He had served on Gallipoli and in Sinai and Palestine with the 5th Light Horse and in 1932 used his diary as the basis of *The Desert Column*, which appeared in many later editions. While the Light Horse embodied a romantic view of Australians in war, evoked by film-maker (and Harry Chauvel's nephew) Charles Chauvel's 1941 film, *Forty Thousand Horsemen*, for decades it attracted scant attention in print.

Besides George and Edmée Langley's *Sand, Sweat and Camels* (1976) on the Imperial Camel Corps, little else appeared until Alec Hill's biography *Chauvel of the Light Horse* (1978), which re-evaluated the Sinai–Palestine campaign. Sadly, it was the only book written by a lecturer at RMC Duntroon who inspired a generation of soldier–scholars.

But the Light Horse attracted enthusiasts, notably Ian Jones, the television producer (instrumental in creating the television series *The Sullivans* and writing and producing the film *The Lighthorsemen*), a great authority on Ned Kelly, and on the Light Horse. He published five books on the subject, three in 1986–87 and two in 2007, including one with Elyne Mitchell (Harry Chauvel's daughter and a beloved novelist) and the evocatively titled *A Thousand Miles of Battles*.

In the 21st century, the romantic legend of the Light Horse became entrenched (exemplified in Lindsay Baly's *Horseman, Pass By* (2003), inspired by his great uncle Jack), not least through the formation of re-enactment troops, a feature of Anzac Day marches. Still, the Light Horse came under serious scrutiny. Jean Bou's *Light Horse* (2010) addressed its war thoroughly without the usual romantic twaddle, using fresh archival sources, and Jeff Grey's last book, *The War with the Ottoman Empire* (2016) presented the Light Horse's war in an imperial context. (Characteristically, he used on the cover a photograph of a Ford light car company, not the expected Lighthorseman-with-Waler shot.)

Some authors present the Light Horse as a rallying cry for evangelical Christians, adding a further layer of meaning to the war in what contemporaries called the Holy Land. Gospel pastor Col Stringer's *800 Horsemen* (1998) represented the Light Horse as *God's History Makers* while Jill Curry's *The Anzac Call* (2016) argued that the charge at Beersheba fulfilled Biblical prophecy which could impel 'spiritual Anzac warriors' to prayerfully initiate 'a new reformation'.

The Light Horse continued to attract popular and often superficial books celebrating rather than investigating the legend, notably by the sporting author Roland Perry, whose books included *The Australian Light Horse: The magnificent Australian force and its decisive victories in Arabia in World War I* (2009 – but Arabia? The Light Horse did not serve in Arabia) and *Bill the Bastard* (2012), the field's only biography of a horse. Naturally, the 'storian Peter FitzSimons piled in with *The Last Charge of the Australian Light Horse* (2023).

Just as the war in the Middle East extended beyond Beersheba, so did authors, with Barry Stone's *The Desert Anzacs* (2014) on the supposedly *Forgotten Conflicts in the Deserts of Mesopotamia, North Africa and Palestine* and Damien Wright's *Churchill's Secret War with Lenin* (2017) which spanned the British intervention in Central Asia, including the Australians in the Dunsterforce mission. Like the North Russian intervention, Dunsterforce was periodically re-discovered to be 'forgotten'.

11

A DIVIDED SOCIETY: AUSTRALIA AT WAR

Ernest Scott's *Australia in the War* (1936) long remained the only substantial book on the war experiences of Australian civilians, though Marilyn Lake's pioneering MA on Tasmania at war, published as *A Divided Society* (1975), anticipated the boom to come. (She seems to have been the first to cite Gammage's *The Broken Years.*) In 1980, Michael McKernan's *The Australian People and the Great War* offered the first general revisionist account of the war. Lake reviewed it, perhaps the first woman to review a book in military history, in *Historical Studies* anyway. She thought, surprisingly given the dearth of studies of Australian society at war, it contained 'little which is new or challenging'. But Lake's review was a long one, and she conceded that it was 'surely the searing divisiveness of this great unifying event which draws historians to wonder at it again and again'. McKernan's book reappeared in 2014 as *Australians at Home: World War I*, informing a further generation of readers and still not superseded as an accessible account.

While popular publishing concentrated on the battle front, academic research embraced what increasingly became known as the 'home front', though, as I never tire of pointing out, as Trove's newspapers show, that term was never used in Australia during the Great War. Regardless, the 21st century especially has seen a succession of mostly scholarly studies which have elaborated Lake and McKernan's pioneering research. Five books largely set in Victoria make the point. John McQuilton's study of north-east Victoria, *Rural Australia and the Great War: From Tarrawingee to Tangambalanga* (2001 – no wonder he didn't sell the film rights) suggested the variety and specificity of civilians' war experience. John Connor's biography of Defence Minister George Pearce, *Anzac and Empire* (2011), emphasised that Melbourne was at the heart of the war effort. Rosalie Triolo's *Our Schools and the War* (2012) is representative of the way doctoral theses present a deeper understanding; in this case of the war's effects on Victorian school children. Michael McKernan's *Victoria at War* (2014) grappled with Victorians' war at home and abroad, while Xavier Fowler's *Not Playing the Game* (2021) dealt with the war's complex relationship with sport.*

Increasingly, scholars deepened and elaborated the simple patriotic narrative of Ernest Scott, in which the official view of the war informed its history. In *Loyalty and Disloyalty* (1987) and *The Red Flag Riots* (1988) Raymond Evans, a Queensland political historian, exposed the strains of war in Great War Queensland. Evans, Jan Bassett wrote in *Australian Historical Studies*, was adding further pieces to the jigsaw which Marilyn Lake had begun to assemble, starting in Tasmania. Evans wrote not of unity of purpose but of bitter divisions which war aggravated, of 'lives blighted by catastrophe', impassioned idealism and violent conservative reaction.

Of the sectarian and ideological tensions that wracked Australian society, none was as divisive as the two plebiscites (usually called referendums) over Billy Hughes's plans to introduce conscription for overseas service, both defeated. Though every study of wartime society discusses it (such as Joan Beaumont's *Broken Nation* (2014), Michael McKernan's *The Australian People and the Great War* (1980), Bobbie Oliver's *War and Peace in Western Australia* (1995), Philip Payton's *Regional Australia and the Great War* (2012), and Robert Bollard's *In the Shadow of Gallipoli* (2013) revealing *The hidden history of Australia in World War I*), the literature specifically dealing with conscription is much thinner than the issue deserves. Frank Bongiorno, Rae Frances and Bruce Scates edited a collection of essays, *Labour and the Great War* (2014) and Robin Archer and others' edited collection, *The Conscription Conflict and the Great War* (2016), which represent

* Curiously, for a nation obsessed with sport, Australian military history has few books specifically on it, though Peter Rees is working on *The Other Battlefield*, a history of war and sport, commissioned by the Defence Force.

the latest expert scholarship, but there is no single recent study of the war's most important domestic controversy. By contrast, the patriotic but ineffectual 'recruiting marches' of 1915–16 (which demonstrated the failure of voluntarism) have attracted admiring amateur chroniclers, in half-a-dozen books published between 1986 and 2006, including John Meredith's *The Coo-ee March*, Nat McCaughey's *The Dungarees* and Sherry Morris's *The Kangaroo March*. In this the literature of the Great War replicates the wartime struggle between 'loyalist' amateurs and 'dissident' academics. Studies of particular communities, following the example of works such as Janet McCalman's *Struggletown* (1998), on Richmond, Victoria; Peter Yule's on Koroit (*A Green and Pleasant Land*, 1999); Peter Donovan's *Storm* (2011), on Kapunda; Philip Payton's *Regional Australia and the Great War* (2012, on Moonta); or Margaret Warburton's *Bunbury's War* (2021) reveal the full range of Australian responses.

The Great War ended amid the 'flu pandemic which cost a further 12 000 lives, discussed in Ian Shaw's seemingly hastily written but topical *Pandemic* (2020) and Rita Bogna's *Under Siege: The Spanish Flu in South Australia 1919–1920* (2023) but in few other works besides academic articles (notably by Anthea Hyslop); extraordinary given that one-in-six of Australia's war-related deaths came in the year after the Armistice.

12

SHATTERED ANZACS: BETWEEN THE WARS

There was a time, Andrew Moore wrote in 1989 reviewing Michael Cathcart's *Defending the National Tuckshop* (1988), when 'the inter-war years' were given 'a cursory paragraph propping up the narrative between the first and second world wars'. That that neglect has ended is partly because historians became aware of the shadow of Anzac. Just as Marilyn Lake had led research on the strains of wartime (in her *A Divided Society*), her 1987 *The Limits of Hope: Soldier settlement in Victoria 1915–1938* (her Monash PhD) was, as a reviewer wrote, 'a welcome foray into this neglected topic', though not until Bruce Scates and Melanie Oppenheimer's *The Last Battle* (2016) did another major scholarly study of soldier settlement appear.

Shattered Anzacs, Marina Larrson's 2009 study of the effects of war wounds and psychic trauma on 'Returned Men' and their families (who despite the massive Repat bureaucracy bore the burden of care) followed Stephen Garton's lead in examining the consequences of war. Bruce Scates's *World War One: A history in 100 stories* (2015) epitomised the 'Shattered Anzacs' school. One of the few projects explicitly associated with the Centenary of Anzac that did not extol Anzac exceptionalism, Scates and his collaborators easily found a hundred stories of Australia's Great War that left no reader in doubt that the war had been a tragedy. It abounded in stories of death, grief, trauma, mutilation, murder and misery; not a VC hero was to be seen except Hugo Throssell, and he killed himself. This was a salutary corrective to the boosting that generally prevailed in centenary events and products, and one that those responsible for managing the Centenary of Anzac deprecated: 'why was it necessary for the authors to be so brutally honest?', one asked. ('As if a dishonest history would somehow be preferable', Scates retorted.) But Joan Beaumont in her *Broken Nation* – its title a nod to Gammage's book – had taken a less extreme view, arguing that as well as tragedy and trauma, war service brought opportunity and the development of skills (among survivors), arguing (as she later wrote) that we should be 'Remembering the Resilient'. Ian Hodges's prize-winning detailed study of Riverina veterans (*He Belonged to Wagga*, 2022) supported Beaumont's more nuanced portrayal.

The decades between the world wars saw the divisions the war had exposed persist. Keith Amos's *The New Guard Movement 1931–1939* (1976) made clear the degree to which the war had disrupted the progressive trajectory of a federal Australia. The divisions over conscription joined the chasm which separated those who had volunteered from those who had not (the majority of 'eligibles') to drive wedges between Australians. Amos suggested that war service merged conservative politics and imperial loyalty to produce a movement of tens of thousands of aggrieved ex-diggers – one which apparently came within days of challenging the NSW Labor government of Jack Lang. Michael Cathcart followed Amos's lead with *Defending the National Tuckshop* (1988) on *Australia's secret army intrigue of 1931*, as did Andrew Moore with *The Secret Army and the Premier* (1989). These books were based on heroic research into groups which had the means and opportunity to conceal their strength, and indeed which represented Australia's single greatest threat to democracy. That the threat emerged primarily among men who had served in 'the War' reinforces claims to the significance of war experience, if not to its dominance. Andrew Moore, speculating on the 'unpalatable ... thought of Tom Blamey as dictator', wondered how Australian military historians would respond to the revelations that he, Cathcart and Amos had made. The answer seemed to be that Blamey's first biography, John Hetherington's *Blamey* (1973), ignored his political activism, but his most authoritative biographer David Horner did not, in his *Blamey* (1998).

Though often represented as the decades 'between the wars', conflict broke out before 1939, in Asia and in Spain. Amirah Inglis's

Australians in the Spanish Civil War (1987) told for the first time the story of the eighty Australian men and women who volunteered to serve the Spanish republic, about a quarter of whom died. Judith Keene's *The Last Mile to Huesca* (1988) gave the war a human dimension in telling the story of *An Australian nurse in the Spanish civil war.*

In looking at the 1930s it seems impossible to resist seeing the drift towards a second and potentially more disastrous conflict. In this the disastrous Singapore Strategy looms large. John McCarthy's *Australia and Imperial Defence 1918–39* (1976) seems not to have been bettered. The doyen of Australian foreign affairs history, WJ (Bill) Hudson, judged not just that McCarthy had skewered the 'indecision, foolishness and naivety' of successive Australian governments in accepting British assurances ('muddle and deceit') so uncritically, but saw this 'short pungent book for the educated layman', as 'the first in a new wave of scholarship from the deeper waters of opened and better organised archives'. That watershed was not, however vigorously explored until Joan Beaumont's *Australia's Great Depression* (2022), building on the insights of her *Broken Nation.*

With the opening and exploitation of the 'Repat' files, allowing the investigation of the lives of the war's survivors (both former soldiers and their families), we can hope for clearer and more profound insights into the Great War's effects.

13

AUSTRALIA IN THE WAR: OFFICIAL HISTORIES

With the AIF demobilised and the nation's people coming to terms with the physical, mental, emotional and political trauma inflicted by the war, it is fitting to turn to one of the major historical consequences of conflict, which is that for a quarter of a century after the end of major conflicts, authors embarked on the massive task of producing the 'official history', a national institution in Australia more than in most other nations marked by war.*

Charles Bean had narrowly won a ballot among members of the Australian Journalists' Association to accompany the 'first convoy' as the AIF's Official Correspondent. (Keith Murdoch lost: how differently Australian military and media history might have been had Murdoch won remains an intriguing 'might-have-been'.) Bean soon decided to write an account of the Australian part in the war (and kept detailed diaries as his core source), but by mid-war had begun to plan and work towards the approval of an 'official history', and formally took up the position in July 1919. He urged AIF units to keep ample files, including war diaries, and not merely hand over its records to British archives, and to collect 'relics' for the war memorial museum he envisaged on the Somme in 1916. In both endeavours he was helped by the dedication

* It's desirable to explain what an official history is, and is not. As Bob O'Neill explained in his history of *Australia in the Korean War*, it was 'official in the sense it was commissioned by the Australian government, which then provided full access to its records ... It has not been subject to censorship'. With few exceptions, successive official history projects have observed those two essential conditions. Whether the current one continues that worthy record seems to lie in the hands of faceless bureaucrats.

of his clerk, John Treloar, who not only gathered and shipped vast amounts of records and relics, but as director of the Memorial (1920–52) organised and added to them, creating the research collections on which Australian military historians still largely rely.

Bean was contracted to produce six volumes each of 650 pages, expecting the task to take about five years. In fact, he wrote six volumes totalling 6000 pages and edited another six, a further 4000 pages, and it took him twenty-one years. He later described how he sought to answer three fundamental questions:

> ... how did the Australian people – and the Australian character, if there is one – come through the universally recognised test of this, their first great war? Second ... what did the Australian people and their forces achieve in the total effort of their side of the struggle? Third: what was the true nature of that struggle and test so far as Australians took part in it?

Lloyd Robson observed (in the Memorial's *Journal* in 1984) that Bean's history was mistitled: 'it has very little to do with Australia during the war': indeed, it was effectively a memorial to the AIF, its virtues and its heroes.

As Denis Winter pointed out (over tea in the old Historical Research Section) Bean based his official history on the models of the imperial wars of the previous century – William Napier's history of the Peninsular war, Alexander Kinglake's *The Invasion of the Crimea* and the Indian Army's staff histories of its wars, which appeared while Bean was maturing as a writer. He at first thought that he would be able to finish within a few years and return to journalism. In fact, it was to dominate the rest of his life. He soon accepted that while he would write some of the volumes (in the end, half of them), he needed help.

At first working at Tuggeranong, a property south of the nascent capital, Canberra, for the sake of his health in 1925 he returned to Sydney, working from an office in Victoria Barracks. There, he laboured to write the 'army' volumes: two on the creation of the AIF and the Gallipoli campaign (*The Story of Anzac*), and four on the AIF on the

Western Front (one each dealing with 1916 and 1917 and two on 1918). He relied upon his own notebooks and diaries (286 of which he had kept throughout the war) but also on the massive lode of war diaries and official records which John Treloar had gathered and which a devoted team of assistants, notably his wartime assistant, Arthur Bazley, organised and prepared for him. Even so, the effort told on his health and indeed, on the quality of the work: Volume VI (on the AIF in the war's final offensives), dealing with complex operations by a corps of five divisions, is notably less coherent than the earlier volumes. They are distinguished by a paradoxical democratic tone – in contrast to its British counterpart even privates got individual footnotes – but also often as seen from the headquarters where Bean spent most of his time. Bean's focus was on the front line, in which he saw the finest qualities of Australians from the bush ('The Australian was half a soldier before the war'), even though as members of a heavily urban nation most Australians came from the cities.

The other volumes of the series were written by a range of authors: Volume VII on the AIF in Sinai and Palestine by the former war correspondent Henry Gullett, and Volume VIII on the *Australian Flying Corps* by another journalist, Frederic Cutlack (both published in 1923). Wartime intelligence officer Arthur Jose wrote Volume IX on the Royal Australian Navy (1928) and Seaforth Mackenzie, who had served with Tropical Force, wrote on the Australian occupation of German New Guinea (1927). Volume XI *Australia During the War* was finished by Ernest Scott, a history professor at Melbourne University and the only academic. Bean had difficulty getting his authors to deliver: Scott took over a volume from the journalist Thomas Heney, overwhelmed by the task, and it finally appeared in 1936. His authors also contended with meddling – Jose complained that 'the whole blessed history' was 'hung up because the Naval Board ... wants to exercise a severe censorship over my opinions as well as over statements of fact'. Bean did not publish his final volume until 1942.

Bean's achievement was not just to document in often minute detail the AIF's exploits, but also to build on his wartime journalism to shape expectations of the qualities Australians would exhibit in war, the constellation of attributes which became known as the Anzac legend. What was published as the final paragraph of his last volume expresses both the romanticism of his vision but also the vigorous character of his prose at its best. He reflected on the AIF's legacy once 'the familiar faded-green uniform disappeared from the streets':

> What these men did nothing can alter now. The good and the bad, the greatness and smallness of their story will stand. Whatever of glory it contains nothing now can lessen. It rises, as it will always rise, above the mists of ages, a monument to great-hearted men; and, for their nation, a possession for ever.

Although it appeared on page 1096 of Volume VI (1942), by diligent scrutiny of his drafts, research by Martin Ball for his PhD found that Bean had written that paragraph in about 1922. The literary mentor appointed by his publisher, George Robertson, thought it unduly flowery and induced Bean to cut it, but he kept it for twenty years and found its ideal place. Whether flowery or prosaic, Bean's series became immensely popular – bought in huge numbers if not read exhaustively: even Fred Cutlack's volume on the tiny Flying Corps went through a dozen editions in twenty years. Formally published by Angus and Robertson (long the colossus in Australian publishing) the volumes were actually aggressively marketed by the entrepreneurial John Treloar, who had troops of salesmen, all Returned Men, selling subscriptions door-to-door.

Often seen as distinct from Bean's twelve volumes (he published a twelfth Photographic Volume in 1923) was the three-volume set of the Medical History, written by Arthur Butler, who had landed at Anzac as the medical officer of the 9th Battalion. Butler wrote slowly, resisting Bean's urgings. He (and his wife) notoriously lived on porridge for months to continue what Bean called his 'slow though brilliant' writing. Butler's detailed volumes, and the archive of medical records he assembled, continue to stimulate medical and social historians to investigate questions which he barely touched upon, as Stephen Garton pointed out in 1994, such as the extent of 'Repatriation', the Australian jargon for the medical and welfare consequences of war service, a subject only coming into prominence in the 21st century.

In 1946 Bean finally published his distillation of his series, in *Anzac to Amiens*. Appearing after a larger and longer war, it was respected but, as Geoffrey Serle wrote, 'neglected' – no one knew how to even pronounce 'Amiens' – was it 'A'may'*o*' (as the French said) or was it 'Ay-mee-ens' as the diggers had said? Finally, in his *Gallipoli Mission* (1948) Bean reflected on how his field work in returning to Gallipoli in 1919 had helped him solve what he called 'the riddles of Anzac'.

Biographies of Charles Bean have formed a distinct sub-set of military biography. Ken Inglis produced a pamphlet on Bean's life and work soon after his death in 1968, *C.E.W. Bean, Australian Historian* (a further sign of Inglis's growing awareness of the importance of the Great War in the nation's story). He identified Bean's strengths and contribution in just thirty pages better than others in many more. Dudley McCarthy, a former diplomat and official historian, published *Gallipoli to the Somme* (1983), not a biography but a digest of extracts transcribed from Bean's notebooks. After a hiatus, with Denis Winter's selection of Bean's writing in *Making the Legend* (1992), Bean books arrived like buses. The Great War centenary prompted Ross Coulthart's *Charles Bean* (2014), Peter Rees's *Bearing Witness* (2015) and Peter Burness's monumental edition of his Western Front diaries in 2018, complementing Kevin Fewster's selections of his Gallipoli diaries, published in 1983 and 2007. (Compiling this book's bibliography revealed the extent to which books appeared in new editions as publishers realised that the market for 'war books' was expanding.)

Bean's history endures, still an essential jumping-off trench for Great War research. Of course it has been criticised. Jeff Grey and what might be called the UNSW Canberra push used to complain that he emphasised front line heroics in favour of headquarters debates, and that he favoured the infantry's deeds over the technical achievements of the artillery. In following in Bean's footsteps at Quinn's Post and Mont St Quentin I found minor errors and omissions. Kit Cullen in *Jack's Journey* (2013) alleges a 'conspiracy' by Bean and his staff to deny men of the 4th Battalion (including Cullen's own great uncle) credit for rescuing a party of Marines in what Cullen called 'Death Trap Valley' on Gallipoli on 1–2 May, but on investigation it looks like an oversight rather than a deliberate slight.

But Bean's history, for all its richness, seemed to stultify rather than stimulate further enquiry. Michael McKernan observed (in *Australians: A Guide to Sources*, 1987) that 'by amassing such a wealth of detail ... the official histories and the companion battalion histories remained all that was written on Australian military history'. That was about to change. By 1943 – the year after the publication of Bean's final volume – another official project was underway; the largest Australia has ever seen: Gavin Long's series on the Second World War.

PART IV
THE SECOND WORLD WAR

14

THE THIRTY-NINERS: THE MEDITERRANEAN WAR

A million Australians, from a population of seven million, served in the world war which began in September 1939; the nation's largest and most extensive conflict. The first volunteers for a second AIF – known, as Peter Charlton's 1981 book had it, as *The Thirty Niners* – formed the first of three divisions to fight, at first, in the Mediterranean.

The three AIF divisions played a significant and perhaps decisive part in the British campaigns around the Mediterranean from early 1941 to late 1942, but for many years the official history, a few dozen unit histories and a handful of memoirs constituted the bulk of the available literature. War correspondent Chester Wilmot's *Tobruk 1941* (1945) prefigured his even more significant *The Struggle for Europe* (1952), which together demonstrated how a perceptive journalist could indeed lay down the 'first draft of history'.

Books on the Second World War took longer to gain momentum, later impelled by *Australia at War 1939–1945* (1981) by Duntroon historian John Robertson. But few books dealt with the early campaigns. Amazingly, there is no substantial study of the Australian part in the eight-month siege of Tobruk (besides Fitzy's flawed blockbuster), and only one on the Lebanon campaign, Jim McAllester and Syd Trigellis-Smith's *Largely a Gamble: Australians in Syria June–July 1941* (1995) – though the Australian operations actually occurred in Lebanon – the only general study of that campaign. *Alamein: The Australian Story* (2002, by me and Mark Johnston) was the first study of the major Australian battle, and two decades on it has not been superseded (except that Allan Converse's *Armies of Empire* (2011) compared the 9th Division to the British 50th).

There are exceptions, for Greece and Crete and for Bardia. For Greece, there's been Peter Ewer's *Forgotten Anzacs* (2008), Maria Hill's *Diggers and Greeks* (2010), Craig Stockings and Eleanor Hancock's *Swastika over the Acropolis* (2013), Peter Monteath's *Battle on 42nd Street* (2019) and Craig Collie's *Where the Hell Are We?* (2024). Why the Greek campaign should attract so much more attention than Tobruk and El Alamein is a mystery. Greece's battlefields are certainly more congenial to investigate. Libya (Tobruk) was for many years out-of-bounds and is again. The only Australian military historian to have visited it is Garth Pratten. The neglect of Egypt (Alamein) is harder to justify, given the 9th Australian Division's central role in the battle, and its flourishing tourist industry. Fieldwork in Egypt lacks Greece's tavernas or the bistros of the Western Front: that can't explain the neglect, surely?

For Bardia, Craig Stockings's *Bardia: Myth, reality and the heirs of Anzac* (2009) remains the most exhaustive study of a Second World War Australian battle (more than any study of, say, Kokoda). Its 481 pages did not deal just with the two days in which in January 1941 the 6th Division captured the Italian fortress in Libya. Rather, Stockings's achievement was to uncover what he called 'the riddle of Bardia' (echoing Bean's 'riddles of Anzac'). He sought to understand not just the mechanics of battle, but also the relationship between the victory and the expectations of Anzac borne by both the troops involved and later generations of Australians imbued with the Anzac legend. In this, Stockings connected a relatively minor battle with a perennial theme in Australian military history.

Naturally, memoirs, unit histories and biographies complement the thin operational literature, such as Margaret Barter's *Far Above Battle*, which explored the experience of battle in North Africa and Greece in the manner of John Keegan's deservedly vaunted *The Face of Battle* (1976), arguing vigorously that combat can be understood by those who were not present, that 'clichés about front line incommunicability are outdated'. James Mitchell's recent 'social' history of the 2/2nd Pioneer

Battalion, *Men at War* (2023) supports Barter's conviction that the experience of battle can be understood, in this case a study of a unit in Lebanon, from below, as it were.

Biographers have produced valuable studies, such as David Horner's *Blamey* or Brett Lodge's *Lavarack* (1998), on the Australian commander in Lebanon, illuminating the campaign from above. Synoptic works such as Horner's *High Command* of course place Australia's participation in context, but the dearth of operational studies of the Mediterranean campaigns may surprise those who may have assumed that Australia's part in the Second World War would have been abundantly documented. The contrast with the Pacific campaigns, and especially Kokoda, is striking.

15

CHASED BY THE SUN: AIR WAR OVER EUROPE

For all that Australians had been 'air-minded' since the pioneers of aviation swooped down on crowds flocking to showgrounds and racecourses in the years after 1918, not to mention the huge scale of the air war in the Second World War, air force history has never fully taken off. What we might call the 'Bean Effect' also afflicted air force history: the existence of four massively detailed histories of the RAAF's war (see chapter 24) seemed for decades to deter anyone from following their examples, though several notable books appeared.

John McCarthy had published with his colleague John Robertson invaluable foundation documents on *Australian War Strategy 1939–1945* (1985), a collection permeated by the relationships between Australia and its senior partners. In *A Last Call of Empire* (1988), McCarthy examined Australian aircrew, Britain and the Empire Air Training Scheme, considering the implications for Australia of what he called in a related Memorial *Journal* article 'The Surrender of the Aircrew'. In 1993 Eric Fry's *An Airman Far Away* provided a complement to McCarthy. A distinguished labour historian who had been a RAAF pilot officer, in retirement Eric wrote about his brother-in-law, Charlie Williams, who had been killed in May 1943 on the famous Dam Busters raid when his Lancaster struck power lines. Fry's book was not just a labour of love, but connected the individual tragedy of Charlie's death with the bigger picture of the air war.

Ten years on, Hank Nelson, who had gained renown as an historian of Australia's relationship with Papua New Guinea and with Tim Bowden virtually invented the genre of PoW studies (see chapter 18), took the unexpected decision to write on Australians in the bomber offensive. Characteristically, he began *Chased by the Sun* (2002) with Yanco in the Riverina, the birthplace of Arthur Doubleday and Bill Brill, whose service and lives formed the core of the story he told. Just as Nelson's motivation in writing his *PoW: Australians under Nippon* had been to rescue them from obscurity, so he opened *Chased by the Sun* with the declaration, 'Australians do not remember the men who fought in the skies over Europe'. Certainly, the relative dearth of books on the air war over Europe suggests that 4000 airmen killed in the air had made less impact than the 2200 soldiers killed in the Mediterranean campaigns of 1941–42.

Peter Rees's *Lancaster Men* (2013), despite its unpromising, boosting sub-title, *The Aussie heroes of Bomber Command*, offered a nuanced account of the Australian part in the bomber offensive, though like most non-scholarly books, he focused on the experience and losses of the offensive, not on its origins, course or effects. That would be left to Alan Stephens, a RAAF officer in Vietnam who became its most distinguished historian, and who analysed the offensive as a manifestation of the application of 'air power' – see chapter 35.

Otherwise, the burden of Australia's part in the European air war has largely been carried by squadron histories, which almost by their nature attract a specialist readership, meaning that the contribution of RAAF units and aircrew in, say, the air war over North Africa, the Mediterranean, and Italy, the battle of the Atlantic or the liberation of North-West Europe, remains poorly served. Exceptions include former schoolteacher Anthony Cooper's *RAAF Bombers Over Germany 1941–42* (2016) (and, with Thorsten Perl, his 2023 *Dispatches from Berlin, 1943*), retired senior RAAF officer John Quaife's *Battle of the Atlantic* (2022), on the RAAF in Coastal Command and, I'm abashed to say, my own *Air War Europe*, published as part of the Time-Life Australians at War series in 1986, which devoted chapters to most of these surprisingly overlooked aspects. The connection between the air war and the fate of many aircrew was made by former WRANS officer and historian Kathryn Spurling, whose *Fury to Hell* (2022) continued the welcome attention on airmen who became 'Kriegies'; prisoners of war.

16
KRIEGIES: POWS IN EUROPE

Paradoxically, while the 7000 Australians captured by the Germans and Italians long remained overshadowed by those captured in Asia, the experience of Britain's prisoners of the Germans became familiar. At a time when most Australian families went to 'the pictures' at least once a week, and suburban cinemas proliferated, 'war films' became a staple. In the 1950s, these films included not just epics of battle – *The Cruel Sea* (1953), *The Dam Busters* (1955) and *Reach for the Sky* (1956) – but a distinct genre of prisoner-of-war films. They included *The Wooden Horse* (1950), *Albert R.N.* (1953) and *The Colditz Story* (1955). British prisioners of war were seen more often on Australian screens than were, say, Australian infantrymen.

Despite this prominence, prisoners in Europe – who called themselves 'Kriegies' (from the German, *Kriegsgefangener*, 'prisoner of war') remained largely unnoticed. Prisoners in Europe were accorded a sixty-odd-page appendix in the official history, but not until the 1980s did much appear about them. Colin Burgess's *The Diggers of Colditz* (1985) revealed the Australians in the most famous German PoW camp. As a schoolboy, he had been entranced by paperbacks and films, such as *The Colditz Story* or *The Great Escape* (1963). Surprisingly, the Great Escape prompted no interest in writing about captivity in Europe. Not until 2011 was an authoritative book devoted to the European PoWs, in *P.O.W.: Australian Prisoners of War in Hitler's Reich* by Peter Monteath of Flinders University. Very few Australians have written about those held by the Italians, but Katrina Kittel in *Shooting Through* (2019) looked at the 106 men who escaped after the Italian armistice in 1943. This aspect clearly deserves greater attention.

Kristen Alexander, already the author of aviation books, commenced a PhD at UNSW Canberra in 2015, investigating RAAF PoWs in Stalag Luft III (the camp in Poland which saw the Great Escape). At first only seeking to explore what she called 'the camp commonweal', the sources led her to realise that she needed to follow the liberated prisoners home and examine the consequences of captivity for them and their families. Alexander asked new questions of PoW experience, of spirituality and sexuality as well as morale and wellbeing. The first book to emerge from her PoW research, *Kriegies* (2023), opens novel avenues for future research, and has justifiably won book prizes.

In the meantime, the new century saw 'PoW studies' become part of mainstream academic research. Both established scholars (such as Christina Twomey and Joan Beaumont) continued their interest, and newcomers to the field publishing, such as PhD theses by Jennifer Lawless (*Kismet*, 2015, a sympathetic approach to Ottoman captors), Kate Ariotti (*Captive Anzacs: Australian PoWs of the Ottomans* (2018), and Aaron Pegram (*Surviving the Great War: Australian prisoners of war on the Western Front, 1916–18* (2020). *Beyond Surrender*, coming out of a conference at the Australian National University in 2013 demonstrated the vigour of the field.

17

THE JAPANESE THRUST: THE DEFEATS OF 1941–42

The swift Japanese conquest of south-east Asia shocked Australians, precipitating a sense of impending calamity at the time and, in retrospect, fuelling a feeling of betrayal that 'Britain' could have allowed such a threat to arise. The lingering resentment is evident in Peter Ewer's *The Long Road to Changi* (2013) in which he condemned 'British diatribes against the Australians', whom he claimed had been unfairly blamed for the loss of Singapore. While Ewer is perhaps extreme in seeing 'the depth of British hostility toward the Australians at Singapore', it is now commonplace for Australian authors to present the disaster of 1942 as if (like Carlyon and Gallipoli) Churchill had engineered the defeat to humiliate John Curtin. Augustine Meaher, an American-born Melbourne PhD, resisted the trend in his *The Australian Road to Singapore: The myth of British betrayal* (2010), who highlighted a 'failure of Australian leadership'. While nationalist ire grates, British authors blaming Australians for Singapore's fall is equally outrageous.

Early 1942 saw a succession of disasters: the capture of Lark Force on New Britain, and of other 'bird' forces, Gull on Ambon and Sparrow on Timor, and the loss of Java. As well as featuring in the various general treatments of 1942, each generated a clutch of books.

The seizure of Rabaul (three weeks before the fall of Singapore) has produced half-a-dozen books, notably Bruce Gamble's *Darkest Hour* (2006), besides the books on the fate of the force's nurses (see chapters 18 and 36). The loss of almost all the PoWs and interned civilians, killed when an American submarine torpedoed the *Montevideo Maru*, is exemplified by the title of Kathryn Spurling's *Abandoned and Sacrificed*

(2022). The fate of Gull Force on Ambon, whose members after a brief resistance endured a protracted ordeal in captivity, became an early subject of the academic interest in PoW experience, in Joan Beaumont's *Gull Force: Survival and leadership in captivity* (1988). Ambivalence over controversial decisions by the PoWs' officers (who conceded disciplinary control to the Japanese) is reflected in the sub-title of Roger Maynard's *Ambon: The truth about one of the most brutal PoW camps [...]* (2014) demonstrating *the triumph of the Aussie spirit*. The surrender of a small Australian force in Java (foolishly diverted on its voyage to Australia from the Middle East) has not attracted a book in itself, but has been strongly documented in a biography (Andrew Faulkner's *Arthur Blackburn, VC* (2008), and in a recent unit history which demonstrates that the unit history seam is by no means worked out, James Mitchell's history of the 2/2nd Pioneer Battalion, *Men at War* (2023).

Sparrow Force on Timor produced a more complex narrative. Just as Singapore is blamed on British duplicity, so the defeat of the island garrisons of the illusory 'Malay Barrier' is attributed to what Peter Henning described in his history of the 2/40th, *Doomed Battalion* (1995) as 'a magnificent display of very bad strategy'. The strategy (placing the bird forces on isolated islands) was in this case all Australian. This has not deterred Tom Gilling from entitling his book on Blackforce in Java *The Lost Battalions*, its argument summarised by its sub-title: *A battle that could not be won, an island that could not be defended, an ally that could not be trusted* (2019). The untrustworthy ally could be Britain – Churchill gets the usual stick for his bullying of Curtin, but it could be the Dutch; the sub-title may be another product of publishers' marketeers.

Despite Sparrow Force's surrender in Dutch Timor, the 2/2nd Independent Company continued a gruelling guerrilla campaign in Portuguese East Timor, best explained in Christopher Wray's *Timor 1942* (1987). The resistance, though skillful, made no difference to the war's outcome, and took the lives of thousands of Timorese in savage Japanese reprisals, who were then abandoned when the guerrillas were withdrawn. One of the connections between the services was that the effort to sustain the campaign by sea produced several books on

HMAS *Armidale*, lost attempting to reinforce the guerrillas, such as Frank Walker's *HMAS Armidale* (1990). A collaboration between an *Armidale* survivor, Col Madigan, and the artist Jan Senberg produced in *Armidale '42* (1999) a unique reflection upon the tragedy.

The defeats of early 1942 had two consequences. They left Australians feeling apprehensive about a seemingly imminent Japanese invasion, and virtually an entire Australian division, the 8th, became PoWs of the Japanese.

18

POW AUSTRALIANS UNDER NIPPON: CAPTIVES IN ASIA

The conventional view of the history of Australian prisoners of war – and I know because I've helped to propagate it – is that until the 1980s their stories were largely untold. Surrender was regarded as a disgrace – even when involuntary – and seen as a betrayal of the Anzac legend, which stressed aggression in battle. Former prisoners of war met an awkward silence, seemingly excluded from the pantheon of Anzac. There's some truth to this, but also some major qualifications.

Though over 22 000 Australians became prisoners of the Japanese, and while a third of them died in captivity (representing about a fifth of Australia's deaths in that war) they were not accorded a volume of the official history, which was organised by service and by phases of the war. (Unlike New Zealand, which devoted a volume of its official history to its PoWs, but better than Britain's 100 volumes, which practically ignored them.) Instead, Wigmore's 1957 *The Japanese Thrust* included a 130-page appendix, by Bill Sweeting, a Kokoda veteran and Gavin Long's wartime confidential clerk, who had a long association with his history and then became the Memorial's assistant director 1967–79. Given the outrages and atrocities he chronicled, the tone of Sweeting's appendix was measured, a considerable feat of discipline.

'War films' such as *A Town Like Alice* (1956) and David Lean's *The Bridge on the River Kwai* (1957) suggest that prisoners of the Japanese received covert interest as well as embarrassed silence. Indeed, three ex-prisoners' memoirs became bestsellers. The journalist Rohan Rivett, captured in Java, described his experience on the Burma–Thailand railway in *Behind Bamboo* (1946). Selling over 100 000 copies, it became one of the most striking publishing successes in Australian literary history. Some purchasers were surely the families of prisoners of war, desperate – but dreading – to learn what had happened to loved ones who died in captivity or who returned changed forever. Two other books also became bestsellers. Russell Braddon, a gunner captured in Malaya and also a survivor of the railway, published *The Naked Island* in Britain in 1952. It too sold hugely – between a million and two million copies internationally over sixty-odd years. Betty Jeffrey, a nursing sister, published *White Coolies*, her memoir of captivity in Sumatra, in 1954. It too sold widely – 70 000 copies – and became a serial on the wireless. They appeared thirty-odd years before prisoners of war were at last welcomed into the Anzac canon. (We have also forgotten Jessie Elizabeth Simons's *While History Passed: The story of the Australian nurses who were prisoners of the Japanese* (1954), which seems to have attracted little attention.)

Prisoners of the Japanese, then, were hardly ignored. Equally – and this is where the conventional view is justified – they did not become the subject of historical research. Perhaps this merely reflected the widespread neglect or disdain from which all Australian military history suffered. That changed suddenly in the mid-1980s. Hyland Nelson – known to all as Hank – was one of the trio of Australian historians (along with Bill Gammage and Ken Inglis) shaped by teaching at the University of Papua New Guinea. Hank produced books on its colonial period, notably in *Taim Bilong Masta*, a series of interviews with Old New Guinea Hands, which became an ABC radio series and book. That collaboration with the ABC, notably with journalist Tim Bowden, resulted in another major radio series, *P.O.W.: Australians under Nippon* (1985). Lloyd Robson observed that those who heard those interviewed for the series 'will never forget how powerful they were in evoking the prisoner-of-war experience'. Nelson's book he rightly found 'compulsive reading'.

Joan Beaumont, a London-trained Australian academic historian relatively new to Australian military history, picked up on this fertile new field. Her *Gull Force* (1988) did not merely reveal the horrors of captivity on Ambon, but also the ambiguities of the prisoners' irresolute officers. Patsy Adam-Smith, who had already popularised Great War history with *The Anzacs*, introduced new readers to an experience they had barely known in *Prisoners of War: From Gallipoli to Korea* (1992).

Once PoW history had been sanctioned, as it were, these books opened a flood of publications, including memoirs, biographies and studies of particular camps, units or groups of prisoners. The ordeal of the Burma–Thailand railway naturally attracted attention, from former prisoners, their children and historians. Hank Nelson and his colleague Gavan McCormack continued to encourage research on PoWs, hosting a conference at the Australian National University which produced a book, *The Burma–Thailand Railway: Memory and history* (1993), which included participants from Japan and Australia, a moving experience for those present. Other notable books included Gavan Daws's *Prisoners of the Japanese* (1994), unusually comparing the experiences of Australian, British and American prisoners, and *The Men on the Line* (2008) by Pattie Wright (author of *Ray Parkin's Odyssey* (2012), one of the finest PoW biographies). Bestselling authors such as Cameron Forbes (*Hellfire: The story of Australia, Japan and the Prisoners of War* (2005)) and Peter Brune (*Descent into Hell* (2014)) ensured that the PoW story was widely disseminated. Popular interest gained an immense boost from *The War Diaries of Weary Dunlop* (1986) and Sue Ebury's biography, *Weary* (1994), their success measured by how many copies still turn up at community book sales. Rosalind Hearder's *Keep the Men Alive* (2009) reminded readers that there were more doctors than just Weary Dunlop on the Burma–Thailand railway. One of them, Rowley Richards, wrote one of the most powerful memoirs of captivity, *A Doctor's War* (2005).

Though it turned out to be relatively benign compared to the Burma–Thailand railway, Ambon, Japan or especially Sandakan, 'Changi' became a shorthand for 'PoW of the Japanese'. The few books specifically on Changi were Kevin Blackburn's *The Sportsmen of Changi* (2012) and Roland Perry's *The Changi Brownlow* (2010), the former a revisionist scholarly study, the latter *An inspirational story of the Aussie spirit*. They illuminate the contrast between the two approaches. Perry, Blackburn observed, 'resorted to stereotypes to tell his story', and omitted mentioning that guards and prisoners played sport together.

'Changi' is known (with the railway and Sandakan): the other camps are unrecognised.

Christina Twomey emerged as Nelson and Beaumont's academic successor, with her *Australia's Forgotten Prisoners* (2007), on Australian civilians interned by the Japanese, who had shamefully been denied recognition and Repat benefits, and later *The Battle Within* (2018), tracing the effects of captivity on former PoWs. While the first wave of PoW studies had depended crucially on personal testimony, this second wave drew upon newly available records files such as Repat files.

The sixty-odd military and civilian nursing sisters captured attracted particular interest. Catherine Kenny's short book on PoW nurses *Captives* (1986), based on her BA Hons thesis, observed that 'few other works exist on this topic'. In the ensuing thirty-odd years, much changed, with too many books to mention individually. Nurses' memoirs or biographies appeared, including Pat Darling's autobiography, *Portrait of a Nurse* (2001), and Barbara Angell's biography of Wilma Oram, *A Woman's War* (2003). The ordeal of *The Rabaul Nurses*, the title of Claire Marriott's 2006 online book, attracted further attention, prompted by the ABC drama series *Sisters of War* (2010), based on Rod Miller's research, later published as *Lost Women of Rabaul* (2022). Nor does the interest seem to be abating. The years 2023–24 saw the appearance of Georgina Banks's semi-fictional *Back to Bangka* (which painfully exposed what seems to be the truth about the Bangka Island massacre), Grantlee Kieza's *Sister Viv* (Bullwinkel) and Colin Burgess's *Sisters in Captivity* (on Betty Jeffrey and her fellow nurse-prisoners), as well as the novels by Heather Morris (*Sisters Under the Rising Sun*) and Anthea Hodgson's *The War Nurses*, which ends on the beach at Bangka.*

The most compelling episode of captivity is evoked by the word 'Sandakan', the atrocity in which only six of the 2000 Australian and British prisoners held in North Borneo survived 'death marches' in 1945. Peter Firkins's *From Hell to Eternity* (1979) exposed the episode

* Georgina Banks argues convincingly that, as many have suspected, the nurses at Bangka were raped before being massacred. Perhaps the test of a book's reliability will become whether or how authors face the possibility of sexual assault.

for the first time as history, though official records remained largely closed, perhaps to spare families distress but also because official files had remained under the 'fifty-year' rule.

Hank Nelson and Tim Bowden's *P.O.W.* touched on the story, and already Don Wall, himself a former PoW, had begun researching it. He published *Sandakan Under Nippon* in 1987, several times revised and reissued over the next ten years as further details came to light and becoming known and respected as the authority on Sandakan. Wall's lead was followed by a dozen books, among which several stood out. The release of the official records, and especially the war crimes files, enabled further books, notably Lynette Ramsay Silver, a dogged researcher, though often uninformative over sources, who produced *Sandakan: A conspiracy of silence* in 1998. Richard Braithwaite, the son of one of the six survivors, published *Fighting Monsters* (2016), a terrible elaboration of the nightmares that haunted his father's life, his thorough research supplanting Wall as the authority. Academic work included Michele Cunningham's two books on prisoners in Borneo, at Sandakan (who had almost all died) and Kuching (who had mostly survived, among them her father), *Defying the Odds* (2006) and *Hell on Earth* (2013).

So much attention had Sandakan attracted that the sub-title of Paul Ham's massive *Sandakan: The untold story* (2012), seemed at best misjudged, at worst false advertising. (Many titles are devised not by authors but by publishers' marketeers.) These books revealed not just the prisoners' terrible fate, but asked why the plan to rescue them – code-named 'Kingfisher' – had been aborted. *Project Kingfisher* (1989) by Athol Moffitt (a prosecutor in the war crimes trials) and Gary Followill in *Operation Kingfisher* (2023) pursued this question. Followill's, based on American documents previously unseen by Australian researchers, offered a persuasive explanation, connecting covert operations in Borneo with the machinations of inter-allied politics.

To the Sandakan canon must now be added Tom Gilling's two books: *Bastard Behind the Lines* (2021, about Jock McLaren, one of the few to escape to fight with Philippine guerillas), and *The Witness* (2023), a more ambivalent tale, testing whether Bill Sticpewich, one of the six survivors, may have collaborated to save himself, even though his testimony decisively convicted Japanese guilty of war crimes. Gilling, a novelist, brought a sensitivity to the challenge of telling a story about which there remains great ambiguity, but also continuing, appalled fascination.

The next push in PoW studies will surely follow the lead of Christina Twomey and Kristen Alexander in following them home, using Repat files and family memories to understand the full ramifications of captivity, even decades and generations on.

19

AUSTRALIA 1942: END OF INNOCENCE

The fall of Singapore and the Japanese conquest of south-east Asia not only brought Australia's greatest crisis as a nation, but decisively changed its conception of its national identity and brought in time a change in its understanding of history. Just as the debacle of Gallipoli had precipitated among the AIF unease at British command, so 1942 signalled, as schoolteacher-author Brian McKinlay put it in 1985, *Australia 1942: End of innocence*. Australians had long feared the nightmare of Asian, and specifically Japanese, aggression – prey to *Fears and Phobias*, as Neville Meaney had entitled his 1996 study of *The problem of Japan 1909–1939*. Singapore's fall foreshadowed, as Curtin said on the wireless two days after the surrender, a 'Battle of Australia'.

The crisis of 1942 has long sustained a cottage industry of writers eager to dramatise Australia's predicament, exposed (if briefly) to Japanese attack and even invasion. Kristen Williamson, using research she conducted for her husband David's 1982 mini-series, published *The Last Bastion*, which presented a beleaguered Australia abandoned by Britain. Books such as Bob Wurth's *1942: Australia's greatest peril* (2008) and *The Battle for Australia* (2013), Peter Thompson's *Pacific Fury* (2008) or Roland Perry's *Pacific 360°* (2012) presented 1942 as (as Perry's jacket blurb put it) 'Australia's Battle for Survival' – indeed his book was re-issued two years later as *The Fight for Australia*. Thompson echoed Carlyon's *Gallipoli* by arguing that Australia's survival balanced on 'a knife-edge' between 'Japanese aggression ... and British deception'.

Buttressed by tenacious popular memory of the mythical 'Brisbane Line', egged on by the Battle for Australia Society and from 2008 seemingly confirmed by the adoption of the first Wednesday in September as Battle for Australia Day, the more extreme interpretation is now widely accepted. Attempts to provide a more balanced understanding of the crisis of 1942 (such as my 2008 *Invading Australia*) drew the ire of the Battle for Australia Society, which decried my research and called for my dismissal as the Memorial's Principal Historian (I had by that time left anyway). A couple of decades of sensational writing has left the field permanently skewed, as suggested by Sue Rosen's *Scorched Earth* (2017), documenting a defensive plan that was never implemented, or Craig Collie's 2020 *On Our Doorstep* with its sub-title, *When Australia faced the threat of invasion by the Japanese.*

The allure of the sensational in books on 1942 can especially be seen in the treatment of the bombing of Darwin, the subject of two major and many more pinprick raids until November 1943. After Douglas Lockwood's *Australia's Pearl Harbour* (1966) (the first besides the official history to use the Lowe Royal Commission's report), the bombing of Darwin attracted some sensationalist books, notably Timothy Hall's *Darwin 1942* (1982) which Alan Powell, already the leading authority on the war in northern Australia, described as 'cribbing from Lockwood where it hadn't got the story wrong'. While Powell's *The Shadow's Edge* (1988) provided a sober account of the attacks, books long on sensation and light on context or perspective continued to appear, such as Rex Ruwoldt's *Darwin's Battle for Australia* (2005). Books like these have led irresponsible tour guides in Darwin to claim – without evidence – that 750 more dead than were officially reported died in the raid but were dumped in the mangroves to be eaten by crocodiles. Not until Peter Grose's *An Awkward Truth* (2009) did an author get the balance right, between the scandal of unpreparedness and the cost (probably slightly higher than the official history had given, but not the 1000 deaths alleged by conspiracists) and the essential fact that the raids on Darwin were made not as preparation for invasion but to impede Allied retaliation against what the Japanese had already seized.

As naval historians emphasise, the Japanese decision to isolate rather than invade Australia prompted books on its submarine campaign, from Lew Lind's *Toku-tai*, on *Japanese submarine operations in Australian waters* (1992) to Terry Jones and Steven Carruthers, *A Parting Shot* (2013). Japanese defeat in the naval battle of Coral Sea, was long represented as 'the battle that saved Australia' (as the Department of Veterans' Affairs website still presents it). Although the Japanese high command decided not to invade Australia in March 1942 (a fact that MacArthur and Curtin realised by mid-year) the thrust of popular books (and websites) on 1942 was that the Kokoda campaign also 'saved Australia from invasion', and it became the central and almost the only widely recognised Australian battle of the war. The fact is that neither saved Australia: the Japanese decided not to invade, and ordered the exhausted remnants of the invasion force to withdraw from Ioribaiwa Ridge.

Sensational treatments of civilians' response to the crisis rely heavily on anecdotal reports of the digging of slit trenches and the formation of the Volunteer Defence Corps. Few tested the drama against the reality. Peter Grose also wrote a balanced account of the Japanese submarine attack on Allied warships in Sydney Harbour in *A Very Rude Awakening* (2007). In it, rather than just repeat the slur that Jewish residents of the eastern suburbs fled to the Blue Mountains, he checked real estate listings, finding the reports to be a fable. Popular authors especially seem to want to subscribe to the dramatic myth rather than the prosaic reality.

20

KOKODA FRONT LINE: THE PAPUAN CAMPAIGN

'Kokoda' – the usual shorthand for the Papuan campaign of 1942–43 – is now the centrepiece of the popular Australian understanding not just of the war in the South-West Pacific, but of the entire Second World War. It used not to be so. As Peter Williams explained in his *Kokoda for Dummies* (2012), 'when I first went to Papua New Guinea in 1980 ... I went to Buna, Lae, Shaggy Ridge, Finschhafen, Rabaul and Bougainville' but not to Kokoda. But 'I can't now imagine a tourist who ... wouldn't have the Kokoda Trail at the top of the list'. Williams concluded that 'something has changed in 30 years'.*

Despite the fame of Kokoda, the first book on the campaign, by journalist and veteran Raymond Paull, appeared only in 1958. Contrary to the boosting which became obligatory, he gave it the downbeat title of *Retreat from Kokoda*, and it appeared sixteen years after the war, a year before Dudley McCarthy's official history volume appeared. (It too had a prosaic title – *South-West Pacific – First Year.*) Paull's book arose from a conversation he had overheard in 1944 aboard HMAS *Manoora* between two officers who had disparaged the Australian defenders of Papua, inspiring Paull to set the record straight. He inherited Chester Wilmot's wartime notes and spent three years gathering evidence, including contacting those who had served in the campaign (who sometimes co-operated reluctantly: 'I don't want to be in your bloody book!', said one former 39th Battalion man). Even then, Paull was

* But Bill Gammage noted that this was not true for him when he had arrived in Port Moresby in 1966 – Kokoda was at the top of his list of places to visit.

conscious that his was but the first attempt to make sense of a campaign which even contemporaries had misunderstood, aware that others would 'soon detect blank spaces in the narrative'. Even with the appearance of Dudley McCarthy's official history, it would take until the early 1980s for interest to coalesce.

Perhaps prompted by David Horner's *Crisis of Command: Australian generalship and the Japanese threat* (1978 – based on his MA thesis) the Papuan campaign has become the focus of Australian writing on the Second World War. Kokoda's centrality derives not just from the commonsense assumption that if the Japanese were advancing on Port Moresby they must have wanted to keep going, but also from the undeniable drama of the ordeal of ill-trained Militia facing a seemingly unstoppable enemy in atrocious terrain. Damien Parer's powerful film, *Kokoda Front Line*, directly and understandably informs popular interest, seen in every documentary touching on the campaign. *Kokoda Front Line* was not just the title of Damien Parer's Oscar-winning documentary but was also chosen by Neil McDonald for the 2012 expanded edition of his already large 1994 biography of Parer, originally *Damien Parer's War*. (Neil was the world's expert on Parer but he just didn't know when to stop.) The 1983 memoir of Henry Steward, *Recollections of a Regimental Medical Officer*, despite its bland title, offered a vivid account of the ordeal of Kokoda, the written counterpart of Damien Parer's footage. Since about then, Kokoda has consumed much attention, from both scholarly and popular authors. 2004 alone saw Peter FitzSimons's and Paul Ham's *Kokodas*, and Stuart Braga's *Kokoda Commander*, on the hard-done-by Major-General Arthur 'Tubby' Allen. A stream of popular and serious books has appeared mostly over the past twenty years, with at least forty books on the campaign, in addition to memoirs and unit histories.

The Papuan campaign seems to demand bulk. Peter Brune's *A Bastard of a Place* is 619 pages; Peter FitzSimons's *Kokoda* is 506. Perhaps the most exhaustive treatment of the Papuan campaign comes in four books (totalling over 2000 pages) by Canberra forensic anthropologist-turned-military-historian David Cameron, whose fifteen books include the step-by-step narrative of *The Battles for Kokoda Plateau*

(2020), *The Battle for Isurava* (2022), *Saving Port Moresby* (2022) and *Retaking Kokoda* (2022). That the fourth is sub-titled *The Battles for Templeton's Crossing, Eora Creek and the Oivi-Gorari Positions* suggests the exhaustive detail in which he has traced the campaign: and he has more to write, about the 'beach-head battles' that followed.

But the stridently nationalist popular narrative of Kokoda 'the battle that saved Australia' was not the only strand in the campaign's history. Just as Gallipoli became viewed in an international perspective as the campaign's centenary approached, so academic interest turned transnational. One foretaste of this came through the Australia–Japan Research Project, funded by Japanese governments seeking reconciliation through scholarship, hosted by the Memorial from the mid-1990s. At the same time, historians like Hank Nelson at the Australian National University and Jeff Grey and Peter Dennis at UNSW Canberra were approaching colleagues overseas, who increasingly participated in academic, Memorial and Army History conferences. The fruits of that more collaborative approach became apparent in (for example) Karl James's 2014 colloquium, Beyond Kokoda, which featured sixteen contributors, including six from Britain, the US or Japan. The chasm between the more astringent academic approach and the bombastic nationalism of popular writers is perhaps the clearest example of how history serves contemporary agendas as much as it constitutes a simple record of the past.

21

ON THE HOME FRONT: AUSTRALIA'S WAR

Little appeared on Australian civilians' war between the publication of Paul Hasluck's two volumes, *The Government and People*, 1952 and 1970. In his *All-In!* (1983), however, Michael McKernan complemented his book on Australian society in the Great War and opened a second front in the social history of Australia's wars. 'The boom in war studies roars on', Lloyd Robson wrote in a favourable review. While irked that Australia ended the war still in an essentially colonial state in 1939, only to the United States instead of Britain, Robson praised McKernan's enterprise in stimulating interest in wartime social history, especially commending his attention to women in the workforce, the evasion of the 'Manpower' bureaucracy and the proliferation of the black market.

Studies of varied aspects of wartime Australia, with both geographical and thematic emphases, followed *All-In!*. Kate Darian-Smith, in *On the Home Front: Melbourne in wartime, 1939–1945* (1990) brought to wartime history the cultural and political concerns of contemporary historical scholarship. Because the wartime generation was still hale, oral history became a key source, exemplified by *The War at Home* (1988) by Daniel Connell, doyen of the ABC's former Social History Unit, and Joanna Penglase's (with David Horner) *When the War Came to Australia* (1992). A quartet of Queensland historians (Kay Saunders and several colleagues) produced *Australia's Frontline* (1992), on Queensland's experience. Oral history and local history advanced understanding, often in tandem.

Each state had different experiences, not least over the American presence – Queensland was most affected; Tasmania least; Western

Australia hosted American submariners (the subject of Anthony Barker and Lisa Jackson's *Fleeting Attraction* (1996)); New South Wales less than you might think. The presence and impact of the hundreds of thousands of American service personnel posted to or passing through Australia attracted relatively few books. John Hammond Moore's *Over-Paid, Over-Sexed and Over Here* (1981) the first book on the subject, was dismissed by Darryl McIntyre (in the Memorial's *Journal*) as 'poorly organized and argued'. Kate Darian-Smith saw Daniel and Annette Potts's *Yanks Down Under* (1985) as the first to treat the subject with 'scholarly respect', even though she thought they had insufficiently tested the myths (including not noticing that Americans were hardly everywhere). Annette Potts and Lucinda Strauss's *For the Love of a Soldier* (1987) dealt with *Australian war-brides and their GIs*, as did Robyn Arrowsmith's *All the Way to the USA* (2013), both drawing on oral history.

Australian historians' strong tradition of labour history has connected with wartime history, notably through the work of Melbourne historian Stuart Macintyre. The premier historian of the Australian Communist Party, Macintyre traced in his final book *The Party* (2022) its wartime 'heyday' as 'The Leading War Party' and its role in pressing for increased war production and the full commitment of the nation's resources. This is such a contrast to Hal Colebatch's *Australia's Secret War*, which claimed (on slim evidence) that workers 'sabotaged' the war effort, that readers comparing the two might imagine they are dealing with two different countries. (I know whose version I back.) Macintyre's insights suggest how much political history has unfortunately been estranged from mainstream military history. Macintyre had already published *Australia's Boldest Experiment* (2015) on *War and reconstruction in the 1940s*, which traced the transformation of Australia from a war to a peace economy, through changes in work, welfare, health, education, immigration and housing, through the application of rational and humane policies and plans. This too made a novel connection between war experience and the 'peace' which military historians customarily take for granted or ignore. Macintyre, who died in 2021, was a powerful intellectual and even moral force in Australian history, widely admired.

The August 1944 outbreak of Japanese PoWs at Cowra has attracted repeated interpretations, though more novels and mini-series than non-fiction books, which include two by journalist Harry Gordon (*Die Like the Carp*, 1978, and *Voyage from Shame*, 1994) and more recently, Graham Apthorpe's *The Man Inside* (2017) and *The Cowra Breakout* by Mat McLachlan (2022). All three authors exhibit a marked sympathy for the Japanese prisoners. Graham Apthorpe had been involved in building Cowra's relationship with Japan, and all researchers benefited from the work of David Sissons, who as a young sergeant in 1945 had learned Japanese. The relationship between Australia and Japan dominated his life. Though he published little, researchers consulted his papers, finally published in two volumes as *Bridging Australia and Japan* in 2016 and 2020.

Much more remains to be said about the civilian experience of Australia's Second World War, though in the absence of forthcoming anniversaries, it is likely that the mainstream of Australian military history will continue to regard civilians as marginal. The impetus to challenge the dominance of the 'uniformed' story may come from the developing field of community histories, such as Greg Raffin's study of the wartime National Emergency Services in central NSW, *Every Cloud has a Silver Lining* (2022).

22

HELL'S BATTLEFIELD: NEW GUINEA AND THE ISLANDS

Besides the Western Front, the campaigns in New Guinea, 1943–45, were the most extensive in which Australia has ever been involved; in numbers engaged, physical extent and in the challenges posed by the region's terrain, climate and environment, and of course by a tenacious and skillful enemy. As on the Western Front, the campaigns were directed and supported by a dominant ally, one which (contrary to popular belief) took a full part in the theatre.

The New Guinea Offensives, David Dexter's volume of the 1939–1945 official history, documented the 1943–44 campaigns fully, devoting the second largest single volume of the series to the great offensive which liberated much of Australian New Guinea, from Salamaua and Lae to the Ramu-Markham valleys and Shaggy Ridge and on beyond Finschhafen. These operations, planned jointly and executed by Australian troops with massive American air, naval and logistic support, represented the most intensive and extensive in Australia's busy military history. Though fully reported at the time (and notably the subject of Damien Parer's film *Assault on Salamaua*) apart from Dexter's volume and some unit histories, they were also almost completely neglected. Gradually, the litany of names familiar to the war generation – Bulldog, Kaiapit, Madang, Merauke, Wau – became virtually unrecognised; even the phrase 'up in the islands', once so redolent of arduous campaigns, fell out of consciousness. So much had the New Guinea campaigns become neglected that in 1992 I gave a paper at a Memorial history conference describing a 'green hole' in Australian military history. Coincidentally, the deficiency was soon rectified. A decade later I reprised the paper at an Army history conference, 'The green hole re-considered', finding that the picture had largely been reversed.

Perhaps the turning point came with the publication of John Coates's *Bravery Above Blunder* (1999), on the 9th Division in the Huon Peninsula campaign. Coates, who had recently retired as a lieutenant-general, had formed a fruitful partnership with the emerging powerful triumvirate of Roger Lee of the Army History Unit and Jeff Grey and Peter Dennis of UNSW Canberra. In *Bravery Above Blunder* (I wrote in *Wartime*, of which I was then the managing editor), 'traditional military history in Australia has never been done better'. Coates was a wise and humane man and had overcome the obstacle of a shockingly deprived childhood to cap a distinguished military career with significant contributions to history.

Besides soldiers' memoirs, several authors made strong contributions to filling the green hole, notably Mark Johnston and Phillip Bradley, among the most impressive of the non-institutional authors who have been such a distinctive part of the writing of Australian military history. Mark Johnston, the foremost authority on army operational history in the Second World War, besides his magisterial *At the Front Line* (1996; the Second World War equivalent to *The Broken Years*) produced a trilogy of divisional histories, of the 6th, 7th and 9th (2006, 2005 and 2002 respectively) and *An Australian Band of Brothers* (2018), astonishing for how he got 'inside' the otherwise closed world of a company of the 2/43rd Battalion. From the early 2000s, Phillip Bradley produced a series of books on the theatre's most significant phases, Bradley, a scientist by training, became a virtual one-man library, doing for New Guinea what David Cameron did for Papua, publishing half-a-dozen books on the 1943–44 campaigns (plus versions for the Army History Unit's 'Campaign' series). They included *On Shaggy Ridge* (2005), *The Battle for Wau* (2008), *To Salamaua* (2010), and *D-Day New Guinea* (2019). His *Hell's Battlefield* (2012) told 'the whole story of the Australians against the Japanese in New Guinea during World War II, from invasion in 1942 to the brutal end game in 1945'.

The war in the islands involved more than just the army (though you might not think so from the books published, which emphasise not just the army but the AIF in contrast with the Militia). The RAN and RAAF played major roles in sustaining and supporting the campaigns, though accounts of operations tend to be produced by proponents of the separate services, who dine at separate tables.* Norman Ashworth's *How Not to Run an Air Force!* (2000) acknowledged how the RAAF's dysfunctional command structure damaged its operations. David Stevens's account of RAN operations around New Guinea in *From a Hostile Shore*, for example, is better known to fellow naval historians than to the authors of books on campaigns on land. Likewise, the RAN and RAAF both served in the 1944 operations in which American forces advanced into Dutch New Guinea (described in, for example, Mervyn Eather and Bill Galmés's *Taken by Storm*, on the landing ship *HMAS Manoora*) is unfamiliar to most Australian readers.

Air force histories, especially squadron histories, detail its part in the Pacific war, often ranging far beyond the New Guinea battlefront (literally so in Bob Cleworth's *The Night Shift* (2015) and Michael Nelmes's *Tocumwal to Tarakan* (1994) representing a distinct approach to air force history, focusing on a particular aircraft, of Catalina flying boats and Liberator long-range bombers respectively. Mark Johnston's *Whispering Death* (2011), on the RAAF in the Pacific war, is the most recent general account of its most extensive sole commitment. He found the story 'inspiring and disturbing', describing both its members' valour and dedication, but also how it remained dependent upon larger allies throughout the war: not a conclusion that George Odgers allowed himself to admit in his *The Royal Australian Air Force: An illustrated history* (1965; the first book I borrowed from the Viscount Slim Library in Whyalla aged about 13).

Rather than operations in 1945 winding down, after a relative lull in 1944 the Australian campaigns in the South-West Pacific intensified. The year saw Australian formations fighting on a great arc across the islands north of Australia, from New Britain and Bougainville on the east through Aitape-Wewak in north-west Australian New Guinea to three 'Oboe' amphibious landings in Borneo, at Tarakan, Brunei Bay/

* The phrase is Shelford Bidwell's, in his *Fire-power* (1982).

Labuan and Balikpapan. The last was the largest Australian amphibious invasion since Gallipoli, in which the 7th Division fought as hard as ever in the war's final month. Again, though chronicled in Gavin Long's volume, *The Final Campaigns* (1963), these operations waited a further twenty years to attract attention from other than unit historians.

When they did, a book stuck the 1945 campaigns with a label which has proved to be surprisingly durable. Peter Charlton, a senior journalist with Brisbane's *Courier Mail*, had written *The Thirty Niners*, a tribute to his father's generation. Aware that some of the longest-serving volunteers had died in the 1945 campaigns, in 1983 Charlton published *The Unnecessary War*. Criticised by John Robertson of the RMC History Department (in the Memorial's *Journal*) as 'simplistic' though 'readable and well-intentioned', Charlton had popularised a memorable phrase which essentially questioned the value of the loss of at least over 1000 Australians (the figure Robertson had given in his *Australia at War*). While the New Britain and Aitape-Wewak campaigns remain virtually ignored, the large and costly Bougainville campaign has been re-evaluated by Karl James of the Memorial in *The Hard Slog* (2012).

In 1994, in preparation for the Memorial's 50th anniversary exhibition *1945: War & Peace*, I tossed a coin over whether to visit Borneo or New Guinea to experience the jungle battleground of 1945, and Borneo won. After a profoundly influential trip to the locations of the Oboe operations, Sandakan and Labuan war cemetery, I became entranced by the subject and produced both the exhibition and *Tarakan: An Australian tragedy* (1997). Otherwise, besides the interest in Z Special (see chapter 39) the Borneo operations have still not received their due, though Christine Helliwell revealed the relationship between the people of Borneo and their Australian liberators in her *Semut* (2021), which justifiably won the Prime Minister's Prize for Australian History in 2022.

But *Semut*'s quality and success notwithstanding, it is irrefutable and unfortunate that Tarakan and Bougainville remain the only two of the final campaigns to have been accorded full-scale books. Clearly, despite the popularity of Australian military history, interest is unevenly distributed. But the renewed vigour in this field is clear in three collections edited by Peter Dean: *Australia 1942* (2013), *Australia 1943* (2014) and *Australia 1944–45* (2016) which collectively reflected the diversity and maturity of both Australian scholarship on the Pacific war, demonstrating research by developing scholars, but also, as with Gallipoli, Australian engagement with international research.

These were literally and figuratively the battles fought closest to Australia. It is odd that eighty years after 1945, Australians rely for an account of some campaigns on an official history published in 1963.

23

HIGH COMMAND: POLITICS AND STRATEGY

By definition almost, wars are the violent expression of international relations, though military historians tend to leave that discussion to specialists in 'diplomatic history'. Building on the work of pioneers of international relations such as Gordon Greenwood, Norman Harper and the legendary William McMahon Ball, the most influential scholar in this field became Carl Bridge. From the Menzies Centre in London, Bridge has published widely on Australia's international relations in wartime, notably *Munich to Vietnam* (1991) and *A Delicate Mission* (2008), on *The Washington diaries of R. G. Casey*. From London, Bridge fostered scholarship, energetically forming networks between scholars and universities internationally, a notable example of the importance of individual generosity and patronage in stimulating research and publication.

In the 1980s scholars became notably less respectful of the traditional narrative. David Day's *Menzies and Churchill at War*, rightly sub-titled *A controversial new account of the 1941 struggle for power* (1986), explored the clash between the two imperial-minded conservative leaders of democracies at war, a portentous one for Menzies and Australia. A reviewer thought that the episode merited merely an article. The reviewer wrote only one book, but Day, an Australian who had used British sources to good effect in his Cambridge PhD, went on to publish a string of substantial books on wartime politics. They included *The Great Betrayal* (1988), *Reluctant Nation* (1992), *Brave New World* (1996) and, especially influential, *John Curtin* (1999). That Day largely wrote these books while a freelancer was an astonishing achievement, as was the nationalism he espoused in the restrained field of diplomatic history.

The drama of wartime politics has attracted several writers, such as Laurie Fitzhardinge's and Donald Horne's biographies of Billy Hughes, both entitled *The Little Digger* (1979 and 1983). While much attention on Robert Menzies focused on his long premiership from 1949, his short term of 1939–41 was assessed by Allan Martin's *Robert Menzies: A life* (Volume I, 1993). John Curtin has attracted particular attention, not least because he has been seen by admirers as 'the man who saved Australia from invasion'. A complex and contradictory character, Curtin was an anti-conscriptionist who sent conscripts overseas and a champion of Australian nationalism who famously 'turned to America' and subordinated his government to an American general. He's had more attention than any Australian wartime leader, in John Edwards's *John Curtin's Gift* (2005) and two volumes of *John Curtin's War* (2017 and 2018) and David Lee's short but punchy 2024 'biographical monograph'.

Pride that operations in New Guinea saw the largest military forces that Australia had ever fielded should not obscure the degree to which Australia depended upon American support, and indeed operated under the orders of an American theatre commander, General Douglas MacArthur. Roger Bell's *Unequal Allies: Australian-American relations and the Pacific War* (1977), though an early-career book, demonstrated how despite wartime rhetoric (still heard on the podium at the launch of AUKUS in 2022) that the two nations shared a 'Pacific Partnership' (as George Johnston's propaganda book of 1944 put it), the relationship was a severely pragmatic one. Bell showed how the United States supported Australia because it needed a base in the region. John Curtin's celebrated 'turn to America' (in which he sought American aid even before the disasters in the Pacific) merely irritated and embarrassed influential Americans – Roosevelt's administration found it obnoxious and craven. The then naval officer Tom Frame's *Pacific Partners* (1992) cast the relationship in more benign terms.

International relations in wartime long failed to connect with military history. Bean's official history respectfully failed to enquire into Australia's relations with Britain, simply accepting its subordinate position in the empire, a relationship which Eric Andrews subjected to scrutiny in his *The Anzac Illusion* (1993). Gavin Long's official history notoriously failed to deal with the higher direction of Australia's war and especially Australia's relationship with its senior alliance partners. Though thorough in documenting Australian operations, Long lacked both sources and expertise to deal with the complexities of strategic command, and senior figures remained influential politically, deterring awkward exposures. Paul Hasluck's volumes on *The Government and the People* did reveal aspects that politicians and bureaucrats might have wished concealed (such as that Australia, not Japan, had breached Portuguese sovereignty, precipitating the tragedy in which as many Timorese died as Australians in the whole war) but he made disclosures so enigmatically and at a time when interest was at its lowest – during the Vietnam war, at the end of two decades of conservative rule and before the revival in military history. However, David Horner, the rising scholar–soldier, was soon to fill the gap.

Horner, like Bob O'Neill a graduate of RMC but a decade younger (but also a veteran of Vietnam), took up challenges which O'Neill identified in his review of Long's *The Six Years War* (see chapter 24). O'Neill had pointed to Long's lack of interest in the characters or interaction of those responsible for Australia's war effort. (In fairness, not all expectations of an official historian can be met, especially when writing within the lifetimes of many of the major players.) Horner took up the baton from Long. He wrote what can be regarded as the 'missing' official history volume, dealing with the higher direction of Australia's war, which became his *High Command* (1982), based on his prize-winning Australian National University PhD, which John Robertson praised as 'the most substantial book in years on Australia in the second world war' [sic]. In his *Inside the War Cabinet* (1996) Horner continued his revelations of Menzies and Curtin's war leadership, and in his *Defence Supremo* (2000) confirmed his authority as the leading scholar of the direction of Australia's largest war effort.

Latterly seconded by scholars such as Peter Dean, David Lee (formerly of Foreign Affairs and Trade and now of UNSW Canberra) Horner's lead arguably completed Gavin Long's mission.

24

THE SIX YEARS WAR: THE SECOND WORLD WAR OFFICIAL HISTORIES

Gavin Long, another *Sydney Morning Herald* journalist and a protégé of Bean's, proved through his reporting of the brief campaign in France in 1940, and of the Mediterranean campaigns of 1941, that he was a conscientious and reliable correspondent (unlike, say, the talented poet Kenneth Slessor, for a time also a correspondent). In 1942, Bean proposed Long as his successor, conscious that the 'architect' of the next history had the responsibility for 'a greater sequel' to his own but confident in Long's 'capacity and character'. Long's biographer, Garry Hills, observed that 'Long consistently proved himself worthy of Bean's endorsement'. Indeed, 'in many ways', Hills wrote, 'he surpassed Bean', not least in leading a project twice the size of Bean's series. Appointed in 1943, Long eventually devised a schema of twenty-two volumes in five series, devoted to the three armed services, with a 'Civil' and a 'Medical' series. The Army series was the largest, with seven volumes, three of which Long wrote himself (Volume I, *To Benghazi* (1952), Volume II, *Greece, Crete and Syria* (1953) and Volume VII, *The Final Campaigns* (1963)).

Another two volumes were also written by journalists. Volume III, *Tobruk and El Alamein* (1967), was begun by Chester Wilmot, an Australian journalist who became a star war correspondent and who through his book *The Struggle for Europe* (1952) helped to explain the final year of the European war and its implications for the post-war world. After Wilmot died in one of the Comet air disasters in January

1954, his volume was taken up by Barton Maughan, a Sydney lawyer who had served with the 2/13th Battalion, gaining the Military Cross and ending the war as a lieutenant-colonel at Mountbatten's headquarters in Ceylon (now Sri Lanka). The journalist Lionel Wigmore, who had survived the Japanese conquest of south-east Asia, ordered out of Java just in time, wrote Volume IV, *The Japanese Thrust* (1957).

Two diplomats wrote volumes in the Army series – Dudley McCarthy's *South-West Pacific Area – First Year* (1959; the dullest title), and David Dexter, who had served as a commando in New Guinea, *The New Guinea Offensives* (1961).* As was usual until the Vietnam war history (and not all volumes then), Long's was largely written by part-time authors. Dexter, for example, recorded in the preface to his volume that he had written it 'in Canberra, in Colombo and on a tea estate in Ceylon's high country', while he completed it in India as counsellor to the Australian High Commissioner. 'At many midnights over the years I had perforce to leave Private Smith and his patrol in danger along the jungle track – and yet as often as not I went on with him through the night.' Dexter dedicated his book to 'the men who fought'.

Soon after Long's retirement, the distinguished historian Bob O'Neill, head of the Strategic and Defence Studies Centre at the Australian National University, wrote that in contrast to Bean's emphasis on individual gallantry, Long tended to present Australian operations as 'team actions', focussing more on collective achievement than 'the way in which the captain led'. It became clear that Long and his authors were muted in criticising decisions by Australian senior officers – in evaluating disasters such as the collapse of the Australian defence of Singapore, for example, Lionel Wigmore (a journalist writing his first book) was circumspect in describing the actions of men still alive. All the volumes were read in draft by participants, often senior officers tender about their reputations, notably Wilfred Kent Hughes, a pugnacious Liberal politician who had spent years in captivity. At the

* Mark Johnston: 'McCarthy may have the dullest title but if marooned on a desert island I'd take that one with me'.

same time, Long 'pricked the bubble' of MacArthur's vanity (as O'Neill put it) and in his *MacArthur as Military Commander* (1969; the book he wrote in his all-too-brief retirement), put the needle in again.

The two volumes in the Naval series (1939–42 and 1942–45) were by George Hermon Gill, who had served in naval intelligence, had edited the wartime *'H.M.A.S.'* series of 'Christmas books' and who is regarded as having (in contrast to many Australian official histories) set Australia's naval war in a global context. Gill's account of the 1941 *Sydney–Kormoran* fight was shown by later research (including the investigation of the wrecks, located in 2008) to be mistaken – how could it not be?

Given the scale of Australia's air war (by 1945 the RAAF had become the world's fourth largest air force) it received greater attention than had the Flying Corps in the Great War series. Douglas Gillison, an aviation journalist, wrote Volume I, largely an account of the RAAF's expansion, 1939–42. George Odgers, a newspaperman who had served in the Pacific as an army sergeant, later commissioned in the RAAF, wrote Volume II, *Air War Against Japan 1943–1945*. John Herington, a wartime flying boat pilot who narrowly survived when his Catalina crashed in Northern Ireland in 1943, wrote two volumes. He produced Volume III, *Air War against Germany and Italy 1939–1943* and Volume IV, *Air Power Over Europe 1944–1945,* the emphasis in the title indicating the contribution air power made to victory in Europe, and the scale of the RAAF's part in it. Unlike the British official history of the strategic bombing offensive, in which Sir Charles Webster and Noble Frankland made themselves unpopular with the Royal Air Force by criticising its justification and effects, Herington largely chronicled the Australian contribution to air operations.*

* Noble Frankland became Director of the Imperial War Museum 1960–82, influencing key innovations in its engagement with history, including the popular TV series, *The Great War* (1964) and *The World at War* (1973). His autobiographical *History at War: The campaigns of a historian* (1988) frankly detail the RAF's attempts to muzzle or dilute his volumes of the British official history. It's a great pity no Australian official historian has ever spilled the beans in the same way.

Again, reflecting the greater demands the Second World War made on Australian people, Long's series included five volumes in the 'Civil' series. Volumes I and II, *The Government and the People*, 1939–41 and 1942–1945, were commissioned in 1944 from Paul Hasluck. A Western Australian polymath (journalist, academic, social activist and pioneering Australian diplomat and minister under Menzies), Hasluck finally published Volume II while Governor-General, in 1970. His volumes were the longest in gestation of any official history in any series, and seemingly the laziest, largely summarising official files. The brilliant economist Syd Butlin likewise took decades to complete his two volumes of *War Economy*, the first published in 1955, the second completed by Boris Schedvin and published in the year of Butlin's death, 1977. The chemist David Mellor's Volume V, *The Role of Science and Industry* (1958) reflected the sophistication of the Australian war economy, which distinguished the Second World War from the first.

Finally, while Arthur Butler's medical series was seen as distinct from Bean's, Long's included four volumes by Allan Walker, a Sydney pathologist who had served in both world wars. Walker initially declined Long's invitation but changed his mind when he learned that the surgeon Rupert Downes, who had also served in the world wars, had been killed in an air accident in 1945. Like Butler, Walker heroically wrote several volumes individually, on *Clinical Problems of War* (Volume I), on the *Middle East and Far East* (Volume II), and on *The Island Campaigns* (Volume III). A fourth volume on the medical services of the RAN and RAAF, and on women in the Army's services, was completed by other authors after he retired (not surprisingly) from ill health. All appeared within a decade: an extraordinary record, though largely of specialist interest.

In contrast to Bean's *Anzac to Amiens*, Long's *The Six Years War* remains a useful summary, though it was completed by the faithful Bill Sweeting, appearing six years after Long's death – he had died in the same year as Bean, in 1968. Bob O'Neill reviewed *The Six Years War* in 1975. Looking at 'the several feet' of Long's volumes, he wondered 'what more is there to be said' but realised that they constituted 'a strong base from which deeper exploration into the unknown may be made'.

However, as Michael McKernan observed in 1987, instead of 'opening up arguments which other historians could explore, they seem to have stunned their colleagues by amassing such a wealth of detail': and of course, the archives on which the official historians relied long remained closed to researchers without official entrée.

In reviewing John Robertson's *Australia at War 1939–1945* in 1981, Joan Beaumont wrote that the state of Australia's Second World War history remained 'fairly rudimentary', its limitations perhaps a consequence of the small number of historians, the attractive power of the Great War and limited access to archives. But Beaumont also argued that the war lacked drama compared to the first, and that Australia's subordinate role explained its relative neglect (but surely no less than 1914–18?) She thought that Robertson 'fails to make his case convincingly'. I reviewed it too – almost my first published book review. I thought that Robertson 'has surpassed Long's work as a stimulus to future scholarly debate'. I also praised how he 'turns without strain from the considerations of LHQ [Land Headquarters] and Curtin's cabinet to the feelings of the families of men killed in the campaigns of 1945'. I sought the same span when I came to write my *Tarakan* fifteen years later. Still, in 1985 – *forty* years after 1945 – David Kent lamented that 'relatively little has been written about Australia's role in the Second World War'.

Beaumont herself soon contributed to the war's reappraisal in her collection *Australia's War 1939–1945* (1996), as did Michael McKernan in his best-selling *The Strength of a Nation* (2006). As is apparent from this book's chapters on the Second World War, it is among the most fertile stimulants to research and interpretation. Extraordinarily, given the stature, scale and significance of Gavin Long's official history, it has taken until now – over fifty years after his death – for a biography to be written. Thankfully, that regrettable omission will now be filled, with the imminent publication of Garry Hills's *Great at Heart*.

PART V
POST-1945

25

THE FORGOTTEN WAR: BCOF, KOREA AND THE COLD WAR

For six years Australian units, including battalions of what became the new Royal Australian Regiment (RAR), formed part of the British Commonwealth Occupation Force (BCOF). Like the 1919 North Russian intervention, it became one of the perennial re-discovered subjects in Australian military history. Besides Bob O'Neill's official history, it has been documented fully in half-a-dozen works, from Larry Lacey's *Unofficial History* (1995) to Robin Gerster's entertaining and stimulating *Travels in Atomic Sunshine* (2008), surely a contender for best title as well as the most insightful account of the occupation. Keiko Tamura's *Michi's Memories* (2001), the biography of a soldier's Japanese bride, deserves to be noted as an example of how military and social history can productively coincide.

The Australian presence in BCOF ensured that the RAAF's 77 Squadron became one of the first elements of the United Nations to join the Korean war when in June 1950 a rumbling Korean civil war became international. The everlasting cliché about the war in Korea is that it is supposedly 'forgotten', a tag applied before its end by an American journalist. He was referring to how Americans, eager to embrace their nation's emerging consumer society, ignored their forces at war in Asia, but the tag is now applied in every news story about it. Type 'Korea forgotten war' into Google and you'll get 12.9 million hits in 1.83 seconds: it's the most remembered forgotten war in history. The cliché endures. Doug Hurst published *The Forgotten Few* (2008), on 77 Squadron in the war, even though David Wilson had produced a history in *Lion Over Korea* in 1994, and Bob O'Neill's official history had devoted a hundred pages to 77 Squadron's service. The very first paragraph of Tom Gilling's recent *The Diggers of Kapyong* uses the f-word, of course. (And it is one of *two* books to deal with the battle out *this year* – the other is David Cameron's *Let the Bastards Come.*)

Even though Australia was itself enjoying post-war prosperity increasingly shared by European migrants, Korea was hardly overlooked. Journalists such as Harry Gordon reported on it at the time, and the Memorial published Norman Bartlett's *With the Australians in Korea* (1954). (Seemingly emulating Bean, Bartlett thought of his book as 'virtually a short official history': it wasn't.) The 1970s saw an official history begin, *Australia and the Korean War* by Robert (Bob) O'Neill, the most academically distinguished of the clutch of educated soldiers the Australian Army produced from mid-century. An infantry officer who had served in Vietnam (and written a book about it, *Vietnam Task*), O'Neill had already done an Oxford thesis on the German army and the Nazi party and wrote the Korean history in addition to his academic work. His two volumes (published in 1981 and 1985) devoted as much attention to the strategy and diplomacy of the war as to Australia's army, naval and air operations, effectively constituting a history of the entire war with an Australian orientation. His volumes gained high praise, overseas and in Australia. O'Neill went on to a stellar career overseas, as Chichele Professor of the History of War at Oxford, retiring to Australia and dying in 2023, one of the few Australian military historians to have made an impact on the field internationally.

The supposedly forgotten war continued to attract attention, such as Gavin McCormack's *Cold War, Hot War* (1983), which approached it with bracing scepticism, albeit demolished by O'Neill in a stinging review, particularly critical of McCormack's partiality toward Wilfred Burchett, the Australian journalist condemned as a traitor. McCormack reviewed O'Neill's second volume in *Historical Studies* three years later, not surprisingly describing it as 'military history in the narrow sense', and regarding the appendix on prisoners of war, by Phil Greville (a former PoW) as flawed because of its uncritical disdain for Burchett.* Australian history is and always has been a small world. Jeff Grey's UNSW PhD was published in Britain as *The Commonwealth Armies and the Korean War*, an early example of how he resisted parochial tendencies, seeking to connect Australia with the contexts in which it fought.

The Cold War precipitated more than one official history series, both demonstrating David Horner's breadth of vision and the reach of his reputation and influence. As official records were released, books on the Australian Security Intelligence Organisation (ASIO) and on well-known episodes such as the Petrov affair appeared (including Robert Manne's *The Petrov Affair* (1987) and Frank Cain's *The Australian Security Intelligence Organisation* (1994)). Horner persuaded the Rudd government to authorise in 2008 an official history of ASIO, a testament to his standing in the field, reassuring an agency understandably wary of scrutiny. Securing permission to consult the files was a triumph for David Horner. A Defence insider, he argued that 'myths or half-truths' had damaged ASIO's standing and that a candid history would restore trust. As a necessary corollary he demanded and was granted complete access to ASIO's records and accepted neither direction nor censorship, except for the usual caveat of national security. Horner and his colleagues so gained ASIO's confidence that it extended the project's reach to 1989; virtually to the end of the Cold War.

Recognising the importance of intelligence agencies, and citing British histories of MI5 and MI6, his official history comprised three volumes, *The Spycatchers* (dealing with 1949–63, its title a nod to former MI5 member Peter Wright's *Spycatcher* (1987), which the British government notoriously failed to suppress). John Blaxland's *The Protest Years* (2015) covered 1963–75, with a third volume, *The Secret Cold War* (2016) by Blaxland and Rhys Crawley, on 1975–89.

---

* Michael McKernan (who was responsible for liaising with O'Neill over the Korean official history) recalled that 'Bob O'Neill asked me if I could see if Phil Greville would, perhaps, tone down some of the stuff on Burchett. Phil hit the roof advising me that he would withdraw the entire appendix if a word on Burchett was altered. It is probably the single strongest criticism of an individual in any of the official histories.' Greville had been a PoW in Korea and held Burchett responsible for the appalling treatment PoWs received.

Whether the project was allowed to read and report the full story will be for the future to judge.

The British atomic testing saga demonstrates the way important issues move from secrecy, ignorance and indifference, to becoming controversial subjects of political enquiry and investigative and popular journalism, to eventually becoming the focus of substantive historical studies. That process literally took a lifetime. Atomic tests on the Montebello Islands in 1952 and 1956, at Emu Field in 1953 and at 'Maralinga', 200 kilometres south, 1956–63 led to claims of widespread illness, prompting a royal commission in 1984. Elizabeth Tynan's *Atomic Thunder: The Maralinga story* (2016) handsomely won the Prime Minister's Prize for Australian History. (One of the curiosities that Tynan uncovered was that 'Maralinga', though an Indigenous word, did not come from the country blighted by the tests, chosen by an official committee because in Garik (a tongue spoken near Darwin) it meant 'thunder'.)

The Cold War's two other 'hot wars' for Australia, the Malayan emergency (1948–60) and the 'Confrontation' with Indonesia (1964–66), have attracted little attention beyond ex-service circles (with books such as Colin Bannister's *An Inch of Bravery: 3 RAR in the Malayan Emergency 1957–59* (1994) the best example). In a miniature instance of the 'Bean Effect', the very comprehensiveness of the official histories, by Peter Dennis and Jeff Grey (in one volume in 1996), may have deterred inquiry. But David Horner's exposure of the secret 'Claret Operations' (in his *SAS: Phantoms of the Jungle* and *Duty First*) constituted the most dramatic revelation of a surprisingly thin literature. Otherwise, many aspects of Australia's Cold War remain to be explored.

26

THE MINEFIELD: AUSTRALIA'S VIETNAM

As this is a personal history, I have to confess that, as I've said many times, I don't 'do' Vietnam. As it's the first war I remember, and though in 1967 I parroted the 'domino theory' to my Grade 5 class, by 1972 I thought it an unjustified, even immoral, war. But I have a view on its place in Australian military history. Vietnam is the largest of Australia's small wars, and has been the subject of strong and continuing interest, in memoirs, unit histories and books on both the conduct of the war and its implications for Australia, arguably greater than even the long 'War on Terror' of the 21st century.

As Australia's second-longest overseas conflict, and one that aroused serious opposition, Vietnam has generated a disproportionately large and diverse literature, from Lex McAulay's *The Battle of Long Tan: The legend of Anzac upheld* (1986) to Val Noone's *Disturbing the War: Melbourne Catholics and Vietnam* (1993), a literature in which personal involvement long remained a determining motivation. (The personal computer and longer, more active retirement made it easier for veterans to produce memoirs – a genre ripe for analysis.) Authors rightly rely on veterans' memories, and Paul Ham's *Vietnam* perhaps most closely reflected what veterans felt about their war. Mark Dapin, when interviewing them at home for his *The Nashos' War*, found that they often had a 'war alcove' 'with a regimental crest on the wall and Paul Ham's *Vietnam* ... on the bookshelf'.

Several academics in history and literature at UNSW Canberra, Jeff Grey, Jeff Doyle and Peter Pearce, published influential collections of essays, notably *Vietnam Days* (1991), *Vietnam: War, myth and memory*

(1991) and *Australia's Vietnam War* (2002), reflecting the ferment the war aroused; again, it formed part of the lives of many of the contributors – Grey's father had commanded a battalion in Phuoc Tuy. One of the themes of Grey, Doyle and Pierce's work on the war's cultural impact was to argue that much of the 'Australian' view had in fact imbibed an American inflection, especially through films and fiction. Dapin (himself the author of novels set in Vietnam) realised 'how profoundly the truth about Vietnam had been corrupted by post-war fiction'. This makes interpreting Vietnam arguably more complex than other, larger conflicts. Mark Dapin's *Australia's Vietnam: Myths vs history* (2018) contested (and indeed demolished) some of the most persistent fables the war had thrown up (including the furphy of 'no welcome parades' and 'the myth of airport demonstrations'. (Dapin's book begins with an affectionate portrait of Jeff Grey, his doctoral supervisor, one of the finest accolades I've read – and I edited UNSW Canberra's tribute, *Jeff Grey* (2017) following his shocking death in 2016.)

The war became contentious while it was being fought (though not from the beginning; popular opposition developed only around 1970, as the Australian commitment diminished), and arguments soon influenced what was written about it. Michael Sexton's *War for the Asking: Australia's Vietnam secrets* (1983) was based on cables and cabinet papers which came into his hands, arguing that Australia's support was pressed on the United States. Peter Edwards, soon after being appointed official historian, called it 'a provocative book': his own view was more complex and measured. In the same year, Peter King's *Australia's Vietnam* (1983) made 'an attempt to open up scholarly analysis of Australia's involvement', inevitably unevenly. He asked 'whether the controversies surrounding Vietnam will attract or deter the next generation of writers on Australian military and diplomatic history'. The literature on the Vietnam war is vast, and much of it partisan, sometimes in surprising ways. The most trenchant critique of Australian operations came from Greg Lockhart, another former soldier with a PhD, who published *The Minefield* (2007), exposing one of the most egregious failures of Australia's war – the infamous Dat Do mine barrier, which the Viet Cong regarded as '*kho tang vu khi*' ('weapons store house'). Lockhart's former comrades warmly embraced his book, many confirming its argument and congratulating him for revealing the 'strategic self-deception' that led to hundreds of Australians being killed or maimed by their own mines used against them. Lockhart's history was no mere academic product: veterans appreciated his revelations, which incidentally helped some to establish the psychological effects of the mine threat in dealings with Veterans' Affairs.

The *Official History of Australia in Southeast Asian Conflicts* (as it became with the addition of the Malayan Emergency and the Confrontation with Indonesia) became the most contentious official history project ever. The content of the project's volumes, overseen by Peter Edwards, the very model of a diplomatic historian, caused few ripples – surprisingly for a conflict which had been so contentious. But members of the team fell out, and a difference between him and at least one of his authors had to be sorted out – Ken Inglis acted as a mediator. But viewing it from the outside – and even though I worked in the next office the official historians kept largely to themselves – they seemed not to be as harmonious a team as, say, Long's had been or Horner's teams would be. As with other projects, deaths and departures disrupted the even production of volumes, leading to notable delays.

By 1998 almost all of its volumes had appeared (in 1993, Ian McNeill's *To Long Tan* and Peter Edwards's *Crises and Commitments* (1994), Brendan O'Keefe's *Medicine at War* (1995), Chris Coulthard-Clark's *The RAAF in Vietnam* (1996), Peter Dennis and Jeff Grey's *Emergency and Confrontation* (1997), Peter Edwards's *A Nation at War* (1998), and Jeff Grey's *Up Top* (1998) – the latter on the RAN). The final 'Army' volumes, however, caused the greatest angst. Ian McNeill, a former army officer, had published a lauded first volume, *To Long Tan* (the title an echo of Gavin Long's *To Benghazi*) in 1993. In 1998 he died suddenly. Rather than appoint a new writer (with David Horner the expected successor), Steve Gower (the Memorial's director 1996–2012) and Peter Edwards promoted McNeill's research assistant, Ashley Ekins, to complete the second volume, which was supposedly well in hand. As years passed, this became an increasingly tenuous proposition. I found Steve Gower's attempts to justify the delay in completing the project embarrassing. The Memorial's annual reports to Parliament documented its protracted gestation. In 1998 the volume had been expected to appear in 1999. But, year by year, the expected publication date advanced: in 2000 to 2002, in 2003 to 2004, by 2006 to 2007, by 2008 to 2009, and so on.

Ekins revered McNeill as his mentor and insisted on McNeill's name being included on the title page of the two volumes he eventually published. (The second volume grew to three: Ekins maintained that the complexity of operations demanded an additional volume and Gower surprisingly acceded.) He loyally kept his cards close to his chest, never disclosing how much McNeill had written before his death. Whether the alleged complexity justified an extra volume or whether Ekins's perfectionism explained the delay will only be revealed once the official files are fully opened, perhaps not until the mid-2030s. *Fighting to the Finish* (finally published in 2012; the title an ironic comment on Ekins's attitude to those who attempted to expedite his task) came in at 1139 pages, longer than Bean's longest volume, an extraordinary length for a book dealing with what was actually a brigade group in the war's final years. By contrast, Long's *The Final Campaigns* dealt with six campaigns conducted by two Australian armies across the South-West Pacific in 1945 in just 667 pages. My dissatisfaction with what I saw as Gower's uncharacteristically indulgent management of the project contributed to my decision to leave the Memorial in 2007.

Veterans had always been sensitive to opposition to the war, which many construed as hostility to them (another of the myths with which Mark Dapin grappled). They certainly resented books which presented them as killers: at a Memorial conference in 1987 I saw journalist Stuart Rintoul defend his book *Ashes of Vietnam* and his claims that troops had perpetrated atrocities: they vociferously (and understandably) rejected Rintoul's vague charge. But, surprisingly, the most acrimonious consequences emerged from veterans' reactions to the official history. The first, documented by the journalist Frank Walker's *Ghost Platoon* (2011) arose from the Memorial's inexplicable intransigence in refusing to recognise the existence of an improvised 'Defence and Employment Platoon' which in 1969 participated in an ambush at Thua Tich, after which the bodies of Viet Cong dead were dragged to where they were buried or blown up. Ashley Ekins, backed by Steve Gower, seemed to prefer the incomplete official records which, they claimed, denied the platoon's very existence, while its members insisted that they had been organised as a separate sub-unit. Their claim seemed to be backed, ironically, by the discovery of other official records. The argument was unfortunate, raising questions about whether the official history had been receptive enough to veterans' testimony; ironically, the cause of a larger and longer controversy.

An even more contentious aspect of the Vietnam official history concerned the herbicide Agent Orange. Claims that it had contributed to illness and death among veterans of Vietnam and their families had emerged soon after the war. Brendan O'Keefe's *Medicine at War* included an appendix discussing the evidence, both scientific and historical, a matter of epidemiological complexity and one suffused by enduring emotion.

Describing himself as a 'reluctant volunteer', the respected Australian National University medical historian FB (Barry) Smith contributed a 78-page section to O'Keefe's volume, dealing with the effects of exposure to Agent Orange. Its reception caused him to regret accepting the task. Smith endorsed the emphatic findings of Justice Phillip Evatt's 1985 Royal Commission, that 'Agent Orange is NOT GUILTY'. Veterans seeking an explanation for the incidence of cancer, birth defects and other supposed consequences of the war vociferously and understandably disagreed, and Evatt's report was indeed both partisan and flawed – it uncritically adopted text from the herbicide manufacturers. For a further twenty years veterans denigrated Smith (who died in 2015) and attacked the War Memorial Council's support of the history as a 'devious, treacherous ... maliciously ... contrived falsification of fact'. Both epidemiological research and veterans' lobbying continued. Rather than asserting that the official historians had done their best and leave posterity to revise their findings, the Memorial's director, Brendan Nelson, decided to take the unprecedented step of commissioning a study which revisited Smith's work. Soon after Smith's death, the veterans' advocacy prevailed.

Although rightly proclaiming that 'to rewrite an official history ... would set an unfortunate precedent', the Memorial then proceeded to do exactly that, commissioning freelance historian Peter Yule to review and revise Smith's volume. In 2020 Yule produced *The Long Shadow*, its 600-odd pages both a review of the medical evidence but also containing anecdotal testimony from over 120 veterans. It was as sympathetic to them as Smith's had been distant – he had interviewed just two. Yule found Smith's research to be partial and deficient, arguing that veterans 'deserved better of an official history'; a sad conclusion for those who admired Smith – a respected historian of Victorian medical history, he had launched my own 2003 book on 19th-century surgery, *For Fear of Pain: British surgery 1790–1850*.

Many major Australian units which served in Vietnam produced histories. Some, compiled immediately after their tours, were more illustrated mementos than formal histories. Others followed the Commander's Diary with minimal commentary or elaboration. The best appeared decades later. Two, Mike O'Brien's *Conscripts and Regulars* (1995) and Bob Hall's *Combat Battalion* (2000), both written by former officers in their respective battalions, are highly regarded. While O'Brien, 7RAR's intelligence officer in its 1970–71 tour, wrote *Conscripts and Regulars* like many unit histories in collaboration with the battalion association, it was no mere chronicle, but analysed the battalion's effectiveness, notably quoting at length from soldiers' memories (in the Gammage tradition). Bob Hall had served with 8RAR in Vietnam, later completed a history PhD, and held firm views of what good military history comprised. 'Good history', he wrote in the introduction to *Combat Battalion*, 'requires that critical and fearless evaluations be made'. His book was notable for his willingness to acknowledge aspects of combat which previous unit histories had avoided: 'forces of cohesion and disintegration', 'friendly fire', and the killing of enemy wounded or prisoners. Unusually for a unit history, *Combat Battalion* reached outwards and upwards to consider 8RAR's experience in the context of the Australian war in Vietnam as a whole.

The Vietnam war also produced a book which should be regarded as one of the classics of the field, in Gerard Windsor's *All Day Long the Noise of Battle* (2011), an account of an attack on a bunker system during the Tet offensive of 1968. A novelist rather than an historian, Windsor became interested in the story of Mark Moloney, a former schoolmate, because of a conversation with Mike O'Brien, author of *Conscripts and Regulars*. Intrigued, Windsor approached Moloney, who characteristically agreed to him writing about his men, but not himself. The result was one of the most vivid evocations of an Australian day of battle in this or any war.

27

OTHER PEOPLE'S WARS: PEACE AND PEACEKEEPING

After Vietnam the Australian Defence Force (as it became in 1976) withdrew to what White Papers described as the Defence of Australia doctrine, though the posture did not imperil the Anzus alliance, which saw Bob Hawke's government send mostly naval forces to the first Gulf war, 1990–91, documented inevitably by David Horner in *The Gulf Commitment* (1992). The end of the Cold War precipitated both a fresh wave of conflicts (which superpower rivalry had tended to suppress) and a wave of optimism, even idealism, that international co-operation could promote peace.

'Peace' figures much less often than 'war' in Australian military history. Though desired, military history traditionally ignored it. The pairing 'War *and* Peace' seldom appears: in Tom Millar's survey *Australia in Peace and War* (1978), and Bobbie Oliver's *War and Peace in Western Australia* (1995), but few others. Although Australia as a nation has been notably bellicose (with a third of its first century and virtually all of its second spent at war) even the idea of 'peace' has not been a major part of its history.

The (as it turned out) short-lived genre of 'Peace Studies' produced little specifically on Australian history, understandably when an unstable world on the brink of nuclear holocaust needed advocacy and activism. Malcom Saunders published prolifically, notably a short history of *The Australian Peace Movement* (1986) and Bobbie Oliver traced opposition to war in her *Peacemongers* (1997). But although the Centenary of Anzac Commission had recommended the establishment of an institute to examine the causes of war, nothing was provided in a budget of what James Brown (in *Anzac's Long Shadow*) called 'a discordant, lengthy and exorbitant four-year festival of the dead' to fund it. A handful of universities each offer a couple of peace studies courses.

But for a shining moment, especially between the long war of Vietnam and the unending conflict after 2001, Australia became a notable exponent of international peacekeeping. Australians, police and members of the Defence Force, have been engaged in peacekeeping operations across the world, from the major 57-year-long commitment to Cyprus, or the 218 Australians who served in Kashmir 1958–85 to short deployments of individual officers or small parties to, say, Guatemala, Sierra Leone or Zimbabwe. For a couple of decades, especially in the 1990s, and especially under the energetic Minister for Foreign Affairs, Gareth Evans, peacekeeping became one of the Defence Force's priorities, embraced by officers eager to do more than train, and Australia contributed large contingents to Somalia, Rwanda, East Timor, Bougainville and the Solomons.

As ever, memoirs appeared earlier than formal histories. They included Rod Barton's *The Weapons Detective* (2006) or Peter Cosgrove's *My Story* (2006) along with more formal accounts, such as Bob Breen's *A Little Bit of Hope* (1998), his detailed account of the 1993 Operation Solace in Somalia or Kevin O'Halloran's powerful and disturbing *Rwanda: UNAMIR 1994/95* (2012). Australian scholars of international relations investigate the theory and practice of peacekeeping globally, but two historians, Peter Londey and David Horner, have dominated the interpretation of peacekeeping. Londey, a Memorial historian, had curated its first temporary exhibition on peacekeeping, at the instigation of the Army History Unit, its first venture into public engagement. He became interested in a subject previously virtually untouched. Londey produced a pioneering synoptic history of Australian peacekeeping, *Other People's Wars* (2004), and later joined Horner's peacekeeping official history.

Many saw peacekeeping as an aberration – Jeff Grey sternly warned that it 'corrupts armed forces and unfits them for their primary purpose', though his *Military History of Australia* mentioned ten missions. But Horner, with his magisterial understanding of the Defence Force's history, saw that Australia's extensive involvement in peacekeeping needed to be documented. With the support of the Memorial, the Strategic and Defence Studies Centre at the Australian National University and some Australian Research Council funding, Horner cobbled together an official history team, many working part-time, which over a decade produced six volumes, an extraordinary achievement given its minimal resources. Widespread support for John Howard's belated (and somewhat reluctant) intervention in East Timor in 1999 helped to make peacekeeping popular, surely bolstered by Defence Force media managers who saw photographs of soldiers holding babies as palatable. The series's six volumes dealt with a great geographical and temporal range, including the few substantial Australian deployments and the many operations, usually known by baffling acronyms – UNAMET, UNAMIR, RAMSI.*

The first volume of the series, by Londey, Rhys Crawley and Horner, *The Long Search for Peace* (2020), exemplified the project's challenges. It dealt with over thirty 'observer missions' in crises and conflict zones, including Indonesia, Kashmir, the Middle East, the Congo, Cyprus, and Rhodesia/Zimbabwe. Volume 2, Horner's *Australia and the New World Order* (2011) covered peace operations 1988–91 including Namibia, Iran, Pakistan and Afghanistan, the Persian Gulf and Kuwait. Volume 3, by Horner and John Connor, *The Good International Citizen* (2014) covered peacekeeping in Asia, Africa and Europe 1991–93, including Iraq, Cambodia, Western Sahara and the former Yugoslavia. Volume 4, by Jean Bou, Bob Breen, Horner, Garth Pratten and Miesje de Vogel traced *The Limits of Peacekeeping* (2019) in Somalia, Mozambique, Rwanda, Haiti, Eritrea, Guatemala, Sierra Leone and Sudan. Volume 5 by Bob Breen, *The Good Neighbour* (2016), dealt with peace support operations in the Pacific 1980–2006, including Bougainville and the Solomons. Volume 6, *In Their Time of Need*, by Steve Bullard (2017) covered emergency relief operations between 1918 and 2006, including Papua New Guinea, Sumatra, Pakistan, Iran, and in the Pacific. The

* As an indication of the complexity of peacekeeping nomenclature, UN missions in East Timor alone between 1999 and 2012 have successively been called: UNAMET, INTERFET, UNTAET, UNTACT, UNMISET, ISL and UMIT.

peacekeeping official history incidentally demonstrated how official histories foster historical talent. Scholars who worked as research assistants, often during or soon after their doctorates, became authors of their own books, including Jean Bou, Rhys Crawley, Rosalind Hearder, Margaret Hutchison, Tristan Moss, Garth Pratten and Tom Richardson.

Peacekeeping was not all a matter of photo opportunities with grateful locals. The diplomacy and restraint demanded of all peacekeepers imposed pressures, none more than at Kibeho, in Rwanda in 1995, when Hutus massacred perhaps 4000 Tutsis while peacekeepers vainly attempted to save them, a trauma as powerful as any combat experience. But however laudable peacekeeping operations have been, they do not attract the attention which Australians traditionally devote to war. Peacekeeping itself has now returned to the low levels seen before 1990 – only about sixty Australians presently wear the light blue beret – but it will surely continue to attract authors interested in Australia's relationship to the world through peace- not war-making.

28

BORN OF FIRE AND ASH: CONFLICT AFTER 2001

The 21st century brought conflicts and commitments seemingly without end; in Timor, Iraq and Afghanistan especially, becoming the subjects of another official history series, again brokered by David Horner, now the single most influential figure in the field. It opened with Australian troops serving as part of a regional peacekeeping force in the Indonesian province, which after great trauma became the independent nation of Timor Leste. Though widely endorsed by Australian popular opinion, the complexities of the intervention demanded explanation. UNSW Canberra's Clinton Fernandes, an astringent critic of successive Australian governments' complicity in Timor's occupation, explained how Australia came to be, as he put it, *East Timor's Reluctant Saviour* (2004). The official history project, under UNSW Canberra historian Craig Stockings, is devoting two volumes to East Timor, the first published, *Born of Fire and Ash* (2023) revealing not just the problems of Australian operations, but the equivocation which preceded it by successive governments over twenty years. John Blaxland, himself an official history writer, described it as a 'no-punches-pulled account'. Stockings encountered appalling and unprecedented opposition in securing records, despite wielding the official historian's authority. Further volumes in Stockings's series may disclose both how operations were conducted but also whether the century-old independent tradition of the Australian official histories has prevailed.

With the Al-Qaeda attacks on 11 September 2001, John Howard invoked the Anzus treaty and unquestioningly joined the American invasion of Afghanistan, with unintended consequences, all bad. He committed Australian forces to Afghanistan to suppress Taliban terrorist bases, an entanglement ended only in 2021 with the Taliban re-conquest of Afghanistan. Australians also served with coalition forces in adjacent regions, such as the Red Sea, Diego Garcia (in the Indian Ocean), Saudi Arabia and over Syria, though much of the detail of their involvement remains secret. Lewis Frederickson's account of air operations, endorsed by the RAAF Historical Section (which compared them to air operations in the same region in 1918), *Armageddon and Okra* (2020), suggested the value of exposure to what the Chief of the Defence Force, Angus Campbell, called 'the healing light of truth'.

Over 25 000 Australians served in Afghanistan. The commitment involved Australian Defence Force personnel, many in support or training roles, but the main operational burden was carried by the Special Air Service Regiment, many of whose members served multiple tours. Forty-one Australians died in combat, with 261 wounded. The full picture of the Australian commitment will remain obscure until the publication of Craig Stockings's official history. In the meantime, we have a few accounts written by unit historians, such as *War in the Valleys* or *Mentoring and Reconstruction Task Force 2* (both 2012). Journalists' accounts provide a partial framework, both laudatory, such as Sandra Lee's *18 Hours: The true story of an SAS war hero* (2007), or insightful, notably Chris Masters's *No Front Line* (2017).

Several volumes of the continuing official history will deal with Afghanistan. Widely regarded as having failed, Australia's war in Afghanistan has now become clouded by allegations and revelations of misconduct, unlawful killing and possible war crimes, notably by Ben Roberts-Smith, who had been awarded the VC for his courage at Shah Wali Kot in 2010. Acclaimed in hundreds of adulatory articles and TV reports (even spoken of as a possible future governor-general), Roberts-Smith became the focus of allegations that he had unlawfully killed Afghan civilians. A defamation trial in 2023 found the claim upheld as substantially true, among allegations of up to 39 deaths identified in the 2020 Brereton Report and the subject of continuing investigations. In 2023 the journalists exonerated in the defamation action brought by Roberts-Smith himself published complementary accounts of the episode, *Flawed Hero* by Chris Masters and *Crossing the Line* by Nick McKenzie. Tom Frame's *Veiled Valour: Australian Special Forces in Afghanistan and war crimes allegations* (2022), the result of research commissioned by the Department of Defence, provided insightful context into the saga. Coming from a clergyman as well as an historian, and an authority on 'moral injury' inflicted in war, the study was sobering. As Chris Masters wrote in *No Front Line*, 'for Australia there is no more important war to examine in detail. Afghanistan lives in our recent past and will continue to occupy our future'.

During the Afghanistan incursion, between 2003 and 2009 some 2000 Australians also joined the US-led force which invaded and occupied Iraq. The initial euphoria at the ousting of the dictator Saddam Hussein degenerated into insurgency and civil strife. While just four Australians died in the intervention, over 400 000 Iraqis died and the country remains in turmoil. David Horner brought his skill in analysing the decision for war in Iraq in *The War Game* (2022), but until the publication of the two volumes of official history now in train we lack an authoritative account. In the meantime, understanding the commitment depends upon an imperfect blend of official and individual sources. The authorities' perspective could be gleaned from the Department of Defence's *The War in Iraq* (2004) or Jim Molan's *Running the War in Iraq* (2008). Independent views came from journalists (such as Paul McGeough's *In Baghdad: A reporter's war*, 2003), or critics (such as Geoffrey Barker's *Sexing It Up: Iraqi Intelligence and Australia*, 2013) and dissidents. Andrew Wilkie's *Axis of Deceit* (2004) documented his arc from intelligence officer to whistleblower and therefore supposedly a 'national security threat'. The Howard government, which had taken Australia into the conflict on the basis of fallacious claims of 'weapons of mass destruction', attempted to suppress it. A 2010 edition included an appendix by publisher Morry Schwartz describing attempts to block the book's publication. Iraq, Wilkie argued, was undertaken 'All for a lie'; a lie successive governments sought to conceal. Sometimes, in history as in life, truth will out.

'Contemporary history' is notoriously challenging. The interpretation of the conflicts of the 21st century presents even greater difficulties, arguably far greater than for earlier periods, even Vietnam. We live at a time when governments suppress records, when truth is contested in court and when society is disinclined to accept authority. Perhaps we should not expect too much of the historical writing about the post-2001 conflicts; not yet. In a sense, writing about them is in a similar position to writing about the Great War in the 1920s or 1930s. We have a number of participants' accounts, both service people like John Cantwell's *Exit Wounds* (2012) or Mark Donaldson VC's *The Crossroad* (2013), as well as journalists' accounts like Karen Middleton's uncompromising *An Unwinnable War* (2011). We have books questioning Australia's involvement, in Marie-Therese Wisniowski's *Not in My Name* (2003). We have an authoritative official history only just appearing, which has yet to shape public perception. It is, perhaps, too soon to expect the perspective which only time can give.

PART VI
THEMES IN AUSTRALIAN MILITARY HISTORY

29

INVENTING ANZAC: THE PERENNIAL LEGEND

'Anzac' (not 'ANZAC' – it's been a word since before 25 April 1915) remains the single most important idea in Australian military history. Still, it's surprising how few writers have directly addressed its origins, expressions and history: the index to Dietrich Borchardt's authoritative bicentennial reference *Australians: A guide to sources* (1987) contains no mention of 'Anzac'. While about one title in twenty in the bibliography upon which this book is based refers to 'Anzac' in one way or another, this absence is striking. Except for a relatively small minority, mostly of academic authors, Australians writing about war have generally accepted the Anzac legend, and many have endorsed and celebrated it.

When *The Broken Years* appeared, as Carolyn Holbrook reminded her readers, 'the Anzac legend was in clear decline'. In 1974, Australian forces had left Vietnam and the war was in its final throes. But Vietnam alone was not responsible for Anzac's decline – Holbrook argued that traditional Anzac observance was already under strain, with tensions between Great War men and younger Second World War veterans vying for control of ex-service organisations, not to mention friction apparent during what Donald Horne called Australia's *Time of Hope* (1980). The stresses operating in a more liberal and diverse society is suggested by Bruce Ruxton's Anzac Day retort that he did not object to 'poofters in the march', but that 'they must march with their units'.*

* Bruce Ruxton, a 2/25th Battalion veteran and the Victorian President of the RSL, was for a couple of decades a byword for obscurantism, notorious for claiming 'I don't remember a single poofter' in the war. Ken Inglis commented that he only knew Ruxton as 'a maker of public statements which make me wince'.

Anzac and its sacred day were changing, but its essence arguably remained. Bill Gammage's foreword to Janice Pavils's study of commemoration in South Australia, *Anzac Day: The undying debt* (2007), raised questions which, he rightly affirmed, remained perennial. Who was the day for? Who should march? What role should organised religion and, increasingly, the Defence Force play? Should memorials be symbolic or useful? These and other questions, Gammage wrote, 'have been contentious questions since 1915, and they can rankle still'.

Though challenged by social, demographic and other changes (such as further conflicts, now fought by a professional Defence Force), Anzac Day observance, once so diverse and organic, became packaged and managed. Bill Gammage has often pointed out the difference between the informal but dignified marches of Returned Men of the Great War, citizen soldiers respectful but unmilitary, marching past silent civilians, and the more highly organised, military-flavoured marches of today, featuring Defence Force veterans, passing applauding flag-waving crowds and often including militaristic elements such as fly-overs or the involvement of military units. But even as expressions of the idea of Anzac changed, the concept and the word remained pervasive.

The National Library's catalogue contains 1741 entries with the word 'Anzac' in the title. Of them, almost exactly 1000 are books, and of them 275 date from before 1974. Serendipitously but hardly coincidentally, the very first entry from 1974 is Bill Gammage's *The Broken Years* (and the next is Patsy Adam-Smith's *The Anzacs*). Of the thousand items, half have been produced in the past seventeen years, an indication perhaps of how Australia marked the centenary of the Great War – officially named the 'Centenary of Anzac'. Even though the list includes brochures, addresses, printed lectures, reprints and facsimiles (including, for example, a 1984 *Investigation into the working environment of the typing pool on the first floor at the Anzac Park West Building*), and many later editions and duplicates, the list remains extensive.

'Anzac' is such an emotionally loaded idea that often books about it resemble theological texts rather than works of history. Patrick Lindsay, for example, a journalist-'storian, published several books, notably

The Spirit of Gallipoli (2006), which explored 'the birth of the Anzac legend': Lindsay was a believer. It began with the bogus Atatürk quotation, invoking the traditional stations of the Anzac cross, all couched in the antiquated 'high diction' of 'glory', 'the fallen', 'valour', 'feat of arms', 'the heroes of The Nek', language more the product of the propaganda mills of 1915 than of *The Broken Years*. It is telling that the photograph adorning Lindsay's cover, a popular image much used for Gallipoli books, depicts 'an Anzac carries a wounded comrade to safety', though the picture is notoriously a posed propaganda shot.

Various historians have explored aspects of 'Anzac'. Catherine Bond explained the ways the law has been used to safeguard the word and its uses, in *Anzac: The landing, the legend, the law* (2016). Graham Seal examined the many manifestations of 'Anzac' in *Inventing Anzac: The Digger and national mythology* (2004). John Moses and George Davis disclosed both the contested origins of Anzac Day observance and the contrast between the two nations in which it is marked, in *Anzac Day Origins* (2013). Others deal with recent manifestations and mutations of it. In her *Consuming Anzac* (2018) Jo Hawkins traced the way 'Australia's most powerful brand' has been commodified and exploited, notably by tour operators, breweries, supermarket chains, sporting codes and, not least, governments. Carolyn Holbrook's *Anzac: An unauthorised biography* offered the most wide-ranging analysis, spanning crucial aspects across the decades. She discussed how the idea and its expression gradually changed, accommodating new readings; for example, how returned soldiers became regarded as victims as well as heroes; how Peter Weir's film *Gallipoli* and successive prime ministers' acts and speeches, and of course the impending centenary, all influenced Anzac's evolution. Anzac, Holbrook showed, has 'drifted on the currents of Australian history', arguing that now, 'stories of mateship, courage and trauma are greatly amplified' and that 'contemporary Australian war memory is an unlikely amalgam of nationalist sentiment and trauma psychology'; more complex than the simple, raw grief tempered by pride expressed in the first Anzac days.

30

THEY DARED MIGHTILY: HEROES

Until about thirty-odd years ago the popular hero of the Great War was the Digger – simultaneously both familiar and a legendary figure, exemplifying the traditional Anzac virtues: endurance, courage, and above all, mateship. Following the Great War centenary, the representative Great War figures are either Victoria Cross (VC) recipients such as Albert Jacka or generals, and especially John Monash. Vying with commanders for pre-eminence in military biography are 'heroes', a word that appears in about fifty titles. Brendan Murray, in his *The Drowned Man*, on the murder of Stoker John Riley in HMAS *Australia*, observed that Australian military history is invariably viewed through three lenses: overwhelmingly that of the hero, 'the quintessential Australian'; sometimes as victim; rarely as villain.

The most prominent heroes are of course the 101 Australian recipients of the VC; (experts deprecate the idea that gallantry medals are 'won'). Ninety-six of these men – all men – gained the VC awarded under the former 'imperial' warrant, and five the 'Victoria Cross for Australia' introduced in 1991. All but the most recent VCs have naturally been accorded entries in the *Australian Dictionary of Biography*, and all appear in the many reference books relating to VCs generally, such as Craig Blanch and Aaron Pegram's *For Valour* (2018), a revision of Lionel Wigmore's *They Dared Mightily*. *TDM*, as it was known in the old Memorial's history section, was originally published in 1963 and revised at least four times (once by Bruce Harding, who had shown the schoolboy Bill Gammage behind the polished wooden doors of the old Memorial, introducing him to the cache of soldiers' letters). VCs also figure prominently in books on the units in which they served or the actions in which they performed their 'deeds', such as Stephen Snelling's *Gallipoli VCs* (2012). All VCs have Wikipedia pages and often websites.

Surprisingly, though, of the 101, only twenty-one VCs have been accorded full biographies (of whom all but five were officers, a curious inversion of the egalitarianism supposedly characteristic of Australians in war, perhaps because officers generate more sources). Of them, four have been accorded more than one: Howse (four), Jacka (three), Murray and Derrick, two each. Albert Jacka, the recipient of the first Australian VC awarded on Gallipoli, remains a compelling character because of the belief that he could and arguably should have been awarded a 'bar' (a second award) for performing equally gallant deeds on the Somme in 1916, because of his prickly personality (perhaps a clue to why he failed to obtain a second award) and because of his tragic early death, at 39 in 1932. Among the most unusual is Ian Loftus's self-published biography of Martin O'Meara VC, *The Most Fearless and Gallant Soldier I Have Ever Seen* (2016), which deals frankly with his tragic years of 'delusional insanity' before his death in an asylum in 1935.

While VCs have been respected and admired since the award was instituted during the Crimean war and while all but five of Australia's were awarded before 1982, no biography of a VC appeared before that year, and only another ten for the rest of the century. But in the 21st century another fifteen were published. Clearly, individual heroism had become a force in Australian military history. (The exception to the pattern of venerating the hero was, of course, the two critical biographies of Ben Roberts-Smith, but even they were a reaction to the adulation directed at Roberts-Smith in the decade since his investiture, making the revelations of 'unlawful killing' all the more shocking.)

But heroes constitute more than just VCs, and many other books extol the deeds of others hailed as heroes. Few explicitly analyse much less criticise the idea of heroism. Three of the enduring heroic figures in Australian military history are those whose statues occupy positions outside the Australian War Memorial: John Simpson (and his donkey), Edward 'Weary' Dunlop and Vivien Bullwinkel. It's striking that all three were medical personnel: a stretcher-bearer, a medical officer and a nursing sister. Frank Bongiorno observed in *The Eighties*, when the first of these statues was installed, 'a shift from the warrior to the carer and healer'. Australia's greatest war heroes now did not (say) charge machine gun posts or take enemy lives.

Simpson used a donkey (perhaps several) to bring lightly wounded men down from the firing line on Gallipoli for three weeks until he was killed. Already he had become legendary, and has been repeatedly proposed for a VC, unsuccessfully. Simpson confounds central tenets of the Anzac legend: though brave, he was English, and he had no mates, unless it was the donkey. Peter Cochrane's *Simpson and the Donkey* (1992) carefully dismantled the traditional myth, in contrast to Tom Curran's *Across the Bar* (1994), which praised *Australia and Tyneside's greatest hero*. Lest you imagine that only academics took a critical view, Graham Wilson, an historically inclined former warrant officer, published *Dust Donkeys and Delusions: The myth of Simpson and his donkey exposed* (2012), the most trenchant attack on a story he regarded as unduly exaggerated. 'Weary' Dunlop's courage and compassion had been revered among former PoWs long before his published diaries spread his reputation nationally. Vivien Bullwinkel, as the sub-title to Norman Manners's *Bullwinkel* (1999) explained, was *A young Army nursing sister, who was the sole survivor of a World War Two massacre by the Japanese*, symbolising those who did not survive. All three naturally figure in many books about Gallipoli and PoWs of the Japanese.

The relatively recent trend to describe all those who served (not to mention sporting figures) as 'heroes' may force those who write about exceptional individuals to find even greater superlatives to describe their conduct.

31
THE COMMANDERS: BIOGRAPHY

As Jeff Grey observed in his *Military History of Australia*, 'personalities loom large in the discussion of Australia and the Second World War', though the insight applies to every conflict. Accordingly, biography has always been a popular approach in military history, though in Australia it started slowly. In retirement, Bean himself wrote *Two Men I Knew* (1957), an admiring memoir-cum-biography of William Bridges and Brudenell White, but for years no strong biographical focus emerged – even Monash had to write autobiography rather than rely on an admiring biographer; he later attracted at least seven, all published after 1974.

Not until after 1945 did biography become a notable theme in Australian military history. Interest was partly stimulated by the establishment of the *Australian Dictionary of Biography* (*ADB*; first published in 1966) though for its first twenty years it worked through the colonial period. By the time the *ADB* reached the Great War, it found a ready group of biographers largely through the example and encouragement of Alec Hill, whose name appears in a string of his students' books, mainly biographies, acknowledging his 'wise and much appreciated advice', as one wrote. Hill, a lecturer at RMC Duntroon, a 9th Division veteran, gathered a coterie of officer cadets and young officers among whom he fostered an interest in history in general and biography in particular, his own *Chauvel of the Light Horse* (1978) providing a model for commanders' biographies. They included aspiring historians such as David Horner, Brett Lodge and Peter Pedersen. A strong school of military biographers emerged, centred on Canberra, often serving or ex-army officers. Biography remains a notable part of the field: about one book in twelve of my starting bibliography, and the proportion is higher if autobiographies or memoirs are counted. Within a generation, virtually all Australian divisional generals in wartime, and many brigade and unit commanders, had been accorded biographies, many of high quality. Studies of their RAN and RAAF counterparts followed more tardily.

Among the products of this RMC-based push was Chris Coulthard-Clark, whose *A Heritage of Spirit* (1979) provided an astringent counter to Bean's adulation of William Bridges, and Brett Lodge, the Memorial's first postgraduate scholar in 1980, wrote two biographies of Second World War generals, *The Fall of General Gordon Bennett* (1986) and *Lavarack* (1998), both exposing the politics of command. By far the most prolific and influential, soon taking over leadership of the push, was David Horner, who prompted the Army History Unit to publish a biographical series. Another Vietnam veteran who went on to a distinguished career in academia from 1991, Horner's first biographical product was, appropriately, a collective one. He edited and contributed to *The Commanders* (1984). In reviewing it for the Memorial's *Journal*, Alan Gilbert, Chair of RMC's Faculty of Military Studies, noted that of its eleven contributors, more than half were graduates in History at RMC; that two were by the recently retired Alec Hill, that all but two had served in the armed forces and that five had seen active service. Lloyd Robson saw *The Commanders* as 'a more old-fashioned form of war history', a counter-attack on those whom Horner described as 'new military historians' concerned with 'sociological issues': battle-lines were being drawn.

One of the most influential of Hill's protegés was Peter Pedersen, who while an army officer completed a PhD at RMC, published as *Monash as Military Commander* (1985). In his first book review in *Historical Studies*, Jeff Grey identified the perennial Australian contrast between the battles generals planned and the ones soldiers fought. Pedersen's *Monash*, he thought, was 'an important step towards rectifying [the] imbalance' – a theme throughout his career. (Grey himself published *A Soldier's Soldier* (2012), an acclaimed life of Lieutenant-General Sir Thomas Daly, a man admired by generations of his men, and others.)

Monash attracted not only the best of biographers – Alan Martin (biographer of Menzies) thought that Geoffrey Serle's *Monash* (1982) 'push[ed] past Monash the man to assessments of ... the Anzac legend itself' – but also admirers rather than analysts. *Monash* (2015) by the boxing writer Grantlee Kieza was couched entirely in the present tense (a common 'storian trick). Kieza's was not, however, the worst. Former deputy prime minister Tim Fischer ended his tendentious *Maestro John Monash* (2014) with an appendix advising readers 'How to Decure [sic; secure] Posthumous Promotion of Sir John Monash'. The lobbying failed; defeated either by 'knockers and naysayers' – including me – or perhaps rather by the recognition that posthumous promotion of a man who had been amply acknowledged before and after his death was an irrelevance. Still, Monash has more biographies than any other Australian soldier.

Australian military biographies have long championed what might be called the multiple biography. Melbourne independent historian Ross McMullin has written several 'lives', including of the war artist *Will Dyson* (1984) and an acclaimed (and monumental) study of 'Pompey' Elliot (2002), an effective but controversial brigadier-general, one of the war's more notable traumatised veterans – he had killed himself in 1931. McMullin later published two substantial multiple biographies, *Farewell Dear People* (2012) reflecting on the loss of potential leaders, awarded the Prime Minister's Prize for Australian History and *Life So Full of Promise* (2023) – both eloquent testimonies to the Great War's cost in lives cut short, promise unfulfilled and, in the case of the latter, cricket innings never completed.

The phenomenon of 'command' lends itself to multiple biography. Garth Pratten led the way with his *Australian Battalion Commanders in the Second World War* (2009), complemented in 2017 by William Westerman's for the Great War, *Soldiers and Gentlemen*. But Australian military history's strong egalitarian ethos has propelled biographies of lower ranked subjects. In an address to the Military Historical Society of Australia in 1988 I called for studies of small groups – sections or platoons, or aircrew; what has since been called 'microhistories'. I contributed to this form in my *Men of Mont St Quentin* (2009), which looked at the experience of one 12-man platoon of the 21st Battalion on one day of battle – in the taking of Mont St Quentin on 1 September 1918 – and through the rest of the survivors' lives. I was pleased to find other authors examining other small groups, such as Peter Dornan's *The Last Man Standing* (2006) looking at the men of one infantry section in the battle of El Alamein, and Mark Johnston's *An Australian Band of Brothers* (2018). For the RAAF there was Mal Elliott's *Fatal Mission* (2019), dealing with the crew of 'Naughty Nan', a Lancaster bomber of 467 Squadron, or Lex McAulay's *Five Maryborough Airmen* on bomber crew from Maryborough. For the RAN, Peter Jones's *Australia's Argonauts* (2016) told *The Remarkable Story of the First Class to Enter the Royal Australian Naval College*. The most skilful exponents of this approach reveal insights into more than individuals, such as Lucas Jordan's *The Chipilly Six* (2023), who argued that the intrepid men of the 1st Battalion embodied the AIF's traditional bush ethos.

Other biographical genres have emerged in military history, such as books on the lives of relatively humble people involved in war such as Janet Butler's *Kitty's War* (2013, based on a Great War nurse's diary) or Kit Cullen's *Jack's Journey* (2013). Family narratives constitute a distinct sub-set of biography often arising from or resolving domestic drama – George Bevan's *Jum's War* (2007) was a 'dramatised biography', in which an estranged son sought connection with a father through his Great War diary. One of the most compelling stories is told in Michael McKernan's *When This Thing Happened* (2015), dealing with a father's ordeal as a slave labourer of the Nazis and then, after migrating to Australia, his son's wounding in Vietnam.

The revival in military history coincided with a boom in family history, as relatives found, transcribed, copied and often published letters and diaries – perhaps 500 between 1980 and 2005, as I estimated in writing the foreword to Winsome Paul's *Blessed With a Cheerful Nature* (2005). Family histories of the Great War especially have followed the same trajectory as the wider field. Carolyn Holbrook revealed that the National Library received just fifty-one personal narratives of the Great War in the 1970s, but ninety-eight in the 1980s, 153 in the 1990s and 215 during the first decade of the 21st century, the later figure boosted by the increasing digitisation of military personnel files and access to newspapers through Trove. A curiosity that Carolyn Holbrook found was that family historians are largely women. The phenomenon is now so extensive that it too deserves to be studied. Historian of captivity Kristen Alexander argues that family histories, such as those by Carolyn Newman, Georgina Banks and Dick Braithwaite (and not scholarly works) have led the greater exposure of historical trauma.

In this the supposedly distinct genres of family history – the archetypal 'amateur' pursuit – and academic studies of biography coincide to reveal the depth and extent of the experience of war.

32

NO MEMORY FOR PAIN: MEMOIRS

I know I *said* that this book would not include many memoirs, but it became clear how important they've been in comprehending the experience of war (witness the PoW memoirs discussed in chapter 18). They are a distinct genre, revealing the differences and links between their then and our now.

Every former serviceman or woman, and indeed, every older person, regardless of war service, should be encouraged to write or dictate a memoir. Every account of the past adds to our knowledge, but writing a useful memoir demands a capacity for reflection and expression not given to all. Senior army medico Kingsley Norris entitled his breezy recollection *No Memory for Pain* (1970), a much better title than book, though it remains a useful source for military medical history. Norris's title notwithstanding, in order to be regarded as exceptional, their creator *needs* to have a memory for pain and yet be able to transmute otherwise unimaginable experience into prose that can literally speak to readers decades later.

Just as historical novels can teach readers a great deal of history, so memoirs can reveal incalculable insights into historical experience. The best Australian memoirs, many of which long preceded the appearance of formal histories, are worthy of being read, and re-read, made available to generations of readers unborn.

Notable memoirs of the Great War include the larrikin Joe Maxwell's *Hell's Bells and Mademoiselles* (1932) and George Mitchell's *Backs to the Wall* (1937). Among the most notable Australian memoirs of the Second World War, besides the PoWs' accounts, include Peter

Ryan's account of his time behind Japanese lines in 1943, *Fear Drive My Feet* (1959), Marsden Hordern's *A Merciful Journey* (2005; on his service in small craft around New Guinea), Don Charlwood's description of his time as a Bomber Command navigator, *No Moon Tonight* (1956) and Claire Stevenson's *The WAAAF Book* (1984), a valuable collective account of women in the RAAF edited by their director. Jeff Grey rated Jo Gullett's *Not as a Duty Only* (1976), as 'the single finest memoir ever written by an Australian soldier about the nature of Australian soldiers', because it evokes so sharply the experience of war.

The greater willingness to engage with emotion explains some of the war's most impressive memoirs. They include *Dangerous Days* by Ernest Brough of the 2/32nd Battalion, who, captured at Alamein, escaped from German captivity and survived the bitter Balkan civil-war-within-a-war, recounting his experience with a rare humility and humanity. The most unendurably honest memoir of the Second World War must, however, be Jan Ruff O'Herne's *50 Years of Silence* (1994), in which she described her sexual slavery in a Japanese officers' brothel. Her memory for pain produced a book harder to read than many accounts of combat.

Still, memoirs are sources which must be used with care. It's now axiomatic that however moving and authentic a memoir may be, they have been refracted through the prism of memory. For several decades, 'memory studies' has alerted us to the problems inherent in memoirs and their offshoot, oral history. The work of Alistair Thomson especially, in his pioneering *Anzac Memories* (1994 but substantially revised in 2013), showed how Gallipoli veterans' memories changed through time, even taking on scenes from Peter Weir's film. *Anzac Memories* represented a maturity in the understanding of war memory, a stature enhanced by Thomson's revisions, in which he revealed what he felt he could not twenty years before, that his family had been scarred by his grandfather returning from the Great War wounded in the mind, and remaining so.

Alistair Thomson's work warned historians to be wary of simply accepting veterans' claims. Not that such lessons were fully accepted. Though it deals with the Great War for only forty of its 300-odd pages, Albert Facey's 1981 memoir *A Fortunate Life* might be counted among the most influential war memoirs. Written late in life by an

86-year-old Western Australian bushman, Facey had volunteered for the AIF at 20, and been wounded on Gallipoli. Historian John Hirst, known as a discriminating critic, found Facey's direct, artless, 'primitive' style captivating, along with 750 000 purchasers, fascinated by Facey's artless evocation of a very different Australia. (The book made the fortune of the then tiny Fremantle Arts Centre Press.) Though Hirst later saw 'artifice' in Facey's disarmingly naïve style, he missed the fact that Facey could not have been at the landing (his AIF file, not then available, shows that he arrived a week later). Facey's memoir was another marker in what we might see as the 'Anzac turn' in Australian history, his dissembling over his being at the landing an example of the phenomenon Alistair Thomson identified in his *Anzac Memories*. Jeff Grey's wry comment on Richard Williams's pompous 1977 memoir *These Are Facts* – it 'does not always live up to its title' – exemplifies the complexity of memoirs as vehicles for historical understanding.

Even John Laffin, the prolific popular military history author, wrote an unreliable memoir. Already, in the 1970s, Central Army Records staff had detected anomalies and outright falsehoods in claims Laffin was making in print: to have been commissioned and to have been decorated. Chastened by its stiffly worded queries, his book-jacket biographical notes suddenly stopped repeating extravagant claims. But Laffin opened his memoir *A Kind of Immortality* (2000) with a story that as a member of the 2/31st Battalion he had taken part in a secret mission behind Japanese lines, one which neither his own AIF file nor the battalion war diary substantiates.

More recently, Daniel Lane's *The Digger of Kokoda* (2022), presented as a recollection by Reg Chard, supposedly, as the title implied, a veteran of the Kokoda Track, raised questions among historians of the Papuan campaign. David Horner, David Cameron and I all questioned its bona fides (and in Australia, criticising a 98-year-old veteran is seen as being in doubtful taste at least). Some basic research revealed that Chard was a veteran of *a* track in Papua, but not *the* Track, while an alleged massacre of forty-odd European women by the Japanese, evidence of which he claimed to have seen, could not have happened at all. Chard's distorted memory was swiftly detected and challenged, a reminder that, sadly, not all survivors' memories can simply be accepted as history. Amanda Laugesen's forthcoming analysis of war memoirs will, I hope, reveal the full richness and value of memoirs as a way of understanding war experience.

33

HMAS AUSTRALIA: THE ROYAL AUSTRALIAN NAVY

The arrival of the Royal Australian Navy's 'fleet unit' – the battlecruiser HMAS *Australia* and its attendant cruisers and destroyers in 1913 – produced a celebratory flurry of 'navalism'. Before he created the Anzac legend, Charles Bean boosted Australia's inheritance of Britain's naval traditions. His official history included a volume on the Royal Australian Navy, the only one which government – ironically, the navy – attempted to censor, on 'national security' grounds. Apart from wartime propaganda, naval memoirs and two further volumes in Gavin Long's series, little naval history was published until the late 1960s. Under the inspiration of Lew Lind, a public relations officer at Garden Island dockyard, enthusiasts launched a Naval Historical Society in 1970. The society's history acknowledged that Lind, a history enthusiast, wanted to form a body 'which would improve the image of the RAN' – the year before the *Melbourne* had collided, again, this time with the USS *Frank E. Evans*. Impelled by both naval veterans and by a group of naval officers consciously shaping the RAN's awareness of its history, there followed a minor boom in naval history, led by Lind.

Naval history's authors have more often been ex-sailors – such as Alun Evans (*A Navy for Australia*, 1986), Bob Nicholls or Ian Pfennigwerth, though there are some notable exceptions, such as Mike Carlton, Peter Firkins or Colin Jones. Indeed, there has been a distinct tinge of tribalism to the writing of naval history, not entirely explained by its peculiar jargon. Robert Hyslop, one of the longest-serving naval public servants and an authority on the esoteric subject of naval administration, condemned in his autobiography *A Very Civil*

Servant (1998) 'a misunderstanding common to Naval officers, that only someone who has "been there" is capable of writing the history of some Naval events'.* Its luminaries include Vic Cassells, Vince Fazio, Ross Gillett, Lew Lind and Iris Nesdale, with as its senior scholars Tom Frame and David Stevens (who as former naval officers effortlessly spans the worlds of the navy and academia). The recent untimely death of James Goldrick, a retired admiral and the Australian naval historian with the most substantial international reputation, deprived the field of a truly inspirational figure. Because navies operate on a global scale and so often in concert with other nations' fleets, naval historians tend to look outwards: the RAN's Sea Power Centre's library has as many books on international subjects as Australian.

Despite its many proponents and its rich history and abundant sources, naval history remains relatively undeveloped, notably focused on ship histories, many unsophisticated chronicles ('The true story of HMAS *Manoora*'s experiences …', reads the title page of a book). It too has been hampered by the excellence of the several official histories. (Peter Firkins's *Of Nautilus and Eagles* (1975) was heavily based on official histories – whole columns of its notes read 'Jose, p. 100; Jose, p. 104; Jose, p. 124 …' – not to mention special pleading against the Whitlam government, briefed by lobbyists for the RAN's ambitions for more and better ships and aircraft.) Miesje de Vogel of the RAN's Sea Power Centre reflected on some of its potential, noting the absence of 'large swathes of social history' beyond biography, a need for studies of how the RAN has operated with other navies, and the need for studies of major aspects of the RAN's role, such as on 'trade protection' in the Second World War.

The tribalism of naval history reinforced a certain distance between naval history and the mainstream of military history. Perplexingly, for example, the RAN did not form part of Jeff Grey's *Centenary History of Australia and the Great War*, though his series includes a volume on the Australian Flying Corps. The dominance of the idea of Anzac, and the

* This fallacy is not confined to naval officers. Jo Gullett, the author of *Not as a Duty Only*, in reviewing *The Broken Years*, admitted that 'to begin with I was inclined to doubt the value of anyone who had not been a soldier', an opinion that *The Broken Years* dispelled.

easy assumption that 'army' history equals Australian military history fuelled the concern among naval historians to assert that their history was both special and separate, overlain by a nagging resentment of the neglect of naval history. David Stevens, one of Australia's leading naval historians, pointed out in his 2014 *In All Respects Ready: Australia's Navy in World War One* that 'As a nation we have been taught the significance of such foreign place names as Gallipoli, Fromelles and Villers-Bretonneux ... By contrast, our war at sea has never received comparable attention'.

Naval historians often decry that authors are unduly attracted to disasters and losses, notably the spectacular wartime losses of HMA Ships *Sydney* in 1941 and *Perth* in 1942 and the peacetime collisions involving HMA Ships *Melbourne* and *Voyager*. Ambivalence hasn't stopped the flow of books. They also lament that popular writers focus on the spectacular – especially battles – when navies often do their best work by preventing battles – convoy escorts, for example, succeed by deterring attack.

The published and unpublished documentation of the controversy over the loss and eventual discovery of *Sydney* occupies almost an entire compactus bay in the Sea Power Centre library. The most intense attention attended the loss of HMAS *Sydney* to the German raider SMS *Kormoran* off Western Australia in November 1941. The encounter, in which no Australians survived, received fourteen pages in Gill's official history. When I reviewed Barbara Winter's *HMAS Sydney: Fact, Fantasy and Fraud* (1984) in the Memorial's *Journal* I learned that she had established that the official account was 'inadequate' and contested 'persistent rumours or distortions'. One of the most pernicious furphies was floated by Michael Montgomery (the son of the *Sydney*'s navigating officer) who in *Who Sank the Sydney?* (1981) claimed that that the answer was 'a Japanese submarine'. This absurd allegation, demonstrably false from records of the submarines' known locations, merely fanned further speculation. In his 1991 *HMAS Sydney: Loss and controversy*, Tom Frame also criticised Gill's account (necessarily based only on German witnesses) as going 'beyond the reliable and corroborated evidence' available to him. The argument sparked an extensive and expensive parliamentary inquiry (1999), which attracted 200 submissions and resulted in the most detailed research on the loss of any Australian warship (possibly any worldwide), and several further books. The inquiry essentially concurred that German survivors' recollections could be accepted, as Barbara Winter and Tom Frame had argued. Despite Frame devoting his book to 'exposing the alternative theories ... [as] hearsay, speculation and wild imagination', that naturally continued.

Only the discovery of the wreck of *Sydney* and *Kormoran* in 2008 settled the speculation but inevitably, led to further books. David Mearns, an American marine geophysicist, in his *The Sinking of HMAS Sydney: How Australia's greatest maritime mystery was solved* (2009), claimed that locating the wreck would afford 'closure' (though hardly anyone alive today knew those killed in the sinking). The controversy convoy steamed on, to other naval mysteries such as the location of the submarine *AE1*, lost off New Britain in 1914 and finally located in 2017.

Australian naval history might seem to be largely devoid of drama, though no fewer than three books have analysed a sordid murder on HMAS *Australia* in 1942 (arguably a case that spurred the Australian government to ratify the Statute of Westminster) – Judith Crosland's *Murder on HMAS Australia*, Brendan Murray's *The Drowned Man* (both 2016) and Robert Hadler's *Dark Secrets* (2020). Otherwise, much worthy, mostly narrative history has documented the RAN's service in war and peace. Curiously, no one has yet thought to use the RAN's records to write a book called *HMAS Australia* (either the battlecruiser 1913–21 or the cruiser 1928–55, or both) as a microcosm of the navy's relationship to the nation. While Lew Lind and Marcel Payne published a detailed Naval Historical Society book on the first *Australia* (1988), and Mike Carlton has published *Flagship* (2016), a superb chronicle of the service of the second *Australia*, there is scope for a book using naval personnel records to explore how either ship or both reflected the composition and character of the nation.

34

A THOUSAND MEN AT WAR: (ARMY) UNIT HISTORIES

'Unit histories' – often called 'battalion histories' – are a characteristic Australian genre in war writing. The single largest category in the bibliography underpinning this book, they are perhaps the quintessential genre in Australian military history. While British 'regimental' chronicles often span centuries, the typical unit history in Australia is of the battalion. Each deals with the history of (as Malcolm Uren's 1959 history of the 2/16th was entitled) *A Thousand Men at War*, invariably dealing with a few intense years of existence. (The palm for the history of the smallest sub-unit probably belongs to William Park, whose *Beyond Adversity* (2010) documented the men of the short-lived 'U' Company of the 15th Battalion, 1941–42.)

Understanding what unit histories have been written, and how they can help comprehend the course of Australian military history, is complicated by the vagaries of the Australian army's repeated re-organisations. Infantry units, for example, have been organised under at least five major schemes: the ninety-odd Militia regiments of the 'federal' period (which persisted until 1921); the sixty-odd battalions of the AIF, the Militia 'regiments' of 1921–41, some of which survived to 1960, the thirty-six battalions of the second AIF, the up to nine regular battalions of the Royal Australian Regiment formed from 1948, and the many battalions of the six state Army Reserve regiments from 1960. That's not to mention the various pioneer, machine-gun and others regarded as infantry battalions, such as the Torres Strait Light Infantry of 1941–46. The complexity bemuses even specialists, but it explains why typically, an Australian unit history bears date ranges like '1939–46' or 1921–43' rather than (as in Britain) '1758–1968'.

Analysis of seventy-four published histories of the sixty infantry battalions of the AIF in the Great War illuminates the contours of the writing of Australian military history. Four battalions published histories within months of the Armistice. Keeping restive men occupied while they waited for ships home, as well as sending them off to learn dairying or accountancy, AIF headquarters directed units to compile what became the archival series AWM 224, 'Unit Manuscript Histories'. Young officers were told to go through their unit records (starting with war diaries) to précis their service. They naturally represented a mixed bag of talent and motivation, and while some produced simple factual chronicles, others effectively wrote the first drafts of what became published histories. *Under Furred Hats*, George Berrie's history of the 6th Light Horse, was written mostly from memory and published before the regiment came home.

The momentum continued, with another five published in 1920, and a further nine by the end of the 1920s. By 1939, thirty more unit histories had appeared, arguably the golden years of the Great War battalion history. In succeeding decades no more than five appeared – in the 1950s, one; none in the 1970s. The war history boom had little effect in the 1980s (three), but in the 1990s the rate increased dramatically – eleven in the 1990s; eighteen in the 2000s. Surprisingly, the Great War centenary years saw only two published, but by then all but three battalions (the 18th, 26th and 35th) were documented. Fourteen have more than one history: three have three apiece. Just three authors have written nearly a quarter of them: Ron Austin seven, Neville Browning six, while Robin Corfield published histories of all four battalions of the 15th Brigade. The subject deserves a thesis and even a book, exploring their authors' and publishers' motivations and methods, the decisions and dilemmas of their creation, the complexities of their production and publication, and the circumstances and consequences of their reception.

The most fortunate authors cultivated the official historian and his staff, and ex-diggers dropping in to his office at Victoria Barracks,

Sydney, to chat with 'Dr Bean', as he became in 1931, must have delayed the production of the final volumes by months. They manifest a great range of sophistication and style, from cheap booklets distributed on Anzac Day to substantial formal histories, though virtually all produced by former comrades for fellow association members. One exception was Newton Wanliss's *The History of the Fourteenth Battalion* (1929), written by the father of Captain Harold Wanliss, killed at Ypres in 1917. Understandably infused with pride and tinged with grief, they often resembled battalion reunions in print. Unit histories were often not only written by former members, but for them as well. The 4th Division medical units, holding a reunion in Melbourne in 1933, published *With the Diggers 1914–18*, but it almost entirely comprised songs, poems and cartoons, many humorous, to stimulate comradeship at 'smoke socials' and get-togethers, because, as the editor wrote, 'perhaps we shall never quite be free of the memory of the sinister shadow of yesterday'. In 1988 Lloyd Robson characterised them as too often 'breezy ... long on battle detail and very short on analysis'. Still, the best of the Great War unit histories, such as Thomas White's *The History of the Thirteenth Battalion* (1924) or Eric Wren's *Randwick to Hargicourt* (1935 – the form of 'X to Y' is a characteristic title), remain both worth reading and essential starting points for research.

The last unit history produced by a Great War veteran was Clarrie Wrench's *Campaigning with the Fighting 9th*, published as late as 1985. Clarrie's description of his and his wife's working methods sounds impossibly quaint to a generation of digital researchers: 'together I dictated and Grace wrote down in longhand extract after extract of diary notes and reports'. The authors of the thirty-odd Great War unit histories published after Clarrie's had not served with the unit, though for a transitional period authors checked their drafts with former members, sometimes to the detriment of their independence.

By 1962, when Gavin Long published a list of Second World War army histories which had appeared since 1945, thirty-four had been published with a further eleven known to be in preparation. Given that the Australian Military Forces had grown to literally thousands of units (documented exhaustively in Graham McKenzie-Smith's five thick volumes of *The Unit Guide: The Australian Army 1939–1945* (2018)), the number may be seen as meagre. 'Arms' units (infantry, artillery, light horse or armour and engineers) have always dominated the genre, though unevenly, and 'service' units have tended to produce 'corps' histories, such as Theo Barker's two, on *Signals* (1987) and the *Royal Australian Electrical and Mechanical Engineers* (1992). As Second World War veterans established careers and families, as Great War veterans had before them, they turned to chronicle their units.

Syd Trigellis-Smith, Sergio Zampatti and Max Parsons's *Shaping History* (1996), their exhaustive listing of unit histories, suggests that by the mid-1990s a third of AIF infantry units had published histories in the thirty years before 1974 (sixteen of them) while more than thirty appeared in the twenty years after. Specialists suggest that the best of the Second World War battalion histories written by veterans include Bill Crooks's *The Footsoldiers* (1971, on the 2/33rd), 'Roaring' Reg Newton's *The Grim Glory* (1976, 2/19th) or David Hay's *Nothing Over Us* (1984, 2/6th). The last AIF battalion to produce a history was the 2/9th, in 2005 (ironically, entitled *Never Late*). Chronicles of Vietnam tours aside, histories of regular units are now unusual: why? Perhaps their authors need the perspective, or because (unlike wartime counterparts) they exist beyond the service of individuals, making a less intense collective experience.

Unit histories have often been communal endeavours, typically the product of a committee of a unit association. The Secretary of the 2/8th Battalion Association explained in 1984 the 'tremendous project' its history, *The Second Eighth*, entailed. Even after a five-man committee had worked for 'many years', including despatching a four-man 'task force' from Melbourne to Canberra to gather primary sources, 'it devolved upon Arthur Bentley to write the history'. Australian military history is full of Arthur Bentleys, and their task often involved more than merely chronicling their former unit's triumphs. Many unit histories revisited wartime grievances, virtually re-fighting the war on the page. Norman McNicol's 37th Battalion history, *The Thirty-Seventh*, for example, rehearsed its resentment against 'the higher commanders' (especially Monash, its divisional commander) for the way it had been let down in the days after the attack at Messines. Andy Pirie, author of *Commando Double Black*, the history of the 2/5th Independent Company, had the problem of dealing fairly with Lieutenant-Colonel Norman Fleay who, despite being awarded a DSO, failed in command of the unit (a conclusion confirmed by Phillip Bradley's *The Battle for Wau*). But how should Pirie treat Fleay's failure, especially as he was still alive (he died in 2007). I recall Andy turning over his dilemma over a cuppa after the Memorial had awarded him a research grant.

Other unit historians realised that they could reveal things previously unknown or even secret. Everard Baillieu, who had served with the 2/24th Battalion at Alamein, published in 1985 *Both Sides of the Hill*, a 40-page 'annexure' to the 1963 battalion history, detailing its capture of Rommel's wireless intercept unit, a key coup in the desert war, but the significance of which only became clear after the release of the 'Ultra' secret intelligence files. It did so partly to belatedly connect the battalion to one of the major disclosures of the war, but also to rebut the claims of a kindred unit in the 26th Brigade. Other histories looked beyond the unit – Douglas Hunter's *My Corps Cavalry* (on the 13th Light Horse) offered a brisk critique of the limitations of the Light Horse legend, taking on both Bill Gammage and Ian Jones, though only because Hunter thought that the 13th (which served on the Western Front) had been excluded from the legend.

Syd Trigellis-Smith, doyen of unit history bibliography, himself a former member of the 2/2nd Field Regiment (whose history he did not write) would emphatically count off the essential characteristics of the ideal battalion history. They involved including a nominal roll, a roll of honour, and lists of all casualties and honours and awards. Ron Austin (who wrote at least ten unit histories) included his criteria in his *AIF Unit Histories of the Great War* (2011). His intention was to capture 'the SOUL OF THE BATTALION'. Austin also enjoined unit historians to 'embrace both the 'heroes' and 'villains' of the unit', suggesting that protagonists of military and social history were growing closer. Indeed, as academic authors entered the field, they demonstrated that more could be expected, and gained, from what might have seemed to be simple unit histories. Margaret Barter, who completed a PhD on the history of the 2/2nd Battalion, published it as *Far Above Battle* (1994), its subtitle, *The experience and memory of Australian soldiers in war 1939–1945*, suggesting that it spanned both the particular history of the 2/2nd, but also contributed to a broader understanding. Dale Blair's history of the 1st Battalion in the Great War, *Dinkum Diggers* (also based on his PhD), was likewise sub-titled *An Australian Battalion at War* (2001).

Histories written by other than members of the unit – sometimes after all their members are dead – can be more comprehensive, penetrating and honest. For example, *Battle-Scarred*, Craig Deayton's 2011 history of the 47th Battalion, AIF, is (as I wrote in its foreword) 'the finest battalion history I have ever read'. Deayton, a Tasmanian high school principal, produced a 'post-Bean' history 'respectful of Bean's achievement but not constrained by it'. He showed that Bean no longer dominates the story of Anzac. Deayton also made use of decades of scholarship on the Western Front producing a full and honest account of the men of the 47th, drawing on a full range of official and private records, including, for example, failures in leadership and instances of bullying. In all this Deayton produced a history more insightful, more analytical – and more readable – than its predecessors.

Astonishingly, no one has yet produced a detailed study of this quintessentially Australian form of military writing.

35

THE THIRD BROTHER: THE ROYAL AUSTRALIAN AIR FORCE

Air Force historians tend to be reluctant to own the RAAF's predecessor, the Australian Flying Corps of the Great War. Its chroniclers have been few since Frederic Cutlack's volume in Bean's series. Though popular among amateurs publishing articles (notably on the Red Baron), its most notable interpreter has been Michael Molkentin. He published his popular but authoritative *Fire in the Sky* (2012) while completing the UNSW Canberra PhD which became the basis of *Australia and the War in the Air* (2014), one of Jeff Grey's *Centenary History of Australia and the Great War* volumes.

Air Force history has been dominated by Chris Coulthard-Clark, Alan Stephens and lately Mark Lax. Coulthard-Clark researched *The Third Brother*, also based on his UNSW Canberra PhD, tracing the RAAF's origins and first two decades. Later Director of Air Force History and Heritage, Clark produced several other books on RAAF history, and much more besides. The intellectual heavyweight of airpower history has been Alan Stephens, a former Canberra bomber pilot (and also a UNSW Canberra PhD) who has published both general histories of the RAAF (notably in *The Royal Australian Air Force: A history* (2001), a pioneering history of its post-1945 decades (*Going Solo*, 1995) and analytical studies of the application of 'air power' – a crucial idea underpinning air force operations, such as *Power Plus Attitude* (1992), on *Ideas, strategy and doctrine in the Royal Australian Air Force 1921–1991* (1992). In this, if Chris Coulthard-Clark became the RAAF's principal chronicler, Stephens was its theoretical guru (though basing his analysis on a solid historical foundation). Mark Lax, who coincidentally entered the RAAF in 1974, has joined Stephens as the most active proponent of the historical exploration of the RAAF's history, through books such as *Taking the Lead: The Royal Australian Air Force 1972–1996* (2020) and *From Controversy to Cutting Edge: A history of the F-111 in Australian service* (2021). The Air Power Development Centre, which combines theoretical and historical research, has recently welcomed Lewis Frederickson, another UNSW Canberra PhD and a published historian, now helping the RAAF to renew its commitment to history.

Like army history, two of the motivating forms of air force history are biography and unit (in this case squadron) history. Kristen Alexander's biographies, *Clive Caldwell* (2006) and *Jack Davenport* (2009) exemplify the former. Squadron histories, like battalion and ship histories, often have about them the feel of school magazines, with in-jokes and a clubby informality: James Harding's history of 80 Squadron, for example, was called *It Had to B.U.* (1996 – assisted by the Australia Remembers program), a reference to both the Kittyhawks' fuselage code and the popular wartime song. Their authors, while including former members of the unit, also include familiar names – Leon Kane-Maguire, Mark Lax, and David Wilson. Air force history also revolves around the service of aircraft types, such as Neville Parnell's *Whispering Death* (1980, on RAAF Beaufighters in the South-West Pacific Area), which have few counterparts in army history.

Inevitably, perhaps, RAAF history is dominated by accounts of flying units. This might seem obvious, but air forces need more than fighters and bombers, and indeed, most of those listed in the ten-volume *Units of the Royal Australian Air Force* (1995, curiously sub-titled *A Concise History*) were not flying units. It had over 140 radar units on its order of battle in the Second World War, but only half-a-dozen have a published history. The ground crew who kept aircraft flying have been almost entirely overlooked, with the exception of Eric Johnston's *The RAAF Ground Staff of the Desert Air Force Squadrons* (1992; and even though Johnston himself served in Britain in Bomber Command). The Women's Australian Auxiliary Air Force has a handful of published memoirs and several books, but none later than 1991.

Several small publishers specialise in RAAF history, notably Lex McAulay's Banner Books but also the RAAF itself. The RAAF's historical section has (under several names and organisational guises) played a strong role in recording the air force's history, though notably largely within rather than beyond the service. One of its 75th anniversary projects was to produce *Units of the Royal Australian Air Force*, documenting every unit, while the RAAF's 2021 centenary saw new commemorative books commissioned. While not formally a publisher, the RAAF has sponsored a biennial Heritage Award since 1987 which has fostered a strong body of air force history, though it has recently devoted greater resources to encouraging both history and heritage.

The RAAF, notably dominated by pilots and engineers, has never cultivated an awareness of history as assiduously as has the Army, but its historical programs have survived, quietly contributing to a body of knowledge for decades, encouraging and recognising works offering insights into its past and perhaps pointers to its future.

36

THROUGH WOMEN'S EYES: WOMEN'S WARS

A 1984 polemic book questioning Anzac Day discussed placards carried at demonstrations: 'Nationhood equals Manhood/This Excludes All Women'. Obviously, the claim was untrue. Women have always experienced war, directly or indirectly, invariably personally, and a growing body of work has made the nature of that connection clear. Lola Wilkins's catalogue of a 1994–95 exhibition of women's art at the Memorial, *Through Women's Eyes*, posed questions that extend beyond art: 'Do women see war differently from men?' Jan Bassett, in introducing her anthology *As We Wave You Goodbye* (1998), with its extracts of eighty women's writings from South Africa to the (first) Gulf War, thought that what united all of them was 'a lament that war occurs', a dramatic contrast to the 'fighting words' characteristic of male authors. (She died the following year, but her posthumous memoir, *The Facing Island*, remains a moving reflection on an historian's sadly truncated life.)

The mid-1970s saw the emergence of a women's movement, expressed in history books as much as in changes in workplaces, boardrooms and bedrooms. Founding feminist texts such as Anne Summers's *Damned Whores and God's Police* (1975) had little to say about wartime experience (unsurprisingly, when every day in peacetime seemed like a battle). In 1976, in assessing Beverley Kingston's ground-breaking study of women and work, *My Wife, My Daughter and Poor Mary Ann*, a reviewer observed that Kingston had 'nothing to say' about 'the remarkable impact made on Australian society as a whole by the First World War'. That neglect has since been rectified, abundantly, though military history remains 'gendered', as the jargon has it.

Just as she had helped to quicken interest in Anzac history, Patsy Adam-Smith's *Australian Women at War* (1984) gave a popular account of women and war. Academic historians were already incorporating women's history into their newfound interest in war, exemplified by Joy Damousi and Marilyn Lake's edited collection *Gender and War* (1995). Scholars led the continuing revival of interest in women's history, which in some ways revised awareness of the impact of war beyond women's experience. Melanie Oppenheimer's *All Work, No Pay* (2002) revealed the existence and significance of a previously unappreciated (and mainly female) 'voluntary war effort', while her history of the Australian Red Cross, *The Power of Humanity* (2014), appeared a century after the foundation of an organisation essential to but often taken for granted in Australia's wars. Oppenheimer's handsomely illustrated *Australian Women and War* (2008), commissioned by the Department of Veterans' Affairs, is representative of the way official bodies have in recent years sought to rectify the neglect of earlier decades.

Nurses constitute a major strand of writing about women in war, though they were more revered than revealed until Jan Bassett's *Guns and Brooches* (1992), which did for nurses what Hank Nelson and Tim Bowden had recently done for prisoners of war. In 1989 Marianne Barker could justifiably claim that her *Nightingales in the Mud* told an 'almost hidden side of the war', since besides Butler's official history and memoirs such as May Tilton's *The Grey Battalion* (1933) little had appeared in print. The appearance of the 'returned sisters' on Anzac Day invariably brought cheers and applause: they were not unappreciated, just unknown. Rupert Goodman's detailed chronicle *Our War Nurses* (1988) heralded the dramatic change that was to come. Gay Halstead's *Story of the RAAF Nursing Service 1940–1990* (1994) helped to redress the army bias of much nursing history, but the RAN Nursing Service remains without a full history. An important part of the revelation of nurses' war experience comes through biography, or books based on diaries or collections of letters, among which Melanie Oppenheimer's *Oceans of Love* (2006) and Janet Butler's *Kitty's War* (2013) are the best (each based on the wartime writings of sisters Narelle Hobbes and Kit McNaughton). But the attention devoted to medical women is uneven.

While Heather Sheard and Ruth Lee's *Women to the Front* (2019) extended awareness to twenty-six women doctors in the Great War, the Australian Army Women's Medical Service (essentially nursing aides) still only have the anecdotal history of Enid Herring's *They Wanted to Be Nightingales* (1982). Like many women's service histories, it modestly purports to be little more than, as its foreword put it, 'a collection of personal stories' rather than a formal history, a description also fitting nursing academic Narelle Biedermann's book on Australian nurses in Vietnam, *Tears on My Pillow* (2004). Though not formal or full histories, they often add constructively to recording a neglected group.

Curiously, the three wartime women's 'auxiliary' services have been unevenly served by their former members. Lorna Ollif (née Box, a wartime member of the Australian Women's Army Service) published *Women in Khaki* in 1981 while Joyce Thomson (herself a Women's Auxiliary Australian Air Force member) published *The WAAAF in Wartime Australia* in 1991. Extraordinarily, all the wartime women's auxiliary services still lack substantial histories. The Women's Royal Australian Army Corps, the wartime Australian Women's Army Service's successor, was chronicled by Lorna Ollif in *Colonel Best and Her Soldiers* in 1985 (just as women ceased to serve in a separate corps), and more fully by Janette Bomford in *Soldiers of the Queen* in 2001. As Melanie Oppenheimer pointed out in her *Australian Women and War*, however, the uniformed women's services accounted for just 2.4 per cent of the female population: civilian women remain seriously neglected. Ironically, the neglect is greatest of women who most actively supported the war effort. With characteristic iconoclasm, Joan Beaumont noted in *Australian Historical Studies* in 2000 that while progressive, anti-war and anti-conscription women in the Great War had attracted research, she asked, 'Whatever Happened to Patriotic Women?'

It must be said: literally dozens of books and articles about the women's services invariably begin with the claim that women have been overlooked or otherwise 'forgotten'. Annabelle Brayley in *Our Vietnam Nurses* (2016; the third book on the subject) claimed that Australians had 'disregarded the enormous contribution these nurses had made, but also ignored their very existence'. In fact, any given nurse has a greater chance of being named than her male counterparts in, say, the infantry. For example, the Australian Women's Land Army only numbered about 2000 members, but it has attracted two substantial books, Jean Scott's *Girls with Grit* (1986) and Sue Hardisty's *Thanks Girls and Goodbye!* (1990), though the common assumption is that groups such as the Land Army remain neglected.

It's generally true that historians were slower to notice not so much the experiences of women in war as its effects upon them. In this, women outside the uniformed services were especially neglected. Just as popular works on Australian military history generally increasingly took a heroic turn, so did women's history, exemplified in Susannah De Vries's *Heroic Australian Women in War* (2004), telling *Astonishing tales of bravery from Gallipoli to Kokoda*. The great majority tend to be overlooked. Margaret Geddes's *Blood, Sweat and Tears* (2004) and even more Jacqueline Dinan's *Between the Dances* (2015) (which drew on the memories of 300 'ordinary' women) helped to redress this. As in other aspects of life, however, the gender imbalance remains. The film *Gallipoli*, Ken Inglis observed in 1988, 'is a grand*son*'s perception', but then noted that 'grand-*daughters* are articulate now'. Women plainly constitute a minority in the male-dominated field of military history, but the field's sixty 'aces' who have published five or more books (see chapter 49) include at least five women (Kristen Alexander, Joan Beaumont, Melanie Oppenheimer, Lynette Ramsay Silver and Kathryn Spurling) among whom Joan Beaumont has published almost twenty books, including several edited collections (which, as a senior academic mentor she is more likely to have edited). Increasingly, Australian military history is seen through women's eyes.

37

CELLULOID ANZACS: AUSTRALIAN MILITARY HISTORY IN FILM

Explaining the growing interest in Australian military history in the 1980s, Lloyd Robson's 1988 survey noted the 'astonishing success' recent films had enjoyed. Bruce Beresford's *Breaker Morant* (1980) and Peter Weir's *Gallipoli* (1981) were a vital part of the Anzac revival of the 1980s.

The first 'feature' film dealing with an aspect of an Australian war after the fact was *Mates from the Murrumbidgee* (1911), a melodrama about a love triangle resolved on the South African veldt. The Great War produced propaganda such as *Heroes of the Dardanelles* (1915), documented in Daniel Reynaud's *Celluloid Anzacs* (2007). The comedy 'talkie' *Diggers* (1931), based on a stage hit, played on the already familiar stereotypes of the larrikin citizen soldier, framed as yarns told at a boozy reunion. Cinema also reflected the ambiguities and conflicts of war memory: a hit of 1933 was *Two Minutes Silence*, based on an anti-war play. Soon, 'the pictures' were shaping the recounting of deeds of the Great War and in 1940 Charles Chauvel (nephew of the Light Horse general) made *Forty Thousand Horsemen*. Shot in the sandhills of Cronulla and using Militia Light Horsemen to re-enact a version of the charge at Beersheba, Chauvel's film was praised (in the *Sydney Morning Herald*) as 'the first really great Australian picture'.

The post-1945 decline of the Australian cinema industry saw few war films made, until the 1980s. Those few included Sumner Locke Elliott's *Rusty Bugles* (1965, set in northern Australia in the Second World War; re-made in 1981), *The Mango Tree* (1973), based on Ronald

McKie's novel, set in Great War Queensland and *Escape from Singapore* and *Lindsay's Boy* (both 1974), the latter dealing with the strains of returning from war. Perhaps the most significant was *My Brother Jack*, George Johnston's novel serialised by the ABC in 1965. Much of the attention on war on Australian television screens centred on the Second World War rather than the Great War. Television series included *Spyforce*, sensationalising Z Special's exploits (1971–73) and the ABC's *Over There* (1972–73). The most influential Second World War drama series was the massively popular *The Sullivans*, set in Melbourne 1939–48 and running for 1114 episodes (plus a spin-off 'telefilm', *The John Sullivan Story*) between 1976 and 1983. *The Sullivans* surely introduced millions of younger viewers to a war now a part of their grandparents' lives.

Under the impulse of a new national confidence, a consequence of Gough Whitlam's years as prime minister and facilitated by the '10BA' taxation incentives introduced under Malcolm Fraser in 1981, hundreds of feature films were made by a revivified Australian film industry. Given the centrality of Anzac to the national sense of identity, war naturally became a source for film-makers. The 1980s saw a flood of feature films and television 'mini-series' (a form now supplanted by the 'television event').

Notable mini-series appeared every year through the 1980s, a golden decade of television drama, in which (in the years before video recorders or streaming) friends and families would gather around their sets after dinner so as not to miss the next instalment. Notable series in the 1980s included: *A Town Like Alice* (1981, based on Neville Shute's novel, set among prisoners of war and internees of the Japanese); *1915*, a 1982 dramatisation of Roger McDonald's Gallipoli novel; in 1984 both *The Cowra Breakout* and *The Last Bastion*; in 1985 *The Dunera Boys*, *The Long Way Home* (the aftermath of Vietnam), *Mud, Bloody Mud* (WWII in puppets) and *Anzacs*; in 1986 *Darwin 1942*, *Death of a Soldier* (about Eddie Leonski, the American 'brown-out murderer' of 1942), *A Fortunate Life* and *Sword of Honour* (set in Vietnam); in 1987 *Fields of Fire* (Queensland cane-cutters in the Second World War: two sequels followed), *Fragments of War* (1987) on Damien Parer and *Vietnam* (with the teenaged Nicole Kidman as an anti-war protester) and

Nancy Wake; in 1988 *The Alien Years* and *Always Afternoon* (extraordinarily *both* dramatising the experience of German internees in the Great War); in 1989 *Tanamera*, an Australian–Singaporean co-production, set in wartime Singapore; and in 1990 *The Private War of Lucinda Smith* – an Australian chorus girl in wartime London.

These television dramas reflected as well as fostered popular interest. The five-episode *Anzacs*, produced by John Dixon (a history buff and Army Reservist, a member of the Memorial's Council), was sold to Kerry Packer over an hour-long meeting to be broadcast on his Channel 9 in 1985. It touched upon many of the familiar tropes in Australian war history: questions of identity (British or Australian?), the naïvety of the volunteers of 1914, the forging of mateship in the AIF, British incompetence, the losses of Gallipoli, the horror and futility of trench warfare, and, of course, Monash's genius. Dixon was inspired by Bean's official history (and not *The Broken Years)* but retained Patsy Adam-Smith as 'story consultant'. John Williams, in his *German Anzacs*, dryly described *Anzacs* as 'no *War and Peace* ... essentially a very long "buddy" movie in the form of television soap'. It has never been emulated, though several television series, including *Anzac Girls* (2014, based on Peter Rees's book, on nurses in the Great War and featuring the inevitable romance between Anzac and nurse) echoed Dixon's themes.

The incentive of 10BA film funding built on the success of *Breaker Morant* and *Gallipoli*. The year 1982 saw two films about Z Special-type operations (*Attack Force Z* and *The Highest Honour*, the latter a Japanese–Australian co-production inspired by the 'Jaywick' and 'Rimau' raids on Singapore). *An Indecent Obsession* (1985) dramatised Colleen McCullough's 1981 novel about a nurse in the islands in 1945, and *The Lighthorsemen* (1987) re-imagined *Forty Thousand Horsemen*, made under the impetus of Light Horse buff Ian Jones, whose film was the most authentic-looking. (But on the famous photograph supposedly of the charge at Beersheba Ian was wrong: it showed the 1918 re-enactment of it.) Elyne Mitchell, Harry Chauvel's daughter and the author of the 'Silver Brumby' series of children's novels, who had published her own book on the Light Horse in 1978, wrote the 'novelisation' of the film script.

While this crop of war films might seem to imply a preoccupation with war, in fact, based on the near-complete listing by cinema guru David Stratton in his *The Avocado Plantation*, fewer than a dozen out of about 275 films made in the 1980s dealt with war; about 5 per cent. The proportion of 'tele-movies' and mini-series listed by Scott Murray in his *Australia on the Small Screen 1970–95* was similar (though both missed some – notably the film *Blood Oath* (1990) and the TV series *Over There*).

The decades spanning the millennium saw another spate of films, including *Sahara* (1995, set in north Africa, regarded as one of the worst Australian war films), *The Last Bullet* (1995, set in Borneo in 1945), *Harry's War* (1999, about an Indigenous solder in the Second World War), *15 Amore* (2000, about Italian prisoners of war), and *Broken Sun* (2008), also dealing with PoWs, but Japanese at Cowra. *Kokoda* (2006) failed to repeat the success of Weir's *Gallipoli*; likewise Baz Luhrmann's otiose spectacular *Australia* (2008), which luridly recreated the bombing of Darwin. Another wave followed in the 2010s, in 2010 alone including *Ghosts of War* (in which a man killed on the Somme meets his own ghost), *Sisters of War* (about captive nurses and nuns in New Britain) and *Beneath Hill 60*, on tunnellers at Messines. The crop included *The Water Diviner* (2014), a fanciful father-searches-for-lost-teenage-son notable for embracing Turkish historical orthodoxy. A bizarre outrider was John Doyle's TV comedy–drama *Changi* (2001) which, despite its title, professed to be a generic treatment of captivity, but missed its target, awkwardly mixing Dennis Potteresque mimed songs with a genuinely moving evocation of the trauma of memory.

Contrary to expectations, war films, like military history more generally, seemed at last to be running out of steam. In 2015 the Anzac centenary saw a six-part mini-series (by 2015 a rare phenomenon) in *Gallipoli*, which, despite its notably graphic combat scenes (and the seemingly compulsory nurse-and-soldier sub-plot) failed to attract an audience. The Nine network, sensing a falling market, 'burned' the series by broadcasting the final several episodes consecutively to cut its losses in advertising revenue. *Before Dawn* (2024), a Western Front redemption/buddy film, is neither graphic not gripping, and commits many howlers. Despite Australia having been at war pretty much continually from 2001 we have seen few dramas basing plots on recent military history.

Australian documentary films about war have a long lineage, from Damien Parer's footage (recut for the series 1960s *Anzacs*) to Chris Masters's ABC programs on Crete and Kokoda and beyond. Documentary films are perhaps less influential popularly, but some on military historical themes and stories open research – the premier example is *Angels of War* (1982) by Andrew Pike, Hank Nelson and Gavan Daws, which focused attention on the experience of Papuan and New Guinean carriers. More than feature films, documentaries often have strong links with the authors of books – Sue Hardisty's book on the Women's Land Army, *Thanks Girls and Goodbye* (1990), began as a 1988 film of the same name. Others have had effects beyond their content: Michael Caulfield's eight-part series *Australians at War* (2001) funded by the Department of Veterans' Affairs was notable for taking historical advice seriously – Caulfield convened a 'kitchen cabinet' of historians: Joan Beaumont, Jeff Grey, Michael McKernan, and me. He also parlayed the revenue from the project to fund the massive Australians at War Film Archive, eventually comprising thousands of hours of interviews and now held by UNSW Canberra.

Most documentaries, however, arise from the film-maker's awareness of the subject. In this, Wain Fimeri is an outstanding creator. Fimeri's *Love and War* (2003) told the story of Corporal John Johnson, father of eight who, inexplicably, was allowed to enlist and who died at Tobruk, based on *Love Letters from a War* (2003), by Len Johnson, one of his sons. Fimeri, an historical expert in his own right, extraordinarily recreated the battle of *Pozières* (2000) in a muddy paddock with half-a-dozen actors, and he went on to make *Charles Bean's Great War* (2010), which featured historians debating Bean's legacy juxtaposed with recreated scenes of his life. (Honesty if not modesty impels me to declare that I was the 'Australian' presenter on Fimeri's *Revealing Gallipoli* (2005), a production which had three presenters, from the three national broadcasting bodies which funded it: Australia, Turkey and Ireland.) Along with Michael McKernan and Michael Molkentin

I also participated in Michael Caulfield's innovative series *In Their Footsteps* (2011), which took family members to the places where their forebears' stories could be told. 'Stories' became the watchword of these programs. The popular TV franchise *Who Do You Think You Are?*, which presumes that we're interested in celebrities' family histories, also often features segments exploring war experience, not least because in Australia, abundant military records are so readily accessible.

The years around the Centenary of Anzac were a fertile time for war documentaries, including *Monash the Forgotten Anzac* (2008), *The War That Changed Us* (2014) and *Australia: The story of us* (2015). Taking a leaf from the 'storians' books, many of these documentaries adopted the technique of recounting the past in the present tense, a practice which many directors insisted on and which historians, keen to appear on screen and enhance their claims to 'engagement' (one of the new buzzwords in the academy) were happy to accept.

38

AND THE BAND PLAYED ON: WAR AND CULTURE

War and culture might seem to be poles apart, but art, literature and music contribute to the understanding of its place in Australian history; though less than you might expect. While Charles Bean and later John Treloar took a keen interest in the official war art programs of the two world wars, art has rarely been central to the interpretation of Australia's wars, with the possible exceptions that artists Wendy Sharpe for the Timor intervention and Ben Quilty for Afghanistan helped to convey understanding of the troops' experience. (But Michael Davros's portrait of Ben Roberts-Smith, *Pistol grip*, depicting him in an aggressive stance, also became a key exhibit in the public reaction to the finding in 2023 that he had killed unlawfully.)

Scholars of art have unduly ignored war art, many regarding it as conservative (which it mostly has been), though appreciating innovative work, such as in Richard Haese's *Rebels and Precursors* (1988), on progressive art movements before and during the Second World War. That much of it resides in the collection of the Memorial (which has displayed it to advantage) has paradoxically limited its exploitation. Its curators have, however, promoted and interpreted their collection, in John Reid's pioneering two-volume survey, *Australian Artists at War* (1977). Reid's successors, Gavin Fry and Anne Gray, published *Masterpieces of the Australian War Memorial* (1982) and others including Lola Wilkins and Laura Webster have, rightly, interpreted the collection through dozens of exhibitions over the forty years since John Reid's books.

Art has attracted attention from popular and academic authors, unevenly. The former include Scott Bevan's *Battle Lines* (which deals with fifteen artists) and Betty Churcher's *The Art of War* (both 2004). Scholarly studies include Catherine Speck's *Painting Ghosts: Australian women artists in wartime* (2004) and Margaret Hutchison's authoritative *Painting War* (2019) on the Great War art scheme. There is, surprisingly, no comparable study of the Second World War or of later appointments.

This deficiency has been partly rectified by artists' biographies, including the notable examples of Ross McMullin's *Will Dyson* (1984), and of course Arthur Streeton, subject of half-a-dozen biographies. Despite the biographical details in Richard Travers's *To Paint a War* (2017), two-thirds of Great War artists have no full biographies, including Septimus Power and Frank Crozier. For the Second World War there is Garry Kinnane's *Colin Colahan* (1996) and Anne-Louise Willoughby's *Nora Heysen* (2019). But only sixteen out of thirty-four official artists have biographies, and the omissions include Murray Griffin (who survived Changi) and Alan Moore (who painted Bergen-Belsen).* Official war artists appointed after 1945 tend to be better documented, especially through exhibitions, but 'unofficial' war artists such as the courageous George Gittoes (who seems to be attracted to war and crisis) await published biographies.

Despite anthologies of wartime poetry, the *Oxford Companion to Australian Literature* dismissed many wartime poets as 'rhymesters and balladists in the popular tradition'. David Holloway's anthology *Dark Somme Flowing: Australian verse of the Great War 1914–18* (1987) explicitly sought to challenge Vivian Smith's assertion in the *Oxford History of Australian Literature* that the Great War produced 'little poetry of consequence', unlike Britain's celebrated 'War Poets'. Anthologies – Chris Wallace-Crabbe's *Clubbing of the Gunfire* (1984) and John Laird's *The Australian Experience of War* (1988) – tend to

* Astonishingly, besides Gavin Fry's nine-page introduction to Griffin's brief memoir *Changi* (1992), the creator of the most powerful Australian depictions of captivity has no biography.

confirm the judgment that over a century on, Australian war verse is of greater interest to historians than other poets.

War produced fiction as well as poetry, a great range of it, from literary masterpieces such as Frederic Manning's *The Middle Parts of Fortune* (1929–30), Leonard Mann's *Flesh in Armour* (1932) and Frank Dalby Davison's *The Wells of Beersheba* (1933), seemingly a participant's account of the charge at Beersheba, actually a superb work of imagination. The Second World War prompted even more creative responses, including wartime novels such as Lawson Glossop's *We Were the Rats* (1945), post-war novels like Tom Hungerford's *The Ridge and the River* (1952) and modern creative works such as David Malouf's *The Great World* (1990), Richard Flanagan's *The Narrow Road to the Deep North* (2013) and Gail Jones's *Salonika Burning* (2022). Critical responses have not been equal to the outpouring of creative endeavour.

Robin Gerster's *Big-Noting* (1987) tracing *The Heroic Theme in Australian War Writing* redressed the way war literature in Australia had somehow 'missed the boat', as Richard White put it in a review in *Australian Historical Studies*. Instead of war literature expressing disillusionment with patriotic cant (as in Britain), Gerster showed, as White wrote, how Australian writers about war – the authors of the 'books of the tribe' – succumbed to the tendency to exaggerate; to 'big-note'. Although White thought that the debate 'cannot be the same again', in fact forty years on the field has advanced relatively little. Despite its descriptive power, war literature has been surprisingly little used by Australian military historians. (But not universally; I used Zora Cross's poetry in my *Digger Smith* (2011) and she gave me the title of *The Crying Years* (2017).) Perhaps the abundance of the letters-and-diaries which Bill Gammage exposed has obviated the need; or perhaps military historians are suspicious of creative writing.

Sadly, except for Gerster's *Big-Noting* and Christina Spittel's promising forthcoming *The Great War in the Australian Novel*, literary scholars have been surprisingly reticent in analysing creative writing about war. One of the exceptions has been Kosmas Tsokhas in *Making a Nation State* (2001), who used the literature of the Great War, and especially 'Anzac, Sexuality [and] Otherness' to second the idea that it forged an Australian identity; hardly an original argument. As this book shows, writers about war are mostly male; however Donna Coates's *Shooting Blanks at the Anzac Legend* (2023) goes a step further to claim that women's voices have been actively silenced. I think that that's an exaggeration: women are now prominent in the writing of military history.

Who reads literature in war? That question has been comprehensively answered by Amanda Laugesen, Director of the Australian National Dictionary (an expert on wartime language – *Furphies and Whizz-bangs*, 2015) in her *Boredom Is the Enemy* (2011). The answer is – very many people, both to understand and to escape war.

Wartime music and entertainment generally has attracted some scholarship but few books. Septimus Kelly, the Australian–British composer killed on the Somme, has drawn the greatest attention, and his elegiac music has recently been re-discovered through *Race Against Time* (2004), Thérèse Radic's commentary on his diary and popularised (and played) by musician Chris Latham.

As an entrepreneurial composer, Latham co-ordinated the international Gallipoli Symphony (but only involving Australia, New Zealand and Turkey), first performed in Istanbul in 2015. This, the first of the musical interpretative oratorios Latham would create over the next decade, was arguably the musical counterpart of the transnational Kemalist history that had come to prevail in the popular view of Gallipoli since Carlyon's book. As an Australian War Memorial artist-in-residence (its first) from 2017 to 2022, Latham produced a series of 'requiems', offering musical interpretations of episodes in Australian military history in words and music. His productions included Diggers Requiem (2018), Vietnam Requiem (2021) and PoW Requiem (2022), all notable for their empathetic use of the words of war's participants and victims.

Popular songs, despite their ubiquity, remain largely undocumented. From 'Australia Will Be There' to 'I Was Only Nineteen', songs have exemplified war experience; so far surprisingly unexplored. Robert Holden's *And the Band Played On* (2014), dealt with music in the Great War, especially in the AIF, though, couched as 'paying homage' to the Anzacs' 'camaraderie, innocent enjoyment and spontaneous entertainment', it stayed on the lighter side. Graham Seal's *Echoes of Anzac: The voice of Australians at war* (2005) collated much doggerel verse (often set to music) which preserves valuable evidence of attitudes and emotions, including darker expressions of resentment and protest. The cultural impact of the Second World War, which was perhaps greater, has been surprisingly neglected (except for the impact of American music from 1942–45, which has attracted half-a-dozen studies, from Andrew Bisset's *Black Roots, White Flowers* (1979) to Deirdre O'Connell's *Harlem Nights* (2021)).

'And the Band Played Waltzing Matilda', the Anzac Day anthem (astonishingly, 'covered' in nearly 200 versions within twenty years), has been analysed by Michael Walsh's *Eric Bogle, Music and the Great War* (2023), a model for other discussions of popular music. Clearly – surprisingly – there is more to be done in understanding culture and war.

39

WAR BY STEALTH: SECRET AND SPECIAL

What are today known as 'special operations' became a part of Australian military history arguably with Australia's contribution to Dunsterforce in Persia in 1918, documented in Alan Stewart's *The Persian Expedition* (2006), a story that Vicken Babkenian and I also told, from the Armenian perspective, in our *Armenia, Australia & the Great War* (2016). Dunsterforce was hardly a *Secret Army*, as Barry Stone's 2017 book had it, dramatising the episode as *An elite force, a secret mission, a fleet of Model-T Fords, a far flung corner of WWI.*

The formation of independent companies in 1940, which became commando squadrons later in the war, introduced Australians to behind-the-lines operations, best discussed in Greg Blake's *Jungle Cavalry* (2019) and in their unit histories. But the most significant Australian special force was Z Special (part of a complicated organisation usefully known as Allied Intelligence Bureau), which mounted dozens of secret missions in Japanese-occupied south-east Asia. The best account of Z Special is Alan Powell's *War by Stealth: Australians and the Allied Intelligence Bureau, 1942–1945* (1996), but several Z Special missions have been the subject of books, such as Don Dennis's *The Guns of Muschu* (2006), on an operation in New Guinea that went tragically wrong.

Accounts of some Z Special operations appeared in books on the successful 'Jaywick' and disastrous 'Rimau' raids on Singapore harbour in 1943 and 1944, first in Ronald McKie's *The Heroes* (1960), the inspiration for *Spyforce*, the 1970s TV series. Despite a lack of sources (Powell estimated that only about 13 per cent of those created had survived post-war culling) many further books appeared, on 'Z' in general and on Jaywick and Rimau, including Will Davies's *Secret & Special* (2021), not surprisingly still marketed as *The untold story of Z Special.*

Cognate to Z Special were the naval Coastwatchers, whose contributions to intelligence in the Pacific war – and the risks they ran in evading capture, torture and execution – cloaked the Allies' possession of Japanese signals intelligence. Several books, beginning with Eric Feldt's *The Coast Watchers* (as early as 1946) and most recently Betty Lee's *Right Man, Right Place, Worst Time* (2019) celebrate the Coastwatchers' bravery without fully revealing their real role.

From its formation in 1957 Australia's main special operations unit became the Special Air Service Regiment, one unduly wreathed in secrecy, reprehensibly as events would later reveal. The SAS's secret cross-border 'Claret' operations in Borneo in 1964–66 were first disclosed in Britain in 1974 but an open secret long before. David Horner, notably in his *Phantoms of the Jungle* (1989), disclosed the operations. As the mainstay of the commitment to Afghanistan, the SAS's exploits in that long conflict formed the substance of many of the books published about it, especially by journalist Ian McPhedran, who cultivated a rapport with its notoriously secretive members and produced a laudatory book, *The Amazing SAS* (2005). Revelations of alleged war crimes in Afghanistan diminished admiration for the SAS, though the appetite for the 'secret and special' remains.

40

REVEALING SECRETS: CODES AND CODE-BREAKERS

Secrecy in war has been the subject of books since at least 1915, when Walter Henderson published the sensational (and wholly invented) *Foiled! The enemy in our own land.* By the nature of the subject matter and especially the sources, however, historians were slow to write about codes and code-breaking and espionage.

Wartime secrecy prevailed over codes and code-breaking until the mid-1970s. Australia's premier historian of intelligence, John Blaxland, points out that Gavin Long gave the Allied Intelligence Bureau only a six-page appendix. Long's official history was written without knowledge of 'Ultra' secret intelligence. The existence of Ultra files was disclosed in Britain only in 1974, with the publication of wartime intelligence officer Frederick Winterbotham's *The Ultra Secret.* These revelations were slow to be taken up and exploited – David Horner's *High Command* (1982) was the first synoptic work to use it, and Mark Johnston's and my *Alamein* was the first battlefield history to draw on Ultra files. Australia's own Bletchley-like outfits, especially Central Bureau, came under investigation, presaging a gaggle of books on codes and code-breaking.

Already, Geoffrey Ballard (Australia's Winterbotham) had told the essential story in *On Ultra Active Service* (1991), after seeking permission of the Minister for Defence. Jack Bleakley's *The Eavesdroppers* (1992) expanded the story (securing the Chief of Air Staff's endorsement), while Jean Bou completed a long-awaited history of Central Bureau in *MacArthur's Secret Bureau* (2012). Des Ball, in collaboration with Keiko Tamura, revealed David Sissons's work on codebreakers in *Breaking*

Japanese Diplomatic Codes (2013).* The release of secret files also changed the understanding of Cold War history. Des Ball and David Horner's *Breaking the Codes* (1998) substantiated the long-contested story of the Soviet spy 'Venona' signals, showing that while left-wing historians regarded the 1954 Petrov defection as engineered by Menzies or his agents, the decrypts confirmed the fact of Australian treason. Awareness of naval intelligence deepened following biographies of key naval intelligence officers, Barbara Winter's *The Intrigue Master* (1995) on Rupert Long, and Ian Pfennigwerth's *A Man of Intelligence* (2006) on Eric Nave.

As has often happened, popular authors disseminated pioneering research. A decade on, a run of books on signals intelligence appeared – Craig Collie's *Code Breakers: Inside the shadow world of signals intelligence in Australia's two Bletchley Parks* (2017) and David Dufty's *The Secret Code-Breakers of Central Bureau: How Australia's signals-intelligence network helped win the Pacific war* (also 2017; also suggesting that American-style unduly long explanatory sub-titles had reached Australia). John Blaxland and Clare Birgin produced *Revealing Secrets: An unofficial history of Australian signals intelligence and the advent of cyber* (2023): 'unofficial', because though approved by the relevant senior bureaucrat, it was 'cut off in mid-stride' by his successor. *The Factory* (2023), by Defence insider John Fahey, was billed as *The official history of the Australian Signals Directorate*, raising the question of whether senior spooks essentially quashed a history they could no longer control.

* Though he published little in his lifetime, David Sissons was an extraordinary asset to the understanding of the Pacific war. Admirers published his work posthumously in two volumes as *Bridging Australia and Japan* (2016 and 2020).

41

OUR MOB SERVED: FIRST NATIONS AT WAR

First Nations people have served Australia in war since the Boer War. Harry Gordon. the sporting journalist, Korean war correspondent and newspaper executive, published *The Embarrassing Australian* (1962), a biography of Reg Saunders, whom he had known in Korea where Saunders had served as a captain in 1RAR. Gordon unwittingly helped to promote the idea that Saunders had been the first Aboriginal man to be commissioned. Not until 2015 would Andrea Gerrard's unpublished MA reveal that Alfred Hearps had been commissioned in 1916, and institutions such as the Memorial perpetuated the error, denying primacy to Hearps – who had been killed at Mouquet Farm.

Soon after graduating from RMC Duntroon in 1972, Chris Coulthard-Clark made the first of his many contributions to Australian military history by publishing an article in the *Army Journal* on 'Aborigines in the First AIF'. He identified several hundred Aboriginal men. In 1989, in his *The Black Diggers*, Bob Hall estimated that 'perhaps three or four hundred Aborigines or "part-Aborigines"' served in the AIF, and he wrote as a matter of fact that they 'were excluded from the "digger legend"'. In the Second World War more than 3000 had served, though no one knew – even Queensland, the state with the most rigorous 'protection' regime, 'lamely admitted that the number of Aboriginal servicemen was unknown', Hall wrote. Reviewers immediately saw that Hall's research had uncovered not just a neglected aspect of Australian military history, but that it had implications for what was coming to be called Reconciliation. Jeff Grey ended his review in the *Canberra Times*, 'Would someone please buy Bruce Ruxton a copy!'

About this time the researcher David Huggonson developed a Memorial exhibition, Too Dark for the Light Horse, which toured nationally, welcomed by Indigenous communities (glad to see their contribution recognised) and informing the wider community of service which had formerly been symbolised by Reg Saunders's story. Largely as a result of the pioneering research of Coulthard-Clark, Huggonson and Hall, over the next thirty years, that neglect was fully reversed.

Independent scholar Philippa Scarlett's *Aboriginal and Torres Strait Islander Volunteers for the AIF* (over four editions, 2011–2018) revised the number of identifiably Indigenous AIF volunteers from 815 to over 1000. The Memorial, which from about 2013 vigorously researched Indigenous service (partly out of a belated sense of justice, but perhaps to distract attention from its flagrant refusal to acknowledge Frontier conflict) devoted considerable resources to the quest. One of its mainstays was Margaret Beadman, who as a volunteer contributed hundreds of hours of work to the project, a disinterested effort all the more impressive because she had no personal stake in the outcome.

Researchers approached the subject from the perspective of individuals, communities and states and it is now a busy field. Examples of the three approaches include Peter Rees's biography of Len Waters, the first Indigenous pilot, *The Missing Man* (2018); Doreen Kartinyeri's pioneering *Ngarrindjeri Anzacs* (1996), an early example of the documentation of one First Nations contribution; and Andrea Gerrard's sadly unpublished University of Tasmania MA thesis, 'Overlooked: Tasmanian Aborigines in the First World War', the only state-based study, so far. This research increasingly follows protocols giving Indigenous individuals and communities a voice in how their history is researched and recorded; an understandable development given their history of paternalism and disempowerment, but one which carries the hazard of allowing communities to dictate or censor researchers' interpretations.

In contrast to the disdain of the *Defence Act* of 1903 and the 'colour-blind' acceptance recalled by Indigenous diggers in the world wars, Korea and Vietnam, the Defence Force now celebrates Indigenous service (such as Gary Oakley and others, *First Nations Aviators* (2022)).

Academic researchers have continued their interest in Indigenous service. Outstanding recent books, which tend to be the products of large, grant-funded projects (because they often involve consultation with and the involvement of communities) include Joan Beaumont and Alison Cadzow, *Serving Our Country* (2018) and a product of the larger project, Alison Cadzow and Mary Anne Jebb's *Our Mob Served* (2019). Noah Riseman has published several books, including his *Defending Whose Country?* (2012), *In Defence of Country* (2016) and, with Richard Trembath, *Defending Country* (2016). With First Nations families and communities increasingly eager to re-discover their military heritage, authors are going to need more creative combinations of 'Defending' and 'Country'.

42

SOLDIERS AND ALIENS: ETHNICITY AND ANZAC

In 1988, Ken Inglis, in discussing 'The Australian Military Tradition', posed the question, 'Multicultural Australia – whither ANZAC? [sic]'. Australia's war history traditionally involved non-Anglo participants in walk-on roles – literally so in the case of the 'Fuzzy-Wuzzy Angels' of the Papuan campaign. Until recently they remained marginal.

But war and ethnicity had long been inextricably linked. In 1914, Australians quickly accepted that the Kaiser's Germany posed a threat to Australia. A major element in the ethnic history of Australia's wars has been internment, of subjects of the German, Ottoman and Austro-Hungarian empires in the First World War (about 4500 German-born Australians were interned, including 700 *naturalised* British subjects and even seventy *Australian-born* of German descent). In the Second World War, about 12 000 Germans, Italians and Japanese were interned. Long a subject of embarrassment and even shame among 'enemy' communities, internment did not become the subject of research until the 1980s. Gerhard Fischer published his *Enemy Aliens*, on internment in the Great War, in 1989. Internment in the Second World War has attracted even greater attention.

The most prominent single episode concerned the ship the *Dunera*, which in 1940 carried some 2000 German-Jewish internees from Britain to Australia. Cyril Pearl's *The Dunera Scandal* (1983) was 'not the definitive account', Michael Piggott dryly judged, 'but nor ... will it be the last'. Indeed, Bezion Patkin's *The Dunera Internees* (1979) and Paul Bartrop and Gabrielle Eisen's *The Dunera Affair* (1990) preceded and followed Pearl's book. Ken Inglis's last project, with Jay Winter,

Bill Gammage, Carol Bunyan and Seumas Spark, was to publish a lavish two-volume *Dunera Lives* (2018 and 2020). The first comprised a 'visual history' and the second 'profiles' of the extraordinarily talented cargo of exiles who enriched Australian life despite their unpropitious arrival.* Winter's account (in the second volume) of how Inglis's *Dunera* project evolved provides a masterclass in academic collaboration.

June Factor, a sociologist known for her studies of children's folklore (notably *Far out, Brussel Sprout!*) and whose previous venture into military history had been a study of Army Farms in northern Australia, produced a prize-winning book, *Soldiers and Aliens* (2022). She revealed how 'friendly aliens', including *Dunera* internees, volunteered for the Australian Army's employment companies, a reminder how military history has long been ethnic history. As Gerhard Fischer, historian of German Australia, wrote in *Australian Historical Studies* in 2006, 'Anzac embraces multiculturalism', a result of the fusion of what might be called Australian ethnic history and of the Anzac boom which had begun twenty-five years before.

An early manifestation of this theme was *A Turkish View of Gallipoli* by Vecihi Basaran (assisted by Kevin Fewster) (1985, with a revised edition in 2003) which, though hampered by a dearth of accessible Turkish sources and a slavish adherence to Turkey's prevailing 'Kemalist' ideology, opened the Ottoman experience to readers who had only seen the campaign from the Anzac line. The partial opening of Ottoman sources allowed Harvey Broadbent, perhaps the only Australian military historian to read Turkish, to publish his two books in 2015, the popular *Defending Gallipoli* and the more detailed *Gallipoli: The Turkish defence.*

Though Australians have found themselves at war in over seventy countries since they first went to war overseas in 1860, we

* A formidably synoptic historian of the Great War and memory, mostly European, Winter had first come to Australia through Michael McKernan at the Memorial. Working with Ken Inglis and Bruce Scates, he brought a generation of often young scholars into contact with 'memory studies'. Jay's energy is prodigious – I once saw him literally step off a plane from Paris to give a two-hour more-or-less impromptu lecture: just listening to him is exhausting.

have surprisingly few studies of how they regarded the locals, or how they viewed their guests (welcome or not). Some military historians have written about wartime adversaries – such as Mark Johnston in *Fighting the Enemy* (2000), seen largely through Australian eyes. We have Suzanne Brugger's pioneering *The Australians in Egypt* (published in 1980 and so drawing on the memories of elderly Egyptians; not always positive ones). This encounter has otherwise been told from an Australian (and invariably 'larrikin') perspective: consider the scenes in Cairo of Peter Weir's *Gallipoli*, produced at the same time. We have Mark Johnston's *Anzacs in the Middle East* (2013) and Robin Gerster's frank examination of the complex relationship over the seven years of BCOF's time in occupied Japan in *Travels in Atomic Sunshine*. But we don't really know how Australians at war related to the people of Papua New Guinea and extraordinarily, we still don't have a book on how Australians lived among the people of France and Belgium. In *Diggers and Greeks* (2010), Maria Hill gathered sources opaque to Australians generally and made good use of her perspective as a Greek-Australian. A multicultural Australia needs a multicultural military history.

Several books have highlighted relationships between Australians and ethnic groups in wartime. They include *Armenia, Australia & the Great War* (2016) by Vicken Babkenian and me, and Louise Lindenmayer's *Debt of Honour* (2018), revealing *How an ANZAC* [sic; Stanley Savige] *saved the Assyrian people from genocide*. These books provoke protests from a vociferous pro-Turkish lobby, which presses its claim to be seen as vital to the Anzac legend. Ethnicity also figures in Australian war history by writers uncovering the war experience of former allies, such as Lynette Ramsay Silver's *Blood Brothers: Sabah and Australia 1942–1945* (2010) or Paul Malone's *Forgotten Heroes: The true story of Sarawak people who fought and died assisting Allied Forces in WWII* (2014).

The ethnic composition of Australia's forces has attracted a succession of books over the past twenty years. The trend to write about 'ethnic Anzacs' may be dated from John Williams's *German Anzacs* (2003), which explored the complexity of Australia's largest non-Anglo-Celtic minority, perhaps 20 000 of whose sons volunteered to fight their ancestral homeland. Jeff Kildea's *Anzacs and Ireland* (2007) dealt with another sizeable minority, busting myths cherished by Australian-Irish tradition, suggesting that the tendency to oppose conscription notwithstanding, Irish-Australians had volunteered (and died) at much the same rate as their Anglo or Protestant comrades. Likewise, Rodney Gouttman's *In Their Merit* (2015, on Australian Jews and the Great War) or Mark Dapin's *Jewish Anzacs* (2017) renewed their claim to sharing in the legend, not least through Monash, the community's most conspicuous member. Dzavid Haveric's *A History of Muslims in the Australian Military* (2024) also shows that Muslims have served since the colonial period.

Seeking to explicitly establish a link with their new homeland through a wartime relationship, other groups have attracted their historical champions. Elena Govor's *Russian Anzacs in Australian History* (2005) led the study of smaller groups, such as Khrystyna Misko's *Faded Footsteps, Forgotten Graves* (2016) on Queensland's sixty 'Ukrainian Anzacs' or Bojan Pajic's *Our Forgotten Volunteers* (2018) on Australians serving with Serbs in the Great War. Migrant groups naturally make much of wartime relationships to establish bonds with their new society, most notably the Turkish community, which has encouraged the concoction of a myth that despite tens of thousands of dead, Turks on Gallipoli were, as David Cameron's 2014 book put it, *Our Friend the Enemy*. Greek-Australians have equally seized on the Anzacs' brief time on Lemnos in 1915 as the basis of a connection, expressed in Roger Hawthorn and Tony Whitefield's *A Lemnos Odyssey* (2015). Several abortive attempts have been made by Sikh- and Indian-Australians to connect with Australia through the service of 'Indian' volunteers for the AIF. The ventures are notable not so much for the small numbers of 'Indian Anzacs' – fewer than two dozen – but also because of the belief in the leverage their recognition would afford.

Protestations that ethnic communities are 'forgotten' are perhaps overstated. Will Davies's *The Forgotten* (2020) tells the story of 'Chinese Anzacs', the subject of two earlier books; Alastair Kennedy's *Chinese Anzacs* (2012) and Jo Clyne and others', also entitled *Chinese Anzacs* (2015). (But Davies's book is one of the few books in Australian military history to be simultaneously published in Mandarin.) Journalist John Hamilton published *Gallipoli Sniper* (2008), on the Chinese-Australian Billy Sing, commemorated in a statue in Clermont, Queensland, as long ago as 1995.

Curiously, the largest single non-native group in the AIF, the British-born who constituted between 10 and 20 per cent of its strength, still await their chronicler. Just as British migrants are overlooked in studies of migration, so 'Poms' remain the 'Forgotten Anzacs' – had that title not been snaffled by Peter Ewers's 2008 book on the Greek campaigns of 1941.

43

A STOUT PAIR OF BOOTS: BATTLEFIELDS

Walking Australian battlefields has informed the writing of military history since Charles Bean returned to Gallipoli in 1919, a venture he described in his *Gallipoli Mission* (1948, and reprinted in 1990). After a considerable hiatus, Australian historians have donned boots to 'sniff the ground', as a former Memorial colleague once put it. One of the Memorial's early, intermittent grants gave Bill Gammage an absurdly small amount to visit Gallipoli and the Western Front in 1970 – not the first Australian historian to visit Gallipoli since Alan Moorehead, but one of the two most portentous visits.

With the revival of military history in the early 1980s, Peter Pedersen, then writing a PhD on Monash, visited Gallipoli to understand the failed offensive in August 1915. This trip produced an article, 'Ghosts of Anzac', in the Memorial's *Journal*, and soon serious researchers routinely sought to walk battlefields. Inspired perhaps by Ken Inglis's 1965 visit, other historians travelled to historic sites, sometimes in company with veterans. Hank Nelson, who formed a rapport with former prisoners of the Japanese, returned to the Burma–Thailand railway, 'Travelling in memories', as he entitled an article in the Memorial's *Journal* soon after.

The growing availability of cheap international travel prompted the publication of battlefield guides. One of the earliest, and still among the best, was written by a pair of Victorian teachers, Phil Taylor and Pam Cupper who, while teaching in Britain, adventurously cycled and camped around Gallipoli when doing so involved encountering bunkers and armed sentries on the beaches. Their detailed *Gallipoli: A battlefield guide* (1989) anticipated a slew of such books, including

Glenn Wahlert's *Exploring Gallipoli*, (2008), Richard Reid's *The Anzac Walk* (2009) and Mat McLachlan's *Gallipoli* (2015). Similar guides appeared for the Western Front such as McLachlan's *Walking with the Anzacs* (2015), while Peter Pedersen and Chris Roberts's *Anzacs on the Western Front* (2011), its detailed field research heavily subsidised by the Memorial, was the most authoritative. Gary McKay, the leading writer on Vietnam, produced *Australia's Battlefields in Viet Nam: A traveller's guide* (2003).

Garrie Hutchinson's *Pilgrimage: A traveller's guide to Australia's battlefields* (2006) dealt with almost all Australian battlefields. Still, a day visit, however purposeful, is not the same as battlefield research. Even significant battlefields in the Middle East (such as Beersheba), North Africa (Tobruk and Alamein) and Papua New Guinea, many difficult, somewhat hazardous or even impossible to visit, remain without a detailed guide, though adventurous historians still walk battlefields in North Africa, Borneo, Papua New Guinea and above all Gallipoli and the Western Front. Historians who used the ground as a source include Jean Bou, Phillip Bradley, Peter Brune, David Cameron, David Coombes, Craig Deayton, Andrew Faulkner, Mark Johnston, Peter Pedersen, Garth Pratten, Chris Roberts, Peter Williams and me. Andrew Faulkner described his field work for his *Noreuil* (2024), for which he 'visited Noreuil four times and walked the battlefield from the jump-off tape to the final objective', and incorporated an account of his walk across the battlefield (at the same time of year as the battle) into its final chapter.

The most intensive study of contested terrain remains *Anzac Battlefield* (2006), a collaborative international and interdisciplinary venture which mapped and interpreted Anzac Area on Gallipoli, should influence future research. (It disclosed, for example, that the terraces which I wrote, in *Quinn's Post*, had eroded away could still be found.)

A parallel development to guides was the phenomenon of historical travelogues. In 1956 John Laffin had travelled to the Australian battlefields around the Mediterranean, a trip described in his *Middle East Journey*. Inadvertently impersonating Bob Menzies while circumventing obstructive officials, he was probably the first Australian to visit Tobruk after 1941. Later writers assumed the spirit of *Middle East Journey*. Notable exponents were journalists Tony Wright, with *Turn Right at Istanbul* (2003), and especially Paul Daley and photographer Michael Bowers's *Beersheba: A journey through Australia's forgotten war* (2011), which offered a meditation on both Australian historical experience and on the complex connections between past and present.

By the early 21st century, the range of such work prompted me to write *A Stout Pair of Boots* (2008), offering a commentary on the sources available and suggested techniques which military historians could use in incorporating field research into their understanding. One of the notable features of writing *A Stout Pair of Boots* became that as I drew on the experiences, insights and advice of many colleagues, I realised the extent to which Australian military history constituted not just a field of study, but also a real fellowship.

44

THE COST OF WAR: AFTERMATHS

In 1996 Stephen Garton, an historian of mental illness and social welfare, turned to examining, as his book was called, *The Cost of War: Australians return*. Garton exposed an unspoken ordeal that many families knew: wars' long-lasting impost on Australian society, which became a major theme in Australian military history.

The numbers of dead – and their scale – matter. David Noonan, in his *Those We Forget* (2014), literally re-counted the dead of the Great War, suggesting that Billy Hughes's familiar 'sixty-thousand dead' if anything underestimated the continuing loss. Adding the dead of the 'flu pandemic and Returned Men who died early (some by suicide) suggested the war's full cost. At least 100 000 Australians had died in overseas wars before anyone thought to investigate how their deaths had affected their families and communities. Death had of course been among the most inescapable and enduring effects of war. Acknowledged publicly, in death notices and inscriptions on war memorials, they were largely borne privately: the mourning black so common in Australian streets in wartime essentially deterred comment or inquiry. Recognition was publicly transmuted in the rhetoric of Anzac Day as 'sacrifice' in addresses commemorating 'the fallen', and the rhetoric of Anzac Day still influences how we write about war.

Just as society began to acknowledge and deal more openly with life's emotional costs, so military history changed. In 1994 Bill Gammage had already recognised that *The Broken Years* had really been 'an emotional history of the men of the AIF'. In this he reflected a decades-long progression in historical practice, especially overseas, which had gradually embraced 'social history', 'history from below', and in our field 'the new military history', to come in the 1990s to what theorists called 'the emotional turn'. By this time, historians of war had begun to explore the human effects of war, on all those affected: combatants, civilians, loved ones, later generations and indeed, those who recorded and interpreted history.

In Australia, the emotional turn was especially evident in museums, which from the 1990s seized upon 'personal stories', evident in the selection of artefacts, in words and graphics, and ultimately in whole exhibitions. At the Memorial, our acceptance of the importance of emotion in understanding war was symbolised in the decision in 1995 (inspired by curator Ian Affleck) to include in a 'Sandakan' alcove the paybook photographs of *all* of the 2000-odd victims of the death marches. Museums Victoria's Deb Tout-Smith mounted a large exhibition, *Love and Sorrow* (2014–18), which explicitly approached the Great War through the lens of emotion.

Historians of Australia's wars followed overseas scholars. In the 1980s, Ken Inglis, still working on his great war memorials project, introduced historians from France and the United States such as Annette Becker and Jay Winter, who encouraged Australian colleagues to explicitly address the human costs of war. This sparked a spate of books in which historians asked questions about grief. The notable exponents included Joy Damousi's pioneering *The Labour of Loss* (1999) and her *Living with the Aftermath* (2001) and Pat Jalland (*Australian Ways of Death*, 2002 and *Changing Ways of Death in Twentieth Century Australia*, 2005). Their lead was soon taken up in Tanja Luckins's *The Gates of Memory* (2004), Bart Ziino's *A Distant Grief* (2007) and my own contributions to the genre, *Men of Mont St Quentin* (2009) and *Lost Boys of Anzac* (2014). Most of these books dealt with the dead of the Great War, perhaps because the sources were more extensive or richer. They arrived just too late to disrupt the overwhelming nostalgia and outright triumphalism which Minister for Veterans' Affairs Con Sciacca's Australia Remembers year generated in 1995. (Hank Nelson remarked that '"Australia Remembers" is all very well, but when will we see "Australia Learns?"')

The 'missing' increasingly occupied attention, not just of individual books but of campaigns mobilising community support, with lobbying securing official funding. Writers took on the psychological idea of 'closure', despite sceptics pointing out that hardly anyone seeking closure actually knew the dead, and the notion joined the rhetoric of commemoration. Perhaps the two most significant instances of this phenomenon were the search for HMAS *Sydney* (see chapter 33) and the search for the missing of Pheasant Wood (chapter 10) but there were other groups. For the bereaved families of the sinking of the *Montevideo Maru*, it had been, as Margaret Reeson's 2000 book put it, *A Very Long War*, a powerful and sensitive evocation of what PoW families endured, during the war and for many, long after. Not until 2023 was the ship's wreck found, a more costly tragedy than either *Sydney* or Pheasant Wood but attracting less attention. Scott Bennett (author of *Pozières*, 2011) was only one to follow 'The Missing' of the battle, in *The Nameless Names* (2018), among several such books, like Ian Shaw's *Missing* (2023).

As Margaret Reeson's book hinted, attention soon turned to others affected by war service as well as by grief, with the history of emotions combining with the now established genre of PoW studies. Some groups, of course, had just cause to feel traumatised: those who had experienced intense combat, wounds and death, including virtually all infantrymen, nurses and medical personnel and, pre-eminently, prisoners of the Japanese. Reflecting society's greater openness in speaking of trauma, the writers of two books exemplified the willingness to acknowledge it. Michael McKernan, formerly of the Memorial but by this time a freelance historian, had come to meet and understand PoWs, especially through his friendship with Hugh and Patricia Clarke, both writers. (Hugh had published several memoirs, including *Last Stop Nagasaki* (1985) and *A Life for Every Sleeper* (1986). McKernan used interviews and formerly unused Repatriation files to produce *This War Never Ends*, subtitled *The pain of separation and return* (2001).) Carolyn Newman, with whom I worked at the Memorial and herself the daughter of a PoW, edited a collection of memoirs by other PoWs' children in *Legacies of Our Fathers* in which *Their Sons and Daughters*

Tell Their Stories (2005). Christina Twomey's *The Battle Within* (2018), detailing liberated prisoners' continuing trauma, promises that as Repatriation records become available we will gain further insight into what historians (as well as psychologists and therapists) are now calling intergenerational trauma.

The growing complexity and maturity of studies exploring war trauma was perhaps best seen in the work of Kristen Alexander. Already a respected aviation biographer (with books on Clive Caldwell, Jack Davenport and Australians in the Battle of Britain), her UNSW PhD thesis won the Australian War Memorial's prestigious Gandevia Prize, and formed the basis of her *Kriegies* (2023). Alexander revealed not just the subtleties of the airmen's experience as PoWs (though in that she delved more deeply than any previous researcher, for example, exposing hitherto concealed emotional and sexual relationships) but also looked at the multi-generational dimensions of war experience. In this, Alexander amplified one of the decisive 'turns' in historical writing, which in the 21st century began a much more explicit engagement with the emotional impact of war experience.

The greater awareness of the psychological and social costs of war intensified during the two decades of the nebulous 'War on Terror' fought after 2001. Building on the insights gained from the experience of Vietnam veterans, charities (such as Soldier On and Mates4Mates) and families lobbied governments and the Defence Force to secure acknowledgment that they and their loved ones had suffered as a result of their service, in Iraq and Afghanistan but also in peacetime. This culminated in the current Royal Commission into Veteran Suicide, which promises to at least recognise past errors. The movement has prompted several books. They include Ambrose Crowe's *The Battle After the War* (1999) on Vietnam veterans, Gina Lennox's *Forged by War: Australians in combat and back home* (2005), and most recently Dianne Dempsey's *When He Came Home: The impact of war on partners and children* (2021). They decisively challenge the khaki, masculine focus of much of Australian writing on war and its effects. Margaret Hutchinson's forthcoming study of veterans who killed themselves since the Great War will open another window into war's consequences.

45

SACRED PLACES: MEMORY AND MEMORIALS

Although war memorials became from the early years of the Great War ubiquitous in Australian towns, cities and suburbs, they were so much a part of the streetscape as to be taken for granted. Not until the 1980s were they seen as worthy of investigation. Among the pioneers was Judith McKay, formerly an art curator at the Australian War Memorial, who in 1984 produced (with Richard Allom) *Lest We Forget: A guide to the conservation of war memorials*. Several theses and articles followed, as did the 'memory boom' in which Australian historians – notably Joan Beaumont, Ken Inglis and Alistair Thomson – became interested in what was being 'remembered', and how, especially by generations who had not experienced war, known in the trade as 'post-memory'. The work of Ken Inglis (not usually regarded as a military historian, but an acute observer of Australian society, past and present) was crucial.

The genesis of Inglis's seminal *Sacred Places* (1998) emerged in conversations with Bill Gammage in Papua New Guinea around 1970, but it was precipitated in 1983 by a news bulletin that mentioned a national local government organisation. In an intuitive leap, Ken realised immediately 'by God, every town's got a war memorial ... You could actually do a survey of them'. It sounds miraculous, and indeed, John Lack's bibliography of Ken's writing traces in his *Anzac Remembered* (1998) dozens of items from the mid-1960s revealing his growing fascination with commemoration.

The nation's great war memorials had long been the subject of guidebooks – successive editions of guides to the Memorial turn up at car boot sales all over the nation, brought home by tourists over the generations: I wrote one myself in 1986, now deservedly forgotten. *Here Is Their Spirit*, Michael McKernan's history of the Memorial, commissioned to mark the 50th anniversary of its dedication in Canberra and published in 1991, led the way, with McKernan taking a close interest in Inglis's massive endeavour, and brokering the Memorial's support for it. Bruce Scates's history of the Shrine of Remembrance, Melbourne (*A Place to Remember*, 2009) followed, linking the Shrine to broader themes in Victoria's memory of war. While the Anzac Memorial in Sydney has no official history, John Stace's *The Naked Soldier* (2018; the title a reference to Rayner Hoff's striking sculpture 'Sacrifice') offers an insightful study of Australia's most richly iconographic memorial. Other state memorials are still to be accorded detailed formal histories, though Simon Cameron's study of South Australian memorials, *Silent Witness* (1998), shows their potential.

Liz Reed's curiously uncritical study of the 1995 Australia Remembers program, *Bigger than Gallipoli* (2004) was, Peter Londey found, 'vitiated by ... relatively thin analysis' and larded with jargon. It has unfortunately not been followed by a book-length evaluation of the even bigger Centenary of Anzac, except the critique offered by essays emerging from Honest History and a 2019 paper by Joan Beaumont analysing it as a 'Memory "Orgy"'.

While remembrance – a 'carnival of commemoration', Henry Reynolds called it in *Unnecessary Wars* – may have seemed a static, reflective practice, historians also began to investigate its more active, collective manifestation, the pilgrimage. (If Ken Inglis had published the book he wrote about the RSL pilgrimage he accompanied to Gallipoli in 1965, the theme might have emerged sooner – the manuscript only appeared a few years before his death in 2017.) But from 1990, historians not only began to lead pilgrimages (Michael McKernan advised the Department of Veterans' Affairs on the model, Bob Hawke's 75th anniversary visit to Gallipoli) but also began to interpret them.

Bruce Scates, a labour historian who in the 2000s burst into the field of war memory, led from 2011 a productive investigation into the history of Anzac Day. This came out of the prevailing Australian Research Council's shibboleth impelling academics to devise elaborate and expensive collaborative projects, even though modestly costed, individual projects might be more effective. At least it brought researchers together and funded congenial conferences, which themselves generated ideas and argument. While Scates's proposed ambitious single history of Anzac Day has not yet come off – and it remains arguably the single greatest absence in what might be regarded as Inglis's agenda – he produced a remarkable range of books, consolidating the field of what might be called pilgrimage studies. He published studies of pilgrimages (*Return to Gallipoli*, 2006) and of the Second World War (*Anzac Journeys*, 2014). Along the way he wrote a novel (*On Dangerous Ground*, featuring Charles Bean as a character) and supervised a troupe of doctoral candidates who followed and extended his research agenda in investigating the relationship between how war was experienced and how it has been remembered.*

Academic historians explored the connections between Australian remembrance and the sites of their service; the obverse of the interest in pilgrimages. Notable products of this impulse included Romain Fathi's *Our Corner of the Somme* (2019), asking why and how Australians had invested so much in their relationship with Villers-Bretonneux, and Matt Haultain-Gaull, whose *The Battlefield of Imperishable Memory* (2021) explored and questioned the links between Ypres and the Anzac legend.

Especially impelled by the big anniversary festivals of Australia Remembers and the 'Centenary of Anzac' (which saw substantial funds directed toward commemoration electorate by electorate, and the Department of Veterans' Affairs continuing funding of its 'Saluting Their Service' program), many local communities produced mainly modest books on their participation in war. They often began with, and unfortunately did not go beyond, local war memorials. A few examples, of many, are Di Elliot and Ann Wales's *Boorowa Remembers* (2015) or Ron Mumford's *Echoes of War in Avoca* (2011). I saw the value of this movement, publishing *Whyalla at War* (2004), which, unusually for the

* I've just recalled that I also included Bean as a character in my children's novella *Simpson's Donkey* (2011), and I have another official historian 'Gareth Lang' as a character in my novel of 1945, *The Sherrin* (2025).

genre, combined a history of the town in the war and accounts of those from it who died during the war (including in industrial accidents).

As ever, popular authors followed where academic historians had led for over a decade, such as Carol Rosenhain's *The Man Who Carried the Nation's Grief*, on Major James Lean's work in Base Records (which I'd written about in *Lost Boys of Anzac*), Marianne Van Velzen's account of the War Graves Service, *Missing in Action* (2018), which picked up insights that Bart Ziino had made in his *A Distant Grief*, and Ian McPhedran's *Where Soldiers Lie: The quest to find Australia's missing war dead* (2019), which followed Richard Reid's *He Is Not Missing* of 1997.

46

WHAT'S WRONG WITH ANZAC?: CRITIQUES AND CHALLENGES

In 2014, James Brown, an Afghanistan veteran, published *Anzac's Long Shadow*, investigating *The cost of our national obsession*. Brown offered 'a candid look at our most important national day', dissatisfied that 'Australians compete to find bigger and better ways to commemorate' and – among many other ills – identifying the problem that the veneration of Anzac helped to produce 'simplified Anzac stories [that] communicate that war is black and white when the reality is that war is all too many shades of grey'. Those who know Australian military history best are familiar with the shades of grey, which can depress its practitioners. David Kent, one of those attracted to military social history by the opening of the sources from the 1980s (in his case the unexplored riches of the Memorial's 'troopship serials' collection) acknowledged that he found the study of war experience 'disheartening, depressing and distasteful', and felt disturbed that it was such a popular genre. Not only is it popular, but its popular authors most often celebrate rather than critically assess it.

Perceiving *The militarisation of Australian history*, in 2010 Marilyn Lake and Henry Reynolds published a collection of essays, entitled *What's Wrong With Anzac?* They, with Joy Damousi and Mark McKenna, all senior scholars, expressed their unease about the way the idea of Anzac, its historical and especially its educational interpretation, was being conscripted to serve a patriotic cause. Their starting point was how since 1990 – Bob Hawke's first pilgrimage to Gallipoli – Australia had seen 'an extraordinary increase in the number of books, newspaper articles, documentaries and electronic media programmes' on military history. They objected that the 'unbalanced concentration transforming Anzac Day into a sacred myth' had distorted Australia's understanding of its history.

Soon after, David Stephens and a group of activists (including me) formed Honest History (ironically, after coming together to defend the War Memorial from the construction of proposed huge concrete monoliths on the shore of Lake Burley Griffin) directed toward reminding Australians that the nation's history was more than Anzac. Through the coming Centenary of Anzac, Honest History's website offered a counterpoint to the excesses of the centenary, publishing *The Honest History Book* in 2017. Its main service was to document the massive expenditure on the centenary, calculating it to be higher per head (and indeed in absolute terms) than any other nation. (James Brown thought the centenary budget 'so extravagant it would make sultans swoon'.) What indeed was wrong with Anzac?

Objecting to Anzac Day could be hazardous. In the early 1980s feminist protests on Anzac Day remembering women raped in war met press and public condemnation, police harassment and arrests (over sixty in Adelaide in 1981). Monash University's Community Research Action Centre published a book of clippings, poems, photographs, cartoons, reprinted letters and articles on *Anzac Day 1984: For and against*, documenting the debate. Affronted at the misogynist abuse directed at them, the Melbourne protestors gathered not just as Women Against Rape but as the Anti-Anzac Day Collective. While the atrocity it deplored remained, the movement, a product of its time, lapsed, though, as Frank Bongiorno observed in *The Eighties* (2015) 'an emerging Anzac mainstream ... drew attention to the traumatic impact of war'.

Writing critically about Anzac could also draw the crabs, as the AIF said. Joan Beaumont wrote (in her *Australia's War 1914–18*) that Lloyd Robson had received death threats after his *The First AIF* (1970) which, compared to later revisionist accounts, now seems innocuous. David Kent, who had published (in *Historical Studies* in 1985) a well-documented critique of Charles Bean's editing of *The Anzac Book*, came under attack for daring to question one of the wellsprings of the legend. In 2015 Kent revealed the contumely he suffered, remarking on 'the consistent suggestion that I had no business to ... question ... the popular mythology of Anzac', subjected to insults such as 'Tripe ... traitor ... treason-monger ... the vilest man alive'. The British-born Kent should, one assailant wrote, be on the next boat out with $10 in your pocket', a fate patriots urged on me too when in the early 2000s I had the temerity to agree with the official histories that there was no Japanese plan to invade Australia in 1942. The Memorial's director, Steve Gower, much as he might have found me irritating, backed me and laughingly dismissed calls for me to be sacked as Principal Historian.

As academic history especially challenged cherished myths, conservatives reacted, in an unpleasant episode known among those bruised by it as 'the culture wars'. In 2009 the right-wing magazine *Quadrant* damned historians it claimed had mounted an 'Assault on Anzac'. A retired academic, Mervyn Bendle, published *Anzac and Its Enemies: The history war on Australia's national identity* (2015), listing about twenty historians supposedly inimical to the Anzac legend. Besides me, the list included many of the historians named in this book: Joan Beaumont, Joy Damousi, Peter Dennis, Ashley Ekins, Robin Gerster, Jeff Grey, David Horner, Marilyn Lake, Peter Londey, Henry Reynolds, and Craig Stockings. Like me, many of these scholars took a perverse pride in having been 'Bendled' – we joked about striking a medal with a bar for each mention in *Quadrant*. We must have been doing something right to be in such company. Though as the targets of Bendle's ire straddled world-class scholars and novices, post-modernists and empiricists, old and young, left and right, it seemed meaningless to lump them together. There was no anti-Anzac conspiracy: not only did some of these people not agree, some did not even *talk* to each other.

It was certainly true that books in Australian military history explicitly challenged the comfortable assurance sought by readers of, say, the 'storians. Books such as those on sexually transmitted diseases, by Raden Dunbar (*The Secrets of the Anzacs*, 2014) or Ian Howie-Willis (*VD: The Australian Army's Experience*, 2020), can be seen as seeking to undermine the Anzac legend. I argue that they deepen our understanding of the experience of war. In researching my own *Bad Characters* (2010), I found that while some readers were uncomfortable with revelations of ill-discipline (often on behalf of men long dead; sometimes their relatives) many readers were prepared to see sound research presented sympathetically. At the Memorial in the late 1990s we engaged a social research firm that discovered that while some visited to revel in patriotic stories of Anzac prowess, at least as many others were 'truth-seekers', prepared to consider critical interpretations.

Quadrant's editors – more patriotic romantics than truth-seekers – launched their own counter-offensive in the culture war they had unilaterally declared. In 2013, poet and lawyer Hal Colebatch's *Australia's Secret War*, an hysterical rant based on exaggerated distortion of hearsay and false memory, disgracefully shared the Prime Minister's Prize for Australian History with Joan Beaumont's *Broken Nation*. The decision confirmed that under Tony Abbott the prize had become politicised. Colebatch's tirade (alleging that 'the unions' had 'sabotaged' the war effort) was demonstrably a right-wing political pamphlet masquerading as history – its references were thin, its evidence scant and easily shown to be partial, suspect and often risible.

For a time, the two sides skirmished. One of the targets of *What's Wrong with Anzac?* had been the Department of Veterans' Affairs, and especially its ubiquitous and well-funded schools programs, which, critics charged, promoted an unjustifiably uncritical approach to war history. Its education 'kits' did implicitly foster a patriotic agenda, one endorsing rather than challenging the contribution of veterans who volunteered to visit classes. Veterans' Affairs, however, also employed a group of historians, led from 1997 to 2013 by former teacher and Memorial historian Richard Reid. He and his colleagues, and a stable of well-regarded historians, produced over sixty short, illustrated books over twenty years from the late 1990s (thirty of them by Reid himself). Other authors included Peter Burness, Mark Johnston, Jeff Kildea, John Moreman, Hank Nelson, Melanie Oppenheimer, Philip Payton, Craig Wilcox and me. While they observed the sort of prudent self-censorship familiar to me from the Memorial, Reid and his successor, Ian Hodges, rarely encountered undue direction or censorship.

Douglas Newton, who had taught for most of his career in Britain (and had therefore not been exposed to the virus of Anzackery) published two books which took a very different approach to conventional Great War history. His *Hell Bent* (2014) offered a challenging reappraisal of *Australia's Leap into the Great War*. In *Private Ryan and the Lost Peace* (2021) Newton told the story of Ted Ryan of the 51st Battalion, who denounced the war as an 'abattoir' and condemned the machinations of the politicians who engineered its continuation. Both were superbly researched and amply documented. Curiously, despite the popular admiration for 'larrikinism' and the widespread belief that the Great War was a wasteful tragedy, a soldier who challenged the whole basis of the war at the time attracted little attention. Though Newton's books made little impact on popular views, the endorsements he garnered suggest that those whose views carried weight had been convinced. Frank Bongiorno of the Australian National University found *Hell Bent* 'by far the best ever account of Australia's participation in the world's catastrophic plunge into war'.

In this atmosphere, military history has become a battleground between those who believe in and seek to boost the 'Anzac tradition' and those who value the truth more highly. For example, episodes such as the killings in the Transvaal and in Uruzgan are often explained (and even excused) as occurring in 'the heat of battle'. It is sadly true that unlawful or immoral killing has occurred in every war in history, and by Australians in perhaps every war it has fought. I dealt with this in *Bad Characters*, on Australian discipline and indiscipline in the Great War, as have others – Dale Blair in his *No Quarter*, Mark Johnston in his *Fighting the Enemy* and Tom Frame, who brought the sorry story of Australian atrocities up to date in his *Veiled Valour*, published in 2022. Frame, also a clergyman and concerned about the ethics of conflict, had led the way among historians to considering the *Moral Injury* inflicted upon those who serve, notably in a 2015 collection he edited.

Australian military history is and should be a battleground, of ideas. Just as Australians are proud that AIF officers earned their men's respect rather than taking their authority for granted, if the idea of Anzac is to retain its place as a motivating force in Australian identity, it needs to continually justify that prominence.*

* The busting of myths continues. Craig Stockings and his contributors published two volumes attacking *Zombie Myths* (in 2010 and 2012). Academic essays will surely never defeat popular belief, but idealists persist. As this book went to press, Mark Dapin's *Lest* appeared, attacking *Australian War Myths*, a knockabout demolition of 'No Poofters' in uniform and 'Victimised Veterans' to 'The Shape of Myths to Come': good luck, Mark!

47

THE ONCE AND FUTURE ARMY: THE AUSTRALIAN DEFENCE FORCE

It might surprise some readers, but Australian military history is more than war history, though (as this book demonstrates) war has always been more prominent than the history of the armed services in peacetime. The few histories of Militia units are very much overlooked. Craig Wilcox's *For Hearths and Homes* (1998) offered a history of citizen soldiering in Australia 1854–1945, one of the few studies of one of the major strands in Australia's military history, an experience which Wilcox rightly observed 'later generations have almost forgotten'. The Defence Force's PR machine may also have forgotten, but the world wars were fought largely by citizens in uniform, a phenomenon which shaped decades of Anzac Day marches. Increasingly, James Brown observed in 2014, 'the gap between our soldiers and the society they serve is a chasm'.

In a foreword to his colleague John Blaxland's *The Australian Army from Whitlam to Howard* (2014), David Horner reflected upon changes in the public perception of Australia's military history. Formerly, public memory and attention focused almost exclusively on the world wars, but 1945 is almost eighty years away, and the Defence Force history has seen much in the meantime, with involvements in wars, a flurry of peacekeeping, greater involvement in disaster relief, new alliances and potential threats, along with changes in everything from technology and defence policies to the demographics of the Defence Force's composition. With the drama of conflict, sacrifice and heroism driving much of Australian military history, the less eventful service of the Australian Defence Force offers a less populist history. Phillip Deery's *Labour in Conflict* (1978), on the 1949 coal strike, for example, ought to be seen as part of the services' history, but probably isn't.

In the aftermath of the Second World War the Australian armed services, but especially the Army, undertook a profoundly significant re-casting, not least by becoming more securely enmeshed in the Cold War alliance. The RAN and RAAF had always been largely permanent services – because they relied on ships and aircraft needing constant maintenance, not just on Tuesday drill nights. The Army, though, had always relied on a large citizen force directed by a tiny cadre of regular officers. Having been marginalised in their careers by citizen soldiers until they became vital in wartime, they decided in the immediate post-war years that something had to change. In creating what became an Australian Regular Army, career officers achieved a quiet revolution. From 1948, while retaining a diminishing 'citizen' force, the Army became essentially a regular force supported by reservists. Dayton McCarthy's *The Once and Future Army* (2003, the title adapted from TH White's Arthurian *The Once and Future King*) offered a study of the Citizen Military Forces 1947–74, and documented the erosion of the citizen soldier tradition and the triumph of the regular army. As a soldier, McCarthy was hopeful (as his title implied) that citizen soldiers would again become important in the Defence Force; so far unavailingly.

The history of citizen forces has always been more sketchily recorded, but even after 1948 regulars neglected the history they were gradually creating. While former wartime citizen soldiers had formed the mainstay of the writing of unit histories, regular units offered no 'natural' point at which to commission histories. Even the battalions of the RAR tended to produce books on their tours of Vietnam rather than the duration of their service. Not until 1990 did David Horner edit the first collective history of the RAR, one entitled *Duty First*, the regiment's motto (and with Jean Bou he produced a revised edition in 2008). Other major units and entire corps went for longer without histories. The Royal Australian Artillery, for example, the second largest 'arms' corps, also waited until

1995 for a regimental history (*The Gunners*, also written by Horner). The deficiency is gradually being rectified.

The centenary of Federation provided an opportune moment to consider the *History of Australian Defence*, a series produced by another UNSW Canberra soviet, this time led by Peter Dennis and John Coates. The series (2001) comprised seven volumes, each by leading authorities in the subject: Jeff Grey on the history of the Army, Alan Stephens on the RAAF, David Stevens on the RAN, David Horner on the Australian Defence Force, Eric Andrews on the Department of Defence (with a volume on sources and statistics under Joan Beaumont), and John Coates's ground-breaking *An Atlas of Australia's Wars*. Far more than just an atlas, it was a history, a chronology and a bibliography, and represented a long-held dream: I recall Alec Hill approaching the Memorial to sponsor a 'military atlas' in the early 1980s. Fortunately, he lived to see Coates's atlas appear.

The Australian Defence Force has always had an ambiguous relationship with history, using it as the basis of 'tradition' but sometimes nervous of what it might expose. In *Anzac's Long Shadow*, James Brown criticised the Defence Force's 'very short institutional memory', and authors often acknowledge a reluctance to expose awkward facts. In the introduction to his 1992 *Where Fate Calls*, Tom Frame (then a naval officer) described how deciding to write a book on the 1964 *Voyager* tragedy had been difficult, and that he proceeded against the advice of superiors and friends. He persisted, convinced that the story could best be explained by 'someone "inside" the Navy'. Doing so involved making judgments about individuals and the service he had been a part of since he was 16, but he felt a greater loyalty to the historian's obligation to the truth.

Although the fortunes of the individual service history organisations wax and wane with changes in senior commands, budgets and competing priorities, overall, as Al Palazzo wrote in *The Australian Army: A history of its organisation 1901–2001* (2001), knowledge of the Army's past 'can help illuminate its path forward'. If enough influential members continue to hold that conviction, history has a future in the Defence Force.

48

A MILITARY HISTORY OF AUSTRALIA: OVERVIEWS

As has been clear, general histories of Australia's wars are relatively rare. The outstanding examples are Craig Wilcox's expansive study *Australia's Boer War* (2002), Joan Beaumont's *Broken Nation* (on the Great War; 2013) and John Robertson's *Australia at War 1939–1945* or Michael McKernan's *The Strength of a Nation* (2006). They come in guises other than straight narratives: my *The Crying Years* (2017) offered a survey of the Great War through the National Library's collection, giving a different perspective than from the War Memorial across Lake Burley Griffin. Vietnam has attracted several, perhaps because although it lasted a decade it can be encompassed in one volume – they include John Murphy's *Harvest of Fear*, Paul Ham's *Vietnam*, Michael Caulfield's *The Vietnam Years* and Peter Edwards's distillation of the official history, *Australia and the Vietnam War* (2014). Just as the Vietnam war was one of Australia's most contentious conflicts, so its histories reflect diverse perspectives – Murphy's critical, Ham's and Caulfield's empathetic with the troops; Edwards's authoritative and detached.

Histories spanning longer periods come in three kinds: individual volumes, collections of chapters, and series.

Single-volume treatments of long periods are relatively rare. Notable examples include Peter Firkins's *The Australians in Nine Wars* (1971), Tom Millar's *Australia in Peace and War* (1978), Chris Coulthard-Clark's *Where Australians Fought* (1998, which constituted the first *Encyclopaedia of Australia's battles*) and Peter Cochrane's *Australians at War* (2001), a product of Michael Caulfield's massive Veterans' Affairs-sponsored television series of the same name. Pre-eminently, Jeff Grey's

A Military History of Australia (1990, but twice revised to keep up with the rapidly growing field) both defined history and offered trenchant interpretation. The problem of writing a single volume is, of course, not just that readers' expectations magnify the author's challenge (because a history written today would need to address aspects unimagined by, perhaps unimaginable to, (say) Peter Firkins), but also that the subject expands through time. (Firkins's book, if revised, would need to be re-titled *The Australians in Thirteen Wars* – counting the long Australian wars on the frontier as one.)

Dividing the task between a team of writers in one volume makes sense, not least because it makes the most of individual expertise. 'Edited collections' are a common way for academic historians to not only float and debate new ideas (sometimes arising from conferences), but also to satisfy universities' relentless demand for 'productivity' and 'points' – and to stake out a claim in the hope of one day finding the relief from teaching and administration to write the full book. They are less often directed to subjects as general as a history of Australia's wars. One of the few exceptions was *Australia: Two centuries of war and peace* (1988), edited by Margaret Browne and Michael McKernan, the Memorial's contribution to the Bicentenary (which it otherwise largely ignored). It included chapters exploring not just the subject's chronological span, but also some of its challenging themes. These included Bill Gammage on the Anzac tradition, Eric Andrews on civil–military relations and Richard White on 'War and Australian society'. (Richard White was one of the cohort of Australians historians drawn into military history in its expansionary phase in the 1980s but who were not tempted to remain. In the meantime, he questioned the easy assumptions about why men had enlisted in 1914, and considered the AIF as 'tourists', both in articles published in the Memorial's *Journal*.)

The outstanding example of this approach is the *Oxford Companion to Australian Military History*, in the familiar Oxford mold, which has now appeared in two editions (1995 and 2008). Created by a team of historians at UNSW Canberra under the leadership of Peter Dennis, the companion includes about 800 entries which collectively provide both a factual and a critical summary of the field and its literature. Originally an historian of British military history (with books on the Territorial Army and Mountbatten's South-East Asia Command) Dennis became, often in concert with his colleague Jeff Grey, one of the most influential figures in Australian military history, not so much as an author, but as an editor and mentor, most recently acting as editor and advisor on Craig Stockings's official history project.

An even more expansive (and indeed expensive) option is to commission a series, an enterprise demanding the tenacity and connections to secure funding (a business at least as arduous as actually writing) and the managerial skill to maintain focus and motivation and induce authors to deliver to a schedule set by sponsor or publisher. The challenge is so extreme that it is surprising not just that only a few examples exist but that some of their progenitors took it on more than once. The past fifty years have produced several notable series, the idea naturally an evolution of the idea of the official history.

The first commercial venture in the field was the Time-Life *Australians at War* series (1986–89), the initiative of publishing entrepreneur John Ferguson, who in the mid-1980s saw the potential of hitching the familiar profusely illustrated Time-Life concept to the hitherto unexploited but growing subject of Australian military history. The series comprised sixteen books on Australian military history from the Boer War (*For Queen and Commonwealth*) to *Modern Military Towards 2000*, their authors all men, most either freelance writers, novelists or veterans, some all three. They comprised a roll-call of the talent which Ferguson regarded as the best available, including Colin Burgess, Peter Charlton, Hugh Clarke, Kit Denton, Alun Evans, Ian Jones, and John Laffin, all of whom appear elsewhere in this book – and me. I was much younger than the other authors, given a go as an ambitious young aspiring historian. Colin Burgess and I are the only ones still alive.

At the same time, dozens of Australian historians were engaged in producing the massive, ten-volume, 400-author enterprise *Australians: A historical library* under the general direction of Ken Inglis and UNSW Sydney historian Frank Crowley, notable for approaching Australian history through the 'slices' of 1788, 1838, 1888 and 1938, including an historical atlas, dictionary and guide to sources. By the happenstance of the chosen 'slice' years, military history figured little in the series. Australian military historians followed this model, producing several major series, each connected to major anniversaries and their accompanying funding opportunities, and produced in association with a major publisher.

As well as wrangling a multi-volume series, Dennis and Grey initiated other large, complex projects. Peter Dennis had already begun the huge AIF project, which collated data on the 315 000-odd members of the first AIF, a vast archive of individual evidence, both official and unofficial – he included details gleaned by personal inspection of cemeteries across Australia.* He donated his archive to UNSW Canberra, still available and indeed complemented by a similar New Zealand database. The Dennis and Grey partnership also programmed the annual Chief of Army History Conference and edited the published proceedings: all this in addition to teaching and, indeed, producing other books individually.

The approaching centenary of the Great War prompted Jeff Grey to propose and lead the *Oxford Centenary History of Australia and the Great War* (2014–15) – the 'and' was my own special contribution to the project, instead of 'in'. I urged that the story not stop in 1918, but in the event only the volume *The War at Home* went beyond 1918 and then superficially because of the publisher's word limit. The five volumes, which we initially talked of as 'the new Bean', didn't attempt to reprise his massive series, but instead offered revisionist appraisals of *The War Against Germany* (Bob Stevenson), *The War with the Ottomans* (2015; Jeff himself; his last book), and *The AIF* (Peter Dennis and Jean Bou, largely based on Peter's database) and *The War at Home*, which John Connor, Peter Yule and I wrote on Australia's wartime political, economic and social history respectively. The first volume of the series *The War in the Air*, by Michael Molkentin, based on his PhD which

* The usual figure given for the AIF's members is 330 000, an error which has become hallowed by repetition. A more careful reading of the table in Bean's Volume VI reveals that about 315 000 embarked. The higher figure represents the number of embarkations from Australia, and some embarked more than once.

Jeff and I had supervised, saw the advent of new talent as well as fresh interpretation.

Whether the published series can continue in the era of digital publishing remains to be seen.

49

A DICTIONARY OF AUSTRALIAN MILITARY HISTORY: AUSTRALIAN MILITARY HISTORY NOW

In 1992, Ian Grant, schoolteacher and first biographer of Jacka, VC, bravely published *A Dictionary of Australian Military History*, the first time anyone had ventured to encompass the entire span of the field. This was something that Michael McKernan and I had thought of on a Manly ferry in about 1984. We got as far as drawing up lists of potential entries but hadn't the time or energy to take it further. In any case, by the time Grant's dictionary appeared, Peter Dennis and the UNSW Canberra push were already planning what became the *Oxford Companion to Australian Military History*, the first edition of which appeared in 1995. But the idea of an alphabetical treatment of the subject remains useful.

Aces

It's said that everyone has a book in them, but very often only one. It's surprisingly common for authors to produce just one book; sometimes their PhD, but even journalists often write only one book, usually a subject about which they feel passionate. (Young academics are all-too-familiar with 'the second book problem'. Their first is usually based on their PhD; but how do they find the time to research and write their second when oppressed by teaching and administrative responsibilities?)

A much smaller number of authors produce five or more books. In air-force-speak, an 'ace' is a fighter pilot who shoots down five or more enemy aircraft. Surveying the thousand-odd books on which this book is based, it's clear that a relatively small group of authors has been responsible for a disproportionate number of books. On this measure, about sixty authors have produced about 40 per cent of the books published since 1974. Some fifteen authors have published more than ten books apiece, accounting for about 15 per cent of the books published in the field since 1974. The most prolific, I'm proud to say, have mostly been members of the Military History Section which I led at the Memorial: Richard Reid, Chris Clark and me. Richard Reid has over thirty Department of Veterans' Affairs books to his credit. Chris (formerly Coulthard-Clark) has published over twenty full-scale books. I've published forty-five books; thirty in Australian military history; David Horner, over forty. Through his Mostly Unsung publications, Neil Smith, a retired colonel, has produced almost a hundred books and booklets, some complete unit histories, others medal rolls and short histories of subjects which would surely not otherwise be recorded: balloonists in the Boer War, AIF volunteers' aliases 1914–19, women of Cowra, or Australian concert parties in Vietnam.

Amateurs and professionals

The authors in the field of Australian war writing can be readily – too readily – characterised: academic or amateur; professional writer, journalist or 'storian: everyone can be pigeon-holed. Whether they should be is debateable, but differences and similarities do exist and can be identified. In general, amateurs are often respected for their detailed subject knowledge, while academically trained researchers can be expected to be more analytical, and to consider the nature of the evidence rather just than its content. The assumption that journalists are naturally better 'storytellers' or that academic writing is necessarily 'dry' is simply wrong and offensive. And people change: amateurs become experts; journalists learn skills besides storytelling; students develop into apprentice PhDs; museum professionals may be academically trained or lay authorities. (When I recently described a journalist as an historian, he replied 'I'm not a historian, just a reporter'. I told him that he may have *started* as a journalist but that while writing four books he had become a writer of history.) Over fifty years, I've worn most of these labels, starting as a teenage enthusiast and becoming successively a student, amateur, museum professional, doctoral candidate, published author, academic and freelance writer: labels don't make a great deal of sense.

Military historians know the value of expert 'amateurs', such as Ian Skennerton (on weapons), Geoffrey Pentland (on aircraft) or Anthony Staunton (on VCs). Military history has always been pursued by the very different bodies of amateur researchers, including members of the Military Historical Society of Australia, its New South Wales counterpart, and societies such as the Naval Historical, Aviation Historical or broader-based community groups such as the Family and Friends of the First AIF (founded by John Laffin). Arguably, they came to military historical research sooner than academics – in the early 1980s they could have been excused for thinking of academics as Johnny-come-latelies. One notable non-institutional category has been schoolteachers, such as Peter Brune, Anthony Cooper, Mark Johnston, Lucas Jordan, Brian McKinlay and Michael Molkentin, who have made strong contributions.

The various elements have often seemed wary of each other: amateurs and academics met at Memorial conferences but did not always mix. But notable examples of the two working with each other exist. Eric Andrews of Newcastle University joined Army Reservist Bede Jordan, to reveal (in an article in the Memorial's *Journal*) the reason for the heavy casualties in the second battle of Bullecourt (basically, the placement of German machine guns). Academics and amateurs have often worked together in museums, which especially value subject expertise.

Relations have not always been harmonious. Bob Nicholls, a classic amateur, would dismissively refer to authors with a 'Phud', while the antipathy between high-volume 'storians and uncommercial academic authors was not just driven by jealousy over sales. 'Storians and those they derided as 'revisionists' sniped at each other in reviews, forewords and even acknowledgments pages. In his *Monash & Chauvel* (2017, subtitled *How Australia's two greatest generals changed the course of history*, Roland Perry complained that 'military historians, academics and others' failed to accept that his heroes had influenced the Great War more than even Haig, Ludendorff or Foch, accusing them of 'a desire to push other agendas' – presumably including the agenda of accepting the historical evidence. As I say, relations have not always been harmonious.

Anzacs in the family

Family historians are primarily motivated by their connection to those whose stories they tell. But many other historians, whether academic or otherwise, admit to some degree of association to those who served in war. At the end of a preface in which he confessed a distaste for war history and doubt that 'there is little in the Official History or the unit histories which brings the reader to a closer understanding of ... the ordinary serviceman', David Kent disclosed that of his grandfathers, one had been killed in 1916 and the other 'broken by war'. That motivation seemed to be as compelling as his curiosity over what troopship magazines revealed of men's lives. Nor was Kent alone. Joan Beaumont dedicated her prize-winning *Broken Nation* to her pacifist father and introduced the book with an account of her grandfather, who lost a leg after Polygon Wood and whose experience, she reflected, explained 'why I have written this book'. Rosalie Triolo mentioned great-uncles killed in the Great War in the opening lines of her *Our Schools and the War*, and Narelle Biederman, whose *Tears on My Pillow* derived from her PhD on Vietnam nurses, described her family's military history and her own childhood as an 'Army brat'. Indeed, book-after-book is dedicated to a great uncle, father or aunt. But being aware of having an Anzac in the family is no guarantee of knowledge about them. It's telling that in several of his books 'storian Peter FitzSimons mentioned his father's war service at 'Finchhaven' – that is, Finschhafen – an error first made in his *Kokoda* (2004), and despite his platoon of researchers, the error remained uncorrected for at least a decade in reprint-after-reprint. Nor is the absence of Anzac forebears an impediment to interest in Australian military history; indeed, it may allow a productive disinterest.

Birds of passage

'I am not a military historian in the conventional sense …', Henry Reynolds acknowledged in the introduction to his *Unnecessary Wars* – even though he had done more than anyone to open research into the Australian wars from 1788. Not all who contribute to the understanding of Australia's experience of war can or want to be regarded as 'Australian military historians'. Many authors, especially academics, identify primarily as scholars of other persuasions, who stray into 'military history' for other reasons. In the 1980s, for example, the Memorial supported researchers in other fields working on congruent questions, such as Richard White, advancing his work on soldiers as tourists; social historian Elizabeth Cham to research Australian society during the Great War; the lexicographer Bill Ramson on 'services English'; the radio journalist Tim Bowden on PoW oral histories; Philippa Poole to write *Of Love and War*; and the historian of science Roy McLeod on the mobilisation of university science in the Great War. None of these applicants identified as military historians but they represent the many who over decades have enriched the field. Other notable 'interventions' (as it became fashionable to term them) include Joy Damousi, an extraordinarily versatile historian who, besides making major contributions in histories from female convicts to Freudian psychiatry, produced around the turn of the century two pioneering studies of grief and mourning.

That authors not previously known for writing in the field have won major prizes (*Semut* by anthropologist Christine Helliwell, who won the Prime Minister's Prize for History in 2022, and *Soldiers and Aliens*, by folklorist June Factor, who won the inaugural Anzac Memorial Trustees' prize in 2023) suggests the value of authors bringing fresh insights to the field.

Controversies

Australian military historians rarely explicitly disagree with each other: although clear interpretative differences exist, arguments tend to be avoided rather than embraced. For all its fabled iconoclasm, Australia's historical culture is much more genteel than, say, Germany's (in which scholars take no prisoners) or – surprisingly, perhaps – New Zealand, which has seen some ding-dong rows, though with an even smaller historical community they mainly remain on speaking terms.* Serious controversies are few. Craig Wilcox and John Mordike famously fell out over their incompatible views of whether the AIF was the product of an imperial conspiracy, Peter Williams had to defend his estimates of Japanese numbers in Papua, and Chris Roberts (rightly) took previous chroniclers of the invasion of Gallipoli to task over whether the defending Ottomans used machine guns on 25 April 1915. Most disagreements are of this scale. The criticisms of my argument that the Japanese did not plan to invade Australia came in fragmented sniping (such as websites calling for my sacking from the Memorial) rather than major counter-offensives in print. The most determined arguments have been fought over questions such as whether Breaker Morant and Peter Handcock were murderers or victims, or the reasons for the loss of HMAS *Sydney* in 1941. But, a friend truly confides, 'there may not be many controversies but there is endemic rivalry, involving jealousy and at times spite' among military historians: and who among us is spared that feeling?

Defence Force historians

The Defence Force has also employed historians, though mostly in ones and twos. Its historical sections remain vigorous, and the RAN's History and Heritage branch actually recruited historians as I wrote this chapter.

* The formidable John Moses, one of the foremost scholars of the origins of Anzac Day, trained as an historian in the classic German tradition. Famously pugnacious in arguing that imperial Germany represented a real threat to Australia in 1914, he was frustrated that no one took him on.

The Army History Unit especially forged close relationships with serious military historians, forming an advisory committee and, largely through the influence of David Horner, a growing publications program. Over twenty years it published over a hundred books, from scholarly studies in series published in conjunction with commercial and university presses to shorter, more accessible books published by smaller firms, notably BigSky, whose rise (from one book to fifty a year in less than a decade) may be decisively dated from the Army History Unit's patronage. The key figure in the Army History Unit's ambitious schemes was Roger Lee, an adept bureaucrat who outlasted a rotating roll of two-star superiors and gained a PhD at UNSW Canberra, with Jeff Grey as supervisor. Lee enjoyed a long and productive association with Grey and Peter Dennis, who structured the unit's annual conferences and published their proceedings.

Army History sponsored or published many books of high quality. Its books have included memoirs, campaign and unit histories, and many foundational army histories, such as Al Palazzo's *The History of the Royal Australian Corps of Transport 1973–2000* (2001). But it also produced books which challenged understanding. These included Andrew Ross and Bob Hall's *The Search for Tactical Success in Vietnam* (2015), an analysis of 'Operations Research', and Graham Wilson's iconoclastic (if often unduly pedantic) critiques in *Bully beef and balderdash: Some Myths of the AIF Examined and Debunked*.

The Defence Force also commissions a range of papers and publications, some of which relate to its history, some by historians, though most deal with current issues. When it has commissioned narratives of its role in conflict (such as of the Iraq involvement) the manuscripts have sometimes been classified; understandably to the intense frustration of those responsible for writing them. The continuing official history of the post-2001 conflicts to a degree rectifies this lamentable failure to face Australia's history openly, though the official historian Craig Stockings, his authors and researchers were impeded mightily by nameless bureaucratic apparatchiks eager to avoid embarrassing revelations.

The Great Chain of Being

As I suggested in describing how Bill Gammage drew on Arthur Bazley's advice, there is a Great Chain of Being in Australian military history, though it might defy anyone to map the networks of influence, friendship, emulation and inspiration. We could trace the influence of supervisors, from Manning Clark to Lloyd Robson and on to Jan Bassett; often profound relationships. Bassett wrote that 'the late Lloyd Robson taught me much about the infinite suffering caused by war'. As Lloyd lay dying, Val Noone consoled Jan Bassett, saying 'the flame goes on in other people'. In turn, Jan would pass on that flame, through her books and her posthumous memoir *The Facing Island* (2002), edited by Janette Bomford. Every effective academic historian, besides publishing, supervises postgraduates. They, in turn, publish and in time also supervise, producing not clones and disciples but, ideally, scholars who maintain the great tradition. It's no coincidence that the most prolific academic authors named in this book have also supervised many others mentioned. There are many ways to trace these links: in books' acknowledgments pages, in footnotes, and in dedications, where debts can be acknowledged if not repaid.

'Hot' words

I've lived and worked as a military historian in Canberra for over forty years. My city has more military historians per head than anywhere else in the nation. I often bump into them, not just in obvious places like the café at the National Library, but in my local IGA. Our talk invariably turns to what we're working on, and what other writers are publishing. It became a tired joke to remark on how for a time no book in the field, whether popular or scholarly, could appear without there being, whether in the title, sub-title or 'strap-line' the words 'Forgotten', 'Heroes' or, of course 'Anzac'. Often these 'hot words', known – or at least believed – to ensure visibility and sales, came not from authors but from the anonymous keyboards of publishers' promotions and marketing departments. Seemingly regardless of a book's subject, angle or interpretation, a book would acquire a hotter, more appealing title during its journey from pitch to publication to promotion.*

The National Library of Australia's catalogue lists no fewer than 1042 books with 'Anzac' in the title, the great majority of which relate to Australia (the rest relate to New Zealand, in case you've forgotten). Sixteen titles include 'Anzac Heroes', another twenty-four 'Aussie Heroes', and 246 'Australian Heroes'. Ten are entitled 'Forgotten Anzac', but 'forgotten' is such a common word in titles that sifting out the war books from the 484 'Forgotten Australian' titles is impossible. (I had considered entitling this book 'Incredible Forgotten Anzac Heroes', sarcastically employing words most over-used at present: ironically intended to reflect the parochialism of much of Australian military history writing and perhaps forestall a future book claiming the most jingoistic title imaginable.)

As Bill Gammage once remarked, the word 'forgotten' in a title now means that the *publisher* hadn't heard of something which is, or used to be, well known. Clearly, like familiar clichés of the advertising world, such as 'new' or 'improved', 'forgotten' became a handy way to insinuate that the reader would be getting something fresh, when too often the product was warmed-up hash. How could John Monash, the most famous Australian general ever – the-man-on-the-$100-note – possibly be described as *The Forgotten Anzac*, as he was in the 2008 documentary film (in which I appeared as a talking head)? But there are groups, places, experiences, battles and individuals that could legitimately have been regarded as 'forgotten', episodes dealt with in original books. For example, *Australian Women War Reporters* (the subject of Jeannine Baker's 2015 book), or Richard Guilliatt and Peter Hohnen's *The Wolf* (2010) on those, mainly civilians, seized and carried off to Germany in 1917 by the raider *Wolf*. Among such recent books is Anthony Cooper (with Thorsten Perl), *Dispatches from Berlin, 1943*, on

* Or, indeed, between editions. Paul Daley's *Beersheba* when it first appeared in 2011 was subtitled *A Journey Through Australia's Forgotten War*. When it was re-issued in 2017 (for the centenary of the battle) it was sub-titled *Travels through a forgotten Australian victory*. 'Victory' is a hotter word than 'War' or 'Battle'.

five journalists who flew on a mission in the bomber offensive, only two of whom returned.

Eventually, though, I too succumbed to the lure of the 'hot' words. The strap-line of my *Bad Characters* was 'Some were heroes, some were villains; some were both' – and I dreamed that up; I can't blame it on a publisher's copywriter – and *Lost Boys of Anzac* used not just 'Anzac' but 'Lost' as a kind-of synonym for 'forgotten'. And now when I advise less experienced colleagues on projects and proposals, I'm often candid about them including 'Anzac' in the title and while I still sneer at 'Forgotten', I make clear that if their pitch is accepted, their book may well appear with a strap-line or a title which makes it conform to the universe of Australian military historical publishing. (Recently, a young colleague asked about pitching his book. I urged him to try 'Forgotten Anzac Guerrilla Heroes', because it would mesh with what publishers could most readily see selling.)*

Language

The words used to describe Australian military history are changing, as they always have. After Gallipoli and the Somme, words like 'glory' and 'honour' largely disappeared from serious military writing. But it long remained unexceptional for authors of unit histories to refer to 'Huns', 'Japs' and, indeed, 'Fuzzy-Wuzzies' or 'Natives': our sensibilities are now more tender. (What do we lose by attempting to make history intelligible in our time? The comparison of advising readers that '£1=$2' (which it did, but only in 1966) shows the peril of seeking to impose an equivalence.) We need to learn the language of the past. For example, authors (and indeed participants) before about 1990 used 'front line' – two words – while now most use 'frontline', or even 'frontlines', a change effected by editors also unaware of the historical nuances of language. Sometimes we must accept the past in its own terms.

* The publisher accepted the proposal but seems to want a more sober title, which shows that cynicism isn't always justified.

'Right now', as it seems compulsory to say even when speaking in the present tense, unnecessary and often ugly Americanisms proliferate. We used to speak of 'wounds' (that is, deliberate hurts), whereas now many authors have thoughtlessly adopted the American 'injuries' (that is, accidental hurts). We used to use 'commemorate'. Now many use 'memorialise', not realising that perfectly good Australian terms exist. But Fitzy's attempts to use Aussie slang (especially in his *Tobruk*, with its 'Pommy poofta' officers), came off as gauche. We need to understand the language of *their* past to convey it in our present.

And then there's the inescapable fact that we're writing *military* history. Every field has its jargon, but military history is full of specialised terms, and especially abbreviations and acronyms, and particularly in recent conflicts. My rule of thumb is that the fewer the acronyms the better the book.

The Memorial

As should be clear from the first part of this book, the Australian War Memorial was crucial to the re-discovery of Australian military history, and has played a leading role in stimulating research, opening its collections to researchers, bringing researchers together, publishing their work and defining and contributing to the field. That centrality has diminished in recent years, certainly since Brendan Nelson took the institution in radically new directions, changing the balance between commemoration, collection, display and dissemination, with commemoration and the construction of a vast and hugely expensive physical re-development occupying a disproportionate share of its budget and its staff's energy. While maintaining the collections, the Memorial over the past decade has largely withdrawn from its former role as a clearing house and contact centre for military historians, and its historical staff, while expert, have been preoccupied with both ceremonies and with the development of large new galleries. Like a developing country over-investing in monoculture, this dependence turned into a risk.

While the great majority of visitors would not realise it, the redevelopment involved not just shifting the Memorial's Research Centre to a small demountable located behind the café toilets, but limitations on access to the collection which amounted to effective closure. A limited range of records can be ordered, but only at a month's notice, making serious research, especially by those from outside Canberra, unviable. (Even as a Canberra researcher, it took me three visits over three months to achieve what I could previously have accomplished in a morning.) Irritating and inconvenient as this was, the wider effect was to deter research in Australian military history. What if 2024's Bill Gammage had arrived? She would not easily have been able to read the very same records Bill had used.

Given the centrality of official records held in the Memorial (even if National Archives is their formal custodian) sustained research became virtually impossible.* Doctoral candidates had to modify, defer or even abandon research; who knows how many theses were not started (because potential supervisors honestly advised prospective candidates that research was impractical), or how many books did not appear? The Memorial's own plans perhaps contributed to the ebbing of the boom. One of Australian military history's greatest strengths has turned out, paradoxically, to be (for the time being) one of its greatest weaknesses.

Out soon!

As we have seen, while months could pass in the 1970s before a new book in the field appeared, today a stream appear seemingly endlessly (though especially around Anzac Day and Fathers' Day, a sign of how publishers see their market). In the rapidly developing field of frontier conflicts, Rachel Perkins (with others including Henry Reynolds and Stephen Gapps) is writing a book based on her prize-winning documentary

* Joan Beaumont, who has been as cranky as me over this, wrote in exasperation that if the Memorial wanted to be just a 'semisacred theme park' it should abandon pretensions to support research and return the official records to the National Archives, which actually has custody of them.

The Australian Wars, and Gapps is producing a third book in his trilogy, *The Rising: Resistance wars in the colony of New South Wales, 1838–1845*.

The Army History Unit's publications program, after a hiatus of several years, is returning, with more 'Campaign' books – Mark Johnston on El Alamein and Bob Breen on Kapyong, and in its other series, Lewis Frederickson's *After Anzac*, on infantry on the Western Front, and Daniel and Emanuela Reynaud's *The Anzac Table*, on food in the Great War, and Glenn Wahlert on battlefield intelligence after 1945.

While the wave might be slackening, books now in the works include Peter Rees on sport in war, Tristan Moss on sex and the ADF, Margaret Hutchinson on suicide among veterans, Michael Piggott on the occupation of German New Guinea, Mat McLachlan on the attack on Krithia (naturally, sub-titled *The forgotten Anzac battle*), Alastair Cooper and James Goldrick's *The Navy Chiefs* (Goldrick's posthumous book), Andrew Ross on operational research in Vietnam and *Great at Heart*, Garry Hills's biography of Gavin Long (the first, over fifty years after his death). The boom might be waning, but good books appear.

Publishers

In giving details of books, I've ignored publishers, but their role in fostering military history has been crucial. In earlier decades, established houses such as Angus & Robertson, Halstead Press, and Melbourne University Press were pre-eminent. With the boom from the 1980s, military history became a competitive market, with the burgeoning demand for new titles attracting new publishers to the field. Through the past five decades firms have moved in – and out – as publishing executives saw opportunities and, sadly, risks. In the 1980s UQP (University of Queensland Press) under Laurie Muller published the reprint of Bean's history. In the 1990s William Collins attempted the same, but published only the Army and Navy series of Long's history. Later, Allen & Unwin re-entered the field by publishing the Vietnam and ASIO official histories. Several presses formed seemingly productive relationships with major sponsors, such as John Ferguson with the Memorial, Oxford and Cambridge university presses, and then small publishers Australian Military History Publications and BigSky with the Army History Unit. Some authors, unable to secure commercial publishers (often inexplicably), turn to self-publishing. Ron Austin's Slouch Hat Publications and Lex McAulay's Banner Books brought their books out without commercial support.

Many of these developments followed changes in firms' senior staff – for a time, John Iremonger promised to make Hale & Iremonger a major player, until his early death, while the interest of NewSouth (UNSW Press's commercial arm) in military history peaked under publisher Phillipa McGuinness. I found Murdoch Pier 9 extremely supportive under Diana Hill as publisher, a relationship that ended only after its takeover. Jeff Grey's relationship with Peter Rose at OUP resulted in its involvement in several major series, while under Ian Bowring Allen & Unwin became in the 1990s the single most significant publisher in the field. Small publishers are particularly important in military history. John Burridge of Perth has re-published many rare unit histories, while BigSky, under former Army officer Denny Neave, flourished under the stimulus of the Army History Unit's patronage, now the premier publisher of military history titles by volume. The full story of the role of publishers in promoting the field remains to be told.

Relationships

While writing is characteristically a solitary pursuit, the process of research invariably entails forging and maintaining mutual relationships, as the acknowledgments pages of most works of history attest. For example, in the thirty years in which Mark Johnston has become the premier historian of the Australian Army in the Second World War, he has thanked hundreds of individuals. At first supervisors and the veterans on whose words he drew for his PhD, published as *At the Front Line*, he increasingly acknowledged the help of colleagues. In his *Derrick VC* (2021), he named sixteen individuals, four veterans or members of their families, three archivists, and sixteen colleagues. Every historian could replicate Johnston's experience.

Despite its growth, Australian military history remains a cluster of small, close-knit networks, still unavoidably centred on Canberra. Every Tuesday fortnight a klatch of mostly retired military historians meet at the Memorial's Poppy's café, while the Naval Studies Group meets there every Wednesday. The acknowledgments pages of books would provide grist for a sociologist curious about networks in the field. Jean Bou, in the acknowledgments in his *MacArthur's Secret Bureau* (2012) noted half-a-dozen individuals, most of whom appear in this book: Chris Coulthard-Clark (from whom he inherited the Central Bureau project), Steve Gower (who funded it), and David Horner, Ian Pfennigwerth and Steve Bullard, who offered advice. Jean Bou also thanked his editors, including Robert Nichols, who helped to shape virtually all the Memorial's publications in the period 2001–16. (The role of editors also deserves an article, if not a book.) Networks and relationships are also evident from the covers of books. In the accepted manner, academic historians cheerfully (but with integrity) provided 'puffs' for colleagues' books. Equally, the rise of high-volume publishers created its own webs: a cover puff from Fitzy signals to potential purchasers that the book within is going to reinforce rather than challenge patriotic-nationalist interpretations of Anzac. The two worlds rarely coincided. It is notable that in the four pages of acknowledgments in Carlyon's *The Great War*, he named only one academic historian (Robin Prior, and then only 'to test a few ideas on him').

As is clear from this book, academics played notable roles in the reinvigoration of Australian military history, though whether they can sustain the production of books remains uncertain. Increasingly, driven by the impetus to publish or perish, academics increasingly produced 'chapters' in edited collections. Sometimes these were the proceedings of conferences at which they became conscious of forming part of a network, even a community. The more than a dozen successive volumes of Chief of Army conferences edited by Jeff Grey and Peter Dennis from 1995 offer an outstanding example of the utility of such collaborations. Many were of value in giving younger scholars a chance to try out or demonstrate their work, and to introduce and test new interpretations.

Remembering and forgetting

From the 'memory boom' of the 1990s, much academic writing on war focused on questions of memory; how it had been shaped, how it changed; how it related to other forms of evidence. But remembering also became attached to debates over what is or should be remembered, and book-after-book made claims about what was or was not sufficiently remembered – hence the frequent claims about 'untold' and 'forgotten' stories. Not that anyone could be certain what was or was not 'remembered', and by whom. Still, it was a game we all played, in pitching manuscripts to publishers, in discussing how popular attention seemed to shift, especially in considering how the present thinks of the past (or 'constructs' it, as academic historians would say). Someone should investigate what Australians today 'remember' or not.

Or perhaps we should just stop making these kinds of unprovable claims. As I commented in a review of Maria Hill's *Diggers and Greeks* in 2010, 'how remembered does an event have to be before it stops being "forgotten"?' I called for an end to 'this Dutch auction of "my campaign's more forgotten than yours"'. What, I asked:

> constitutes due remembering? What degree of attention or regard should modest, failed campaigns involving one Australian division deserve? A book a year? An 'iconic' feature film ... an annual day of commemoration? Recognition of, say, the battle of Retimo among a sample of shoppers in any given mall in suburban Australia? It's not Gallipoli or Kokoda, but Greece does better than, say, Lebanon–Syria (for which we can't even get the name right) but not as well as Singapore; that seems about right.

And yet, one of the continuing engines of Australian military history publishing is the belief that aspects are more forgotten than they should be.

Research support

Researchers in Australian military history have always depended upon external support, whether in the voluntary labour of unit association members prepared to sit transcribing routine 'Part 2' orders or the substantial research grants academic researchers seek from funding bodies like the Australian Research Council.

For twenty years from the mid-1970s to the mid-1990s, the Memorial's Research Grants Scheme primed the pump of research in military history, distributing a modest amount of money to assist researchers of all kinds. When it ceased – arguably, when the field was robust enough to stand alone (even though individual researchers still needed help) – happily, the Army History Unit established its own grants scheme, at least for Army research. (The RAAF offered 'heritage awards' which rewarded rather than funded projects; the RAN, while establishing a 'Sea Power Centre' as a research facility, did not directly fund research.) In general, it is now much harder to obtain research funding than it used to be – there is no scheme dedicated to supporting research in this field, and paradoxically, even academic researchers with undeniably viable projects face rejection rates which would demoralise all but the most disciplined and desperate applicants.

The impact of the increasingly rigorous research support schemes imposed upon academic researchers especially has yet to be seen. In the acknowledgments to their *The Last Battle*, Bruce Scates and Melanie Oppenheimer thanked their institutional 'industry partners' – Veterans' Affairs and State Records New South Wales – for their support: not that it was clear what that support constituted, since the archival records ought to have been open to all. In fact, like dozens of researchers, Scates and Oppenheimer were obliged to court 'industry partners' not to conduct the research, but merely to obtain the grant in the first place. The system imposed by a dysfunctional Australian Research Council, rather than distributing funds on merit, subjects researchers to often futile rounds of sounding out institutions seeking 'support' which costs energy to secure, detracting from their productivity. How such a regime can be justified eludes me.

Top ten topics

It's clear that while military history as a whole has been popular among readers and publishers, our interest in the field is uneven: some subjects attract repeated books while other aspects remain neglected. The top ten seem to me to be (in alphabetical order):

Codebreakers
Fromelles
Gallipoli
Kokoda
Long Tan
Monash
Nurses
Sandakan
The loss of HMAS *Sydney*
Z Special

Critics might ask, where is the Air Force? I'm reflecting what has been published, and except for the *Sydney* the RAAF and RAN fare poorly. Some of these subjects clearly arose from particular historical circumstances (notably the search for the Pheasant Wood remains). If a survey of the course of Australian military history over the past half-century tells us anything, it is that the future will develop its own preoccupations and questions, as fresh sources emerge and as new questions are posed by researchers perhaps yet unborn.

Universities

Universities have been crucial to the development of military history, at least since the early 1980s, though not always easily. In a review of the Australian National University's achievements in military history, David Horner observed that a 'focus on military history did not win wide approval [because of] ... the view of some "mainstream" historians that military history was not a legitimate academic discipline'. As his university employs the nation's largest and most productive cohort of military historians, more isolated colleagues must indeed feel beleaguered. The two main groups of players are in Canberra, among the historians employed in what had been the History Department of RMC Duntroon but which became in 1983 the Australian Defence Force Academy, part of UNSW and eventually known as UNSW Canberra. At the Australian National University, another group of scholars, both those part of the Strategic and Defence Studies Centre (which pursued both military history and contemporary defence studies) and its Research Schools formed another productive nexus. At least as many academic historians who would identify as doing military history exist across most of Australia's forty-odd universities, sometimes the only 'military historian' in their school or department.*

The changing world of universities – demanding greater energy simultaneously in administration, teaching, research and publication, often unsustainably – imposed pressures on academic historians. The full effects of the pressures upon younger academics are not yet clear, but it seems that while many can publish a book based on their PhD, many struggle to find energy to write books, but contribute 'chapters' instead. Sadly, the limitations of focus have prevented me from noticing many of the more influential edited collections to appear in the field, including my own. Exceptions relating just to the Great War include Ashley Ekins's *1918 Year of Victory* (2010) and *Gallipoli: A ridge too far* (2013), John Lack and Judith Smart's *Victoria and the Great War* (2015), Jean Bou's *The AIF in Battle* (2016), Rae Frances and Bruce Scates's *Beyond Gallipoli* (2016), John Lack's *1919: The year things fell apart?* (2019), Carolyn Holbrook and Keir Reeve's *The Great War: Aftermath and commemoration* (2019) and Joy Damousi's (and others') *Museums, History and the Intimate Experience of the Great War* (2021).

* Military historians are often regarded as approving of war. I say that no one thinks oncologists approve of cancer.

Veterans as sources

Historians are somewhat unusual in the humanities in developing close relationships with their sources, especially the human ones. This became especially evident as oral history came into its own (Wendy Lowenstein's pioneering oral history, *Weevils in the Flour,* was published in 1978, coinciding with the boom in military history). In this Bill Gammage also led the way, and like him many researchers sought out and valued contacts with those who were by the 1980s invariably called 'veterans' (the Repatriation Department had been re-named the Department of Veterans' Affairs in 1976). Researchers approached them as sources, but often remained in close contact. Many examples come to mind: the Melbourne University historian John Lack, who introduced generations of undergraduates to former members of his father's old battalion, the 2/29th; Hank Nelson of the Australian National University who had (with Tim Bowden of the ABC) revitalised interest in PoWs, many of whom he knew as friends; Jan Bassett formed close relationships with many returned army nurses, while Alistair Thomson had a particular rapport with his *Anzac Memories* informants. Mark Johnston, who had contacted dozens of veterans for the thesis which became *At the Front Line*, dedicated his *An Australian Band of Brothers* to the three members of the 2/43rd Battalion whom he especially admired and whose experiences formed its substance. Bill Gammage, who had known hundreds of Great War men in researching *The Broken Years*, warned younger colleagues that their sources and friends would inevitably age and die.

The wave

As the presence of books in shops and publishers' sales figures suggest, for much of the past forty or so years, interest in military history has been a mainstay of Australian publishing. From the 1980s it seemed that not only was it the most popular non-fiction genre (challenged only by 'true crime') but that the market seemed endlessly elastic: the wave would not break. Half a century on from *The Broken Years*, that confidence seems less certain. The rewards of writing are meagre for all but the bestselling 'storians. Authors, for example, are routinely expected to provide their own images and often maps, meaning that conscientious authors see their royalties consumed in such costs, and it is as hard to find a publisher as it has ever been. But military history is like the world of small business, with a constant stream of aspirants wishing to give it a go, regardless of how many do not succeed in completing or publishing their cherished book.

Who's who

Surveying the course of the writing of Australian military history over the past fifty years or so (regarding the preceding century as its pre-history, in which every writer was a pioneer of one sort or another), it's clear that we can discern various features in the landscape. Most authors write one or two books – most unit histories are written by authors with only one book to their credit: rarely more than two or three. Some authors' influence is profound despite having only published one major book in the field – the example of Bill Gammage standing out. At the other extreme, there are the colossi of the field: the giants of Charles Bean, Gavin Long, David Horner or Ken Inglis, whose influence spreads to many others, whether because they define a field, create an archive (both in the case of Bean and Inglis), or provide a framework for interpretation (Long), found an entire school of strategic and biographical scholarship, as with Horner, or introduce a new approach to understanding the impact of war on Australia. Then there have been influential figures over decades, such as Joan Beaumont, Jeff Grey, Bruce Scates or, I suppose, me, who have written books which have challenged or shifted the way we think about, write or practise Australian military history. Included in this group would be figures such as Michael McKernan, who besides writing several foundational books, also facilitated the boom whose effects we are still enjoying (during his thirteen years at the Memorial, McKernan was behind virtually all its innovations and achievements, from reforming the Research Centre to creating the Murdoch oral history collection, to writing its first history). And then there are the ones who do the heavy lifting, as the cliché goes; the ones who teach and inspire undergraduates, who supervise and mentor postgraduates, whose teaching duties may prevent them writing lots but who hold the community together: John Lack, John McQuilton, Craig Stockings and my colleagues at UNSW Canberra. Beyond the academy, there are independent scholars or freelance writers, often wrongly described as amateurs who, despite their writing outside the formal structures of learning, make decisive contributions: Phillip Bradley, Peter Brune, David Cameron (to take three who between them have published over two dozen books on the New Guinea campaigns alone). These figures include biographers such as Andrew Faulkner, Ross McMullin, Peter Rees or Pattie Wright, and Anthony Staunton (the expert on Australian VCs) or Craig Wilcox, whose books have done more for colonial military history than anyone else.

50

THIS WAR NEVER ENDS: THE FUTURE OF AUSTRALIAN MILITARY HISTORY

Because this book looks back at who has written history and forwards at what they will write, it can't say much about those who will produce the next crop of histories. Most of the theses by my own UNSW doctoral candidates should be or are being published (besides those that already have been). They include Liam Kane on US–Australian relations in the Second World War, James Morrison on the Militia (also in the Second World War), Kerry Neale on facial wounds, Nicole Townsend on Australia and the Mediterranean war, Glenn Wahlert on battlefield intelligence since 1945 and Neil Westphalen on the RAN's medical service.

Beyond UNSW Canberra, there must be a dozen or two doctoral theses in military history in train at various universities. For a Canberra writer it's important to look beyond the ACT. The program of the Australian Historical Association's 2023 conference offers insights. Among the several hundred papers presented, about two dozen were scheduled in a stream on 'War, conflict and military history', sponsored by the Army History Unit. Of the speakers, only about four have been mentioned in this book. Most were doctoral or 'early career researchers' (ECRs in academic-speak), eager to try out ideas and solicit responses. Three-fifths of the speakers were women, and their sessions dealt with themes such as suicide, sexuality, memory, frontier violence and commemoration; few with traditional military history. My colleague Tristan Moss (author of *Guarding the Periphery* (2017), a pioneering study of the defence of colonial Papua New Guinea (who spoke in the conference on sexuality and the Defence Force)), wondered how many of the other speakers identified centrally as 'military historians'. The absence of traditional military historians may simply reflect the character of the Australian Historical Association's predilections. If this complexion means a greater connection between military history and the concerns of a more diverse investigative wider historical culture, so much the better.

The next decade will disclose whether by 2020 we saw 'peak Australian military history'. The absence of major anniversaries until the late 2030s (2039 will see the 125th anniversary of 1914 and the centenary of the Second World War) means that the field will not be given the external boosts of Australia Remembers, the centenary of Federation, or the 'Centenary of Anzac'. And the authors of the history books published in the 2030s will be writing for a very different Australia, unlike the society which first opened *The Broken Years*. Who could have foreseen in 1974, for instance, that we might have several books on the sexuality of members of the Defence Force, such as Noah Riseman and Shirleene Robinson's *Pride in Defence: The Australian military & LGBTI service since 1945* (2020), a book supported by the Department of Defence? Who would have expected a book arguing that the Bangka Island nurses were raped before being murdered? Who could have predicted that 2023 would see the publication of two books detailing the misdeeds of a VC? Who could have foreseen Don Watson's *The Passion of Private White*, a book about the positive relationship between a Vietnam veteran and an Indigenous community in Arnhem Land?

Clearly, Australia's military history is changing. It reflects not just what we know, but what we believe. As Australia changed, so its historians and writers changed their minds about what its wars meant. Many memorials erected after 1918 bore the inscriptions 'KING' and 'EMPIRE', as memorials after 1945 did not. Charles Bean's view that the Great War created the idea of an Australian nation long prevailed. From the mid-1990s the idea gained popular traction that the Second World War was fought and justified not to prevent the triumph of militarism and fascism, but to save Australia from certain invasion. The Vietnam war was explained at the time as a crusade against Communism, though later generations, and even some veterans, began to doubt the cause. The Iraq and Afghanistan invasions were widely believed at the time to be based on a falsehood, and then proved to be so. By the end of the 20th century historians had exposed the long series of conflicts for possession of the continent which few non-Indigenous people before about 1980 had known about or admitted.

War has been and may yet be as significant to Australia as is environmental, demographic or political developments. Frontier violence endured for a century after 1788, Australia was at war for a third of the 20th, we have been in a state of war for much of the 21st and, unless we buck up our ideas, we may well be gulled into yet another needless, disastrous American war, next time with a rival superpower which happens to be our major trading power.

Society is changing demographically. If having an Anzac in the family has been a driver of amateur and family history, and even an element in leading academic interest, then as the great conflicts of the 20th century recede in personal and popular memory we may see correspondingly less interest among writers and readers. For all the rhetoric of continuing remembrance, time will blur and dim. I'm conscious of the poem by George Essex Evans, the Queensland journalist and poet whom Alfred Deakin eulogised in federal parliament, who celebrated the colonial contingents' stand at Elands River in South Africa in 1901:

> On Australia's page for ever
> We had written Eland's River—
> We had written it for ever and a day!

But who today has heard of Elands River (or, outside Toowoomba, where he is handsomely commemorated, George Essex Evans)? The Australian War Memorial's decision to devote a large proportion of its newly constructed galleries to conflicts after 2001 (though they cost few lives and did not impinge greatly on the nation), a decision effectively diminishing conflicts in which tens of thousands of Australians died, makes the point: wars long ago are of less interest. But we may see books which investigate the effects of memories of the war experiences of, say, Palestinian or Ukrainian migrants, just as Nathalie Nguyen wrote of former *South Vietnamese Soldiers* (2016), who had arrived in Australia as refugees from war forty-odd years before. Many of the veterans she interviewed are now Australians: is their experience part of Australian military history? I say it is, but the question needs to be debated. Why should Serbian or Sudanese memories of war not become a part of Australia's complicated relationship with conflict?

The uncertain world and region in which we live may also affect the future of Australian military history, not just in the nightmarish possibility that we may see conflict with China, or wars arising from climate change, water shortages or population movements. The shadow cast over the failed Afghanistan intervention appears to have taken the edge off the simplistic celebration of Anzac, even when over the past twenty years it has always been freighted not just with mourning for those killed in distant wars, but apprehensions for those serving in continuing conflicts. And we should not forget that the first quarter-century of the boom in Australian military history occupied the peaceful years between the end of the Vietnam war and the beginning of the continuing war on 'Terror', which has now morphed into anticipating future conflicts, the very preparations for which surely make war more likely. Insecurity about the future may not make a propitious climate for reading about the glories of past wars.

The long boom in Australian military history is now, if not ending, then falling in amplitude. It was notable that, surely for the first time in years, the 2023–24 'Summer Reading' supplements published in the Sunday newspapers included not a single 'Anzac' history book. It's notable that among the Christmas book catalogues in 2022 Paperchain featured no military history titles, while QBD and Harry Hartog included only two war books each. Tellingly, while one in both was the latest by Fitzy the populist 'storian, the others were Nick McKenzie's exposé of the Roberts-Smith scandal, *Crossing the Line*, and David Marr's truth-telling *Killing for Country.* Clearly, Australian military history is a broad church, and while old believers may find comfort in the familiar certainties of slouch-hatted mateship, other questions and concerns now intrude. And publishing is at bottom a business. It is undeniable that books need to find readers, and that ultimately those readers need to include a proportion of purchasers. Luis Emilio's history of the 54th Massachusetts Infantry (the 'coloured' regiment immortalised in the 1989 film *Glory*) appeared in 1891. Already, just a generation after the American Civil War, Emilio felt obliged to acknowledge that 'almost a surfeit of war literature' had appeared in the quarter-century after Appomattox. 'Every new book issued today', his publisher wrote in a preface, 'ought to be able to give a good reason for its existence'. Could the authors of new books in Australian military history give 'a good reason for its existence'?

This is a short and personal history and, knowing so much of the story and so many of those who have told it over so many years, I am especially conscious of what I have omitted. I hope that other authors will take up the challenge of writing books about so many of the aspects I have merely hinted at. As Gerard Windsor wrote in *All Day Long the Noise of Battle*: 'There is always more to be said'.

But the last word should be left to Bill Gammage, and the epilogue to his *The Broken Years*, published in 1974. Sixty years after the beginning of the Great War in August 1914, he wrote that 'what began to happen on Gallipoli nine months later is with us yet'. One hundred and ten years after the outbreak of the Great War, with the world facing in Gaza and Ukraine the consequences of its remaking of the Middle East and the former Russian empire, sadly, it is certain that an understanding of military history remains relevant.

ACKNOWLEDGMENTS

I'm glad to be able to thank for advice, suggestions and criticism a great many colleagues. For this book they include: Kristen Alexander, Joan Beaumont, John Blaxland, Frank Bongiorno, Steve Bullard, Anne-Marie Condé, Alastair Cooper, Will Davies, Miesje de Vogel, Andrew Faulkner, Tom Frame, Lewis Frederickson, Bill Gammage, Garry Hills, Ian Hodges, David Horner, Margaret Hutchison, Martin James, Mark Johnston, Greg Lockhart, Peter Londey, Michael McKernan, Michael Molkentin, Tristan Moss, Michael Piggott, David Pearson, John Perryman, Daniel Reynaud, Richard Reid, Chris Roberts, Andrew Ross, Christina Spittel, Tony Stimson, Craig Wilcox and the staff of the Petherick Room at the National Library of Australia, and especially the anonymous book retrievers who've delivered hundreds of books on dozens of trolleys over the past year. Beyond those who have advised or helped directly, I'm grateful to the hundreds of authors whose work I have read over the past year. I calculated while compiling the index that I have known personally about half of the living authors named in this book. In that sense, it has been in gestation for over forty years.

More immediately, at NewSouth, I'm grateful to Elspeth Menzies for accepting my proposal, to Paul O'Beirne for his immensely efficient management of the publication process, to designer Peter Long for his wittily apposite cover, to book designer Josephine Pajor-Markus for her handsome design of the pages, and especially to editor Jocelyn Hungerford for her consideration and comradeship in finding the right words.

INDEX

FSC
www.fsc.org
MIX
Papier | Fördert gute Waldnutzung
FSC® C083411

Zeitfracht Medien GmbH
Ferdinand-Jühlke-Straße 7
99095 Erfurt, Deutschland
produktsicherheit@kolibri360.de